Business and Religion in the American 1920s

Recent Titles in
Contributions in American Studies
Series Editor: Robert H. Walker

Mechanical Metamorphosis: Technological Change in Revolutionary America
Neil Longley York

Prologue: The Novels of Black American Women, 1891–1965
Carole McAlpine Watson

Strikes, Dispute Procedures, and Arbitration: Essays on Labor Law
William B. Gould IV

The Soul of the Wobblies: The I.W.W., Religion, and American Culture in the Progressive Era, 1905–1917
Donald E. Winters, Jr.

Politics, Democracy, and the Supreme Court: Essays on the Frontier of Constitutional Theory
Arthur S. Miller

The Supreme Court and the American Family: Ideology and Issues
Eva R. Rubin

Heralds of Promise: The Drama of the American People during the Age of Jackson, 1829–1849
Walter J. Meserve

The Line of Duty: Maverick Congressmen and the Development of American Political Culture, 1836–1860
Johanna Nicol Shields

The Course of American Democratic Thought
Third Edition with Robert H. Walker
Ralph Henry Gabriel

The Golden Sword: The Coming of Capitalism to the Colorado Mining Frontier
Michael Neuschatz

Corporations and Society: Power and Responsibility
Warren J. Samuels and Arthur S. Miller, editors

Abortion, Politics, and the Courts: *Roe v. Wade* and Its Aftermath
Revised Edition
Eva R. Rubin

The Secret Constitution and the Need for Constitutional Change
Arthur S. Miller

Business and Religion in the American 1920s

ROLF LUNDÉN

CONTRIBUTIONS IN AMERICAN STUDIES
NUMBER 91

Greenwood Press
New York • Westport, Connecticut • London

Library of Congress Cataloging-in-Publication Data

Lundén, Rolf.
Business and religion in the American 1920s.

(Contributions in American studies, ISSN 0084–9227 ; no. 91)
Bibliography: p.
Includes index.
1. Business—Religious aspects—Protestant churches—History—20th century. 2. Protestantism—History—20th century. 3. Protestant churches—United States—History—20th century. 4. United States—Civilization—1918–1945. I. Title. II. Series.
BX4817.L83 1988 306′.6′0973 87–17597
ISBN 0–313–25151–7 (lib. bdg. : alk. paper)

British Library Cataloguing in Publication Data is available.

Library of Congress Catalog Card Number: 87–17597
ISBN: 0–313–25151–7
ISSN: 0084–9227

First published in 1988

Greenwood Press, Inc.
88 Post Road West, Westport, Connecticut 06881

Printed in the United States of America

The paper used in this book complies with the Permanent Paper Standard issued by the National Information Standards Organization (Z39.48–1984).

10 9 8 7 6 5 4 3 2 1

Copyright Acknowledgments

The author gratefully acknowledges the receipt of permission to quote material from the following sourccs: Roger W. Babson's *Religion and Business* (1926), by permission of Babson College; two versions of the poem "Business Is Business," by Berton Braley and by Everett W. Lord, both published in *Nation's Business* (1917 and 1924), by permission of the U.S. Chamber of Commerce; B. C. Forbes's *Keys to Success* (1926), by permission of Forbes, Inc.; the song "Onward in Kiwanis!", reprinted with permission from *Kiwanis Magazine* (July 1924), copyright 1924 by Kiwanis International; lyrics to "In Rotary There Is No East or West" from the play *The Heart of the World* by Frank H. Lamb, originally published in *The Rotarian* 21 (August 1922), and the poem by Tom J. Mathews, "One Blood in Rotary," which first appeared in *The Rotarian* 31 (December 1927), by permission of Rotary International.

Every reasonable effort has been made to trace the owners of copyright materials used in this book, but in some instances this has proven impossible. The publishers will be glad to receive information leading to more complete acknowledgments in subsequent printings of this book, and in the meantime extend their apologies for any omissions.

To my father
and the memory of my mother

Contents

Illustrations

Acknowledgments

During the past six years, while working on this study, I have incurred debts of gratitude to numerous persons and institutions. The University of Uppsala gave me a sabbatical leave in 1979–1980, a year that I was fortunate enough to spend at the University of Virginia. To both these universities, and their university libraries, I am deeply grateful.

Many friends and colleagues have discussed the topic of this study with me and have read parts of the manuscript; I have profited greatly from suggestions made by Professor Olov Fryckstedt and Professor Alf Tergel of Uppsala University, and Professor David Levin and Professor Harold Kolb of the University of Virginia. I feel a special gratitude toward Professor Watson Branch, the University of Cincinnati, who has read several drafts of the manuscript and who has given constructive and inspiring criticism. I am also indebted to the American Philosophical Society, to the Hilda Kumlin Fund, and to the Wallenberg Foundation for generous financial support. Finally, my most deeply felt note of thanks goes to my wife Susanne, my severest critic and my closest friend.

Business and Religion in the American 1920s

Introduction

When the archbishop of Sweden, Nathan Söderblom, visited the United States in 1923, he observed that if there was anything that characterized the American it was his business mind. "Everything becomes business" in this country, he sighed, even religion.[1] Söderblom's remark was in no way original. Ever since American independence, numerous European visitors had commented that, in contrast to Europe, American society was a business civilization. Pavel Svin'in found in 1815 that at the heart of the young national character was a passion for "mercantile enterprises"; the Jesuit scholar Giovanni Grassi wrote at the same time that in the United States "the spirit of trade and avidity for profits" distinguished all classes. Two decades later Alexis de Tocqueville found that the whole American nation was engaged in productive industry and that it carried its business qualities into other social sectors, such as agriculture. Francis J. Grund from Austria, who also visited the United States in the 1830s, observed that "business is the very soul of an American." In midcentury the Hungarian revolutionary Ferenc Pulszky and his wife Theresa stated in their book *White Red Black* that "business is a passion with the Americans, not the means, but the very life of existence." Some thirty years later James Bryce pointed out that, whereas in Europe the ablest men go into civil service or the political arena, in the United States "much of the best ability, both for thought and for action, for planning and for executing, rushes into a field which is comparatively narrow in Europe, the business of developing the material resources of the country." Coming back to America in 1905, after twenty-five years, Bryce felt that business had come "to overshadow and dwarf all other interests, all other occupations."[2]

The impressions of the European visitors have been confirmed by later historians, who have pointed to the many differences between Europe and the United States concerning business dominance and attitudes towards entrepreneurship. Even if these distinctions have been leveled during the last four decades, in part due to an American influence on European business, scholars agree that before World War II the United States was molded by business interests to a much greater extent than Europe.

This basic difference between Europe and America has been explained by the relative absence in the latter of traditional social patterns and hereditary institutions, that is, of a "feudal" European system characterized by aristocratic values, a strong centralized state, a petty-bourgeois economy, and peasant agriculture.[3] Some have proposed that Calvinism and its work ethic had a greater impact in the United States than in Europe; that the migration to America and within the country led to innovation and modification of traditional values; and that the geography of America, with its vast areas of rich soil, turned people more into real estate operators than farmers.[4]

According to John Sawyer, the European "feudal" system, at least in France, affected business recruitment, motivation, and behavior. As Bryce had also observed, in Europe the ablest were discouraged from going into business, and preferred to go into the diplomatic or military services, the civil service, the professions, politics, or the arts.[5] European businessmen became less motivated in their enterprises because their societies did not regard material progress as a primary goal and because the accumulation of money gave less prestige than on the other side of the Atlantic. The European entrepreneur was never allowed, like his American counterpart, to feel that his work was a "calling" or a "mission."[6] The *manorialism* of Europe, as Sawyer calls the system, also left its imprint on business behavior by making it more static, more afraid to take risks and to sacrifice unprofitable enterprises, less willing to enter into mergers and mass production.[7]

By comparison, America from the start adopted a system that was favorable to industrial capitalism, and during the nineteenth century business molded an institutional pattern that forwarded its interests. American society favored, as Sawyer states,

> not only the more abstract patterns such as universalism, rationality, specialization, transferability of resources, worldly orientation, and the like; but also those most directly related to entrepreneurship—individualism; competitive economic activity within an impersonal market; mobility, social and geographical; achieved as against ascribed statuses, with economic achievement the main ladder of advancement; emphasis on "success" in a competitive occupational system as the almost universally prescribed goal; money income as a primary reward and symbol of success; the institutionalization of innovation, risk-taking, change and growth.[8]

Even when the comparison to Europe is left aside, the United States has been seen as a business civilization in the sense that business has had such a prominent position in American society that it has often exerted considerable influence over other social sectors. Historians have made clear that entrepreneurism had great impact as early as in the colonial period and that since around 1815 business values have been dominant at the expense of other value systems.[9]

From this time up to at least 1929, as Cochran says, "entrepreneurs dominated and largely shaped the American physical and social environment."[10] Krooss and Gilbert point out that it has become a cliché to say that America is a business civilization but that the cliché rests on solid ground. American culture and mores, they claim, have been shaped more by business than by any other institution.[11] Krooss, in another context, attempts a general analysis of American civilization:

> From its beginnings, the United States was devoted to the business ideal. Business influenced the American's habits, customs, manners, folklore, and way of thinking much more than politics, philosophy, or religion. The American spirit was a business spirit; the American system was a business system.... Even the farmer... and the labor union ...were imbued with the business spirit.[12]

It is obvious to any student of American history that, even though business may continuously have molded the American experience, the strength of its impact has varied in different periods. The traditional view of the Progressive Era and the New Deal, for instance, has been that they were characterized by declining business domination, but some scholars claim that even these periods of seeming government regulation were in effect products of business influence.[13] There is little disagreement, however, about the fact that in such eras as the latter part of the nineteenth century and the 1920s business had a decisive impact on American society.

In this study I want to investigate how business, as a dominant institution, influenced a less forceful social sector, religion and particularly Protestantism, in matters of ideology, organization, and methods. I could equally well have studied the business impact on government, labor, education, or the military; but I have chosen religion because, together with the quest for material gain, the religious experience has also extensively molded the American character. The study is limited to the relationship between business and Protestantism and excludes other churches. The period selected for my investigation is the 1920s, that is, 1920–1929, a decade when business was invested with an authority unusual even in the American tradition.

The Swedish archbishop Söderblom was not only struck by America's entrepreneurism but equally so by its idealism; and he was puzzled, like most Europeans, by the combination. Since colonial times business and religion have put a special imprint on America, and they have existed in a special interdependent relationship. It would, for instance, be difficult to imagine, in Europe today, such religious phenomena as Robert Schuller's gospel of success and abundance or the business methods of Jerry Falwell's Moral Majority. Furthermore, religion in America has not only contributed to the emergence of the capitalistic spirit, as Max Weber claimed, but it has also lent an idealistic and spiritual dimension to entrepreneurial activities. The second half of this study will be devoted to how religion influenced business in the twenties, and how business appropriated religious values and became a pseudoreligion.

NOTES

1. Nathan Söderblom, *Från Uppsala till Rock Island: En Predikofärd i Nya Världen* (Stockholm: Svenska Kyrkans Diakonistyrelses Bokförlag, 1924), p. 251.

2. Marc Pachter, ed., *Abroad in America: Visitors to the New Nation, 1776–1914* (Reading, Mass.: Addison-Wesley Publishing Company, 1976), p. 16; Oscar Handlin, ed., *This Was America* (Cambridge, Mass.: Harvard University Press, 1949), pp. 143, 239; Alexis de Tocqueville, *Democracy in America*, Vol. 2 (1840; New York: Vintage Books, 1945), pp. 165–67; Thomas C. Cochran, *Challenges to American Values: Society, Business, and Religion* (New York: Oxford University Press, 1985), p. 26; James Bryce, *The American Commonwealth*, rev. ed. (New York: Macmillan Company, 1919–1920), I, pp. 77–78; II, p. 72; Allan Nevins, *America Through British Eyes* (New York: Oxford University Press, 1948), p. 385.

3. Thomas C. Cochran, *American Business in the Twentieth Century* (Cambridge, Mass.: Harvard University Press, 1972), pp. 4–5; John E. Sawyer, "The Entrepreneur and the Social Order: France and the United States," in William Miller, ed., *Men in Business: Essays in the History of Entrepreneurship* (Cambridge, Mass.: Harvard University Press, 1952), pp. 11–13.

4. William S. Schlamm, "European Business Is Different," *Fortune* 41 (February 1950), p. 98; Cochran, *Challenges to American Values*, p. 8.

5. Sawyer, "The Entrepreneur and the Social Order," p. 14; see also Herman E. Krooss, *American Economic Development: The Progress of a Business Civilization* (Englewood Cliffs, N.J.: Prentice-Hall, 1974), pp. 66–67; and Arthur H. Cole, *Business Enterprise in Its Social Setting* (Cambridge, Mass.: Harvard University Press, 1959), pp. 105–6.

6. Sawyer, "The Entrepreneur and the Social Order," p. 16; Thomas C. Cochran, *Business in American Life: A History* (New York: McGraw-Hill Book Co., 1972), p. 27.

7. Sawyer, "The Entrepreneur and the Social Order," pp. 17–19; Schlamm, "European Business," pp. 184–85.

8. Sawyer, "The Entrepreneur and the Social Order," p. 21.

9. Cochran, *Business in American Life*, pp. 9–10, 43; Perry Miller, *American Character: A Conversion* (Santa Barbara: University of California Press, 1962), p. 23.

10. Cochran, *Business in American Life*, p. 245. For discussions on how business dominated American society in specific periods, see Thomas C. Cochran, *200 Years of American Business* (New York: Basic Books, Inc., 1977), pp. 13–14; Herman E. Krooss and Charles Gilbert, *American Business History* (Englewood Cliffs, N.J.: Prentice-Hall, 1972), pp. 144, 162; Elisha P. Douglass, *The Coming of Age of American Business: Three Centuries of Enterprise, 1600–1900* (Chapel Hill, N.C.: University of North Carolina Press, 1971), p. 537; Louis Galambos, *The Public Image of Big Business in America, 1880–1940* (Baltimore, Md.: Johns Hopkins University Press, 1975), p. 5.

11. Krooss and Gilbert, *American Business History*, p. 7.

12. Krooss, *American Economic Development*, p. 167.

13. See Gabriel Kolko, *The Triumph of Conservatism: A Reinterpretation of American History, 1900–1916* (Glencoe: Free Press, 1973); Melvin I. Urofsky, *Big Steel and the Wilson Administration* (Columbus: Ohio State University Press, 1969); James Weinstein, *The Corporate Ideal in the Liberal State, 1900–1918* (Boston: Beacon Press, 1968); Paul D. Conkin, *The New Deal* (New York: Thomas Y. Crowell, 1967).

1

Business Enthroned

The American 1920s has been defined as an "age of business" or the "halcyon years of business prestige."[1] There have undoubtedly been other "ages of business" in American history. The period 1800–1840 has been called "the business revolution," and the latter half of the nineteenth century has been termed "the age of enterprise."[2] The business dominance is thus not exclusive to the 1920s, but this period, historians agree, was one of the most business-oriented in the American tradition. In this decade after the Great War, business ideology "permeated the churches, the courts, the colleges, the press," as Schlesinger says.[3] Almost everyone, according to Krooss and Gilbert, "was happy with business. Intellectuals who had always been the first to challenge its hegemony offered little opposition. The antibusiness writers had all but disappeared. A few of the academicians and lawyers remained critical, but not bitterly so, and articulate though they were, they were drowned out in the general swell of business adulation."[4] The American businessman emerged, as Bernstein makes clear, as the hero of the period with an influence by no means limited to economic matters.[5]

The Great War has been seen as a watershed between a prewar reformist era of government regulation and a postwar era of free enterprise and business hegemony. The more studies have been devoted to this period, however, the clearer a picture of continuity and progression has emerged. The business ideology and methods that came to be so influential in the twenties had all been introduced before the war. The war only served as a catalyst speeding up an economic development that was already underway.

The form of business that emerged in the postwar period was based in mass production, achieved by a more efficient exploitation of natural resources and by a continued development of technology and scientific management. It was further characterized by managerial capitalism, which had slowly replaced the financial and family capitalism of the turn of the century.[6] This shift from owner to manager created a need for more competent managers, which resulted in a considerable growth in business education.[7] Moreover, after having been pummeled by members of the progressive movement, business had gradually become more sensitive to public opinion. This sensitivity led to a courtship of employees in the forms of welfare programs, employee stock ownership, and personnel counselling.[8] It also resulted in a growth of business publicity and advertising as means of increasing consumption and of spreading business values to large sections of the people.[9]

The situation in postwar Europe was different. The war had left the European economy in shambles. The British, French, and German societies were characterized by instability, inflation, and unemployment. The German economic structure was worn out after the war effort. Austria-Hungary broke into fragments at the end of the war. The economy of France was in disarray; its northern provinces were devastated. As a result the United States took over the role as the world's economic leader; the economic center of the world moved from London to New York. After 1924, and partially due to the appointment of the Dawes commission, the European economy improved considerably. In this restoration of Europe, businessmen were asked to be the prime movers. The influence of business over European societies consequently grew in the 1920s, and so did the prestige of the businessman, but by comparison to the United States these countries were still fairly unaffected by the business spirit.

As we have seen, American society at large has always had a comparatively favorable view of business. In the 1920s this positive attitude was at a peak. Business was seen as the force that had made the world safe for democracy, that had transformed the United States from a debtor to a creditor nation, that was producing an ever-spreading prosperity, and that was responsible for the growing industrial peace. In general, in this decade business dominated the other social sectors not by coercion but by consent. The business civilization was founded on the principles of voluntarism and contract. Obviously, business did not completely refrain from coercive methods—in its relations to labor, for instance—but during this period it could rely more on its authority and did not need to exert its power.

THE IMPROVEMENT OF BUSINESS

Becoming more conscious of the demands of the public, business launched a campaign to win friends. By improving its performance even more and by persuading the public through mass media, business intended to cleanse its escutcheon from whatever stains remained from the robber baron and trust-busting ages.[10] It is impossible to determine to what extent other social sectors voluntarily accepted business as social leader and to what extent they were manipulated into such an acceptance. One can safely say, however, that the campaign to sell business to the American people would not have been effective if it had not been based on a fairly general popular belief. Frederick Lewis Allen is right in stating:

> The business propaganda of those days is not to be thought of as the dark device of a minority to convert or bamboozle a skeptical majority. It merely reflected and intensified the views of the crowd, merely added somewhat to the size and velocity of a snowball which was already rolling downhill.[11]

A common practice in the campaign to improve the reputation of business was to draw attention to the poor ethics that had characterized American business during the latter part of the nineteenth century, and then compare those to the high business morals of the 1920s. E. E. Calkins wrote, for instance, that business before the turn of the century had been no place for a man with scruples or ideals: "Buying and selling retained the character of bartering, with all that the word implied of haggling, misrepresentation, deceit, trickery, short weight. *Caveat emptor* was the unofficial slogan.... Sharp practice was taken for granted and even applauded." Now, however, in the 1920s, Calkins continued, even "the most jaundiced observer" had to admit that business was ethically better than it used to be. Business had learned the "priceless truth" that "honesty is really the best policy." The old idea of a bargain was that one of the parties must lose. "The modern idea is that both parties must be satisfied, and that the exchange of goods or service for money can be carried on successfully and profitably with clear consciences on both sides. The golden rule is not only good ethics but a workable business axiom."[12]

Alfred P. Sloan, president of General Motors, preached the same message. The old attitude of "the public be damned" had altogether changed, he claimed. "The great modern corporations live, as it were, in glass houses, open to the public gaze, and of course no one who lives and works in such a situation can afford to be other than honorable, humane, and strictly obedient to economic law." The big corporation had justified itself as an instrument for the production of goods and as a social force. According to Sloan, "it has corrected the evils that seemed years ago to be inherent in it; and, as to-day conducted, it is a good employer, a good neighbor, and a good citizen."[13] The president of the American Telephone & Telegraph Company, Walter S. Gifford, made a similar comparison when stating that the old business rule, "every fellow for himself," and the old business law, "the survival of the fittest," had become obsolete. The new business leader knew the limits of his power and recognized his responsibilities to the public. The corporation manager of the twenties had "civic sense, a broad human understanding, administrative ability, sound judgment based on analysis of facts, as well as courage, initiative, and leadership." The old "captains of industry" with their selfish, arbitrary, and semicrooked rule, had been replaced by "statesmen of industry" who had entered the game not primarily to acquire wealth but to be able to accomplish something and to be of service to the public.[14]

Many people from the rest of society shared the view that business had undergone a moral rebirth. Compared to the old style businessman, Walter Lippmann stated, the modern executive of a great corporation could not play the monarch. He must cope with so many "stubborn and irreducible facts" and adjust his own preferences to the preferences of others to such an extent that he became a "relatively disinterested person." He was no longer driven by an acquisitive spirit. The sheer complexity of the modern business corporation, Lippmann meant, made it regulate and discipline itself.[15] The editor of *The Saturday Evening Post* wrote that the "inequitable practices which were once familiar routine and an unconsidered part of the day's work" had become extinct in most of the larger business organizations. The business leaders had cleaned their house thoroughly. "First, they proved that honesty pays. Presently they proceeded to demonstrate that the golden rule pays even better."[16] In a similar comparative fashion, Arthur Train's novel *The Needle's Eye* (1924) pitted the old relentless industrialist against the modern democratic businessman.[17] Thornton Graham is the old-fashioned, paternalistic owner of a West Virginia coal mine who refuses to let his workers enter the union and who opposes every form of democratization in business. He lives in New York far away from the mine and devotes much time to collecting valuable paintings that he donates to various museums. When Graham suddenly dies, his son John, the hero of the story, takes over. Influenced by Christ's teachings and by socialism, he tries to give away his fortune of $100 million to the poor, but discovers that it cannot be done. He is stuck with his holdings and realizes that he has a responsibility towards people dependent on him. He comes to understand that both the old businessmen like his father and the blue-eyed socialists are wrong. Towards the end of the book, he shoulders his responsibility towards "his men" and comes to the conclusion that business must be a service that benefits all; that the workers have a right to organize; that business must be profitable; that there must be cooperation between employers and employees; and that absentee ownership is evil. John Graham becomes the epitome of the enlightened businessman of the twenties.

Even in quarters where one would have expected the business culture to be criticized, its accomplishments were often acknowledged and even praised. The intention of Harold Stearns's *Civilization in the United States* was to denounce the whole of American culture. Since the volume was so censorious in general, it would only have been natural if it had dismissed American business culture as superficial, acquisitive, and at bottom dishonest. However, Garet Garrett's contribution, "Business," did nothing of the sort. Garrett took exception, it is true, to the speculative abuse of credit, "those alterations of high and low prices, inflation and deflation, which produce panics and perilous political disorder,"[18] but his overall attitude towards business was very appreciative, implying that such abuses were already on their way out. He compared the state of commerce at an earlier period to the one of the twenties and was favorably impressed on the one hand by the fantastic change that had turned America from a debtor nation into a creditor nation and on the other by the essential honesty that characterized American business in the 1920s. Stuart Chase was another person who had long seen American business as a "steadfast enemy," but who now had to admit that it had undergone an impressive improvement in the twenties. American commerce and industry, he wrote, had

> in the past few years increased production, increased the real wages of the wayfaring man, reduced the hours of labor, made inroads in the blight of child labor, adjusted for the better the position of women in industry, improved working conditions in the shop, and introduced an energetic campaign against industrial waste and loss.[19]

THE HERO OF THE AGE

As business gained increased authority in the twenties, the American businessman assumed an influential role. He became the nucleus around which society was grouped, the authority to whom men and women paid attention, a hero, often idolized and romanticized (see illustration 1). He reached this position not only through his achievements as a creator of prosperity but also by means of the campaign referred to previously.

One may wonder why there was a need for a campaign in favor of the businessman at all, if the American public generally approved of him. First, the muckrakers of the prewar era had done their job well, and the image of the rapacious man of business was still lingering in the back of the American mind. Secondly, several intellectuals and artists refused to toe the line; they zestfully continued to lampoon the man of commerce as a childish, grasping ignoramus. And even though the H. L. Menckens and the Sinclair Lewises presumably did not have the influence that their book sales might indicate, and even though other intellectuals disagreed with these "self-constituted guardians of the higher sophistication" and "dabblers in dainties," as Charles A. Beard called them,[20] business still felt that it should do what it could to counteract the evil forces of ridicule. It did not feel threatened by such lampoons as George S. Kaufman's and Marc Connelly's *Beggar on Horseback* (1924), which according to the preface only wanted to be "a small and facetious disturbance in the rear of the Church of the Gospel of Success,"[21] but such infamous assaults as Lewis's *Babbitt* had to be met with a counteroffensive.

Whether reflections of altered values or expressions of conscious indoctrination, the pictures of the American businessman in the 1920s portray him in different roles and emphasize his sundry qualities. He is depicted as the uncut diamond, or the new social authority, or the sophisticated thinker, or the professional man, or, finally, the mythical hero of the twentieth century.

The first group of portraits conceded that satirists like Lewis were partially right in saying that the American businessman was uncivilized and mercenary. But this rough surface, they argued, only hid the gem buried beneath. In spite of his apparent crudity, the businessman embodied a steadfastness, courage,

Illustration 1

The American businessman—the hero of the age. (*The Christian Herald*, January 1, 1927. Used with permission.)

and vitality that were worthy of admiration. Numerous articles and short stories exalted the simple man of ambition who rose to success. Robert A. Long, for instance, was a poor farm boy with scanty education and, according to himself, with no "business genius," but who possessed the virtues of industry and "absolute honesty," through which he eventually became the biggest lumberman in the Southwest.[22] William E. Peck, the hero of Peter B. Kyne's bestselling story *The Go-Getter* (1922),[23] also belongs in this category of unpolished-but-indomitable successes; and so does Andy Grayson, in a short story called "Graysons, Unlimited," who through thrift, industry, "the angle of his jaw," and a certain amount of education manages to get the "impossible" order from the "impossible" client and is rewarded with a much-coveted territory.[24]

Maybe the best example of this Silas Lapham–like businessman is Mr. Tinker in Booth Tarkington's *The Plutocrat* (1927). Going to North Africa on a vacation, Mr. Tinker is initially seen through the eyes of the refined, anemic Boston playwright, Mr. Ogle. Ogle is repelled by the backslapping, guffawing Tinker who dominates every company, and he cannot understand how the sophisticated Mrs. Momoro, another fellow traveler, can be attracted to such a vulgar specimen of the human race. By the end of the novel, however, the effeminate Ogle has dwindled into a midget, while the uncouth Tinker has grown into a giant, and Ogle is forced to acknowledge the greatness of this American businessman:

> And, in the end, what *was* the man? "Barbarian," "Carthaginian," "Goth," he had been called; but with qualifications: a barbarian, but a great one; a Carthaginian, but a great one;—a Goth, the little old English lady had just said; but she called him a magnificent one.

In case somebody missed the message, Tarkington gives us one last glimpse of Tinker, in a "cloud of dust against the sun," riding away as "the New Roman," as a "mockingly triumphant charioteer riding home to glory in the arena of the Circus Maximus."[25]

The businessman was also portrayed as the new social leader who had replaced all former authorities. Many articles and books paid homage to him, and his abilities were favorably compared to those of professional men. Stuart Chase, skeptical of the new position of businessmen, wrote: "They have ousted the philosopher, teacher, statesman, editor and preacher as the spiritual leader of the mass of men. They dominate government, press, university, church, the arts."[26] Charles A. Beard agreed as to the businessman's new authority:

> College presidents wait in his outer chambers until he finds time to consider their prayers. Clergymen pay court to him in the interest of cathedrals, missions, and good works. Advertising agents tell him that Christ was created in his image and intimate that the angels are a little bit lower in the firmament than his most excellent self.[27]

The preachers, who earlier had been regarded as "first citizens," according to Winthrop Hudson,[28] had been superseded by the men of business. The businessman's contact with actualities had made him "an honester man and a straighter thinker," said one clergyman, who also confessed that he would rather leave his case in the hands of ten successful American businessmen than in the hands of ten bishops.[29] Others felt that the big business executive had greater opportunities to "influence the lives of thousands of men and women" than the professional preachers had and that they could be of greater service.[30] One minister left his calling for one he considered even nobler; he went into business. "In my new work," he wrote, "I have found greater opportunity for real service than I had in all my nine years as a minister. . . . Above all, I am happy in my work. I am happy because I am doing something vital, and because I am serving, in the larger sense of the word."[31] Eugene O'Neill's *Dynamo* also reflects these changing values when Reuben Light's mother vows that her son shall never become a minister like his father, grandfather, and greatgrandfather but will go into business and earn money.

Politicians were also looked upon as being less competent than businessmen. Many were convinced that the commercial class was much more suited than the politicians to run the country. Edward A. Filene, a representative of business interests, gave reasons why business was a better instrument than politics to achieve a better social order. Business operates all the time, he pointed out, while politics is efficient only at intervals. Business deals with concrete things that affect our daily lives, while politics deals too much "in airy abstractions" that are inadequate to live by. Business determines the careers of most people; politics determines chiefly the careers of officeholders.[32] E. E. Calkins agreed that politicians had played out their role; this meant that it was time to acknowledge the businessman as the true leader of society. He was doing more for social progress than anyone else: "No king, or general, or priest, is accomplishing as much, even in the terms of his own métier, as the captains of industry."[33]

It was also argued that the businessman had greater ability and greater insights into things that really mattered than intellectuals and artists. Aldous Huxley's "On the Margin" was quoted as proof that it was more difficult to compose an advertisement than to write a sonnet. Businessmen were poets, one admirer held; they did not express themselves in words, but "in deeds and action every day of their lives." They were also philosophers who took the best of philosophy and put it to work with the result that "in real wisdom the intelligent business man has far outdistanced the theoretic philosopher."[34]

Still another way of trying to improve the status of the businessman—apart from depicting him as coarse-but-capable or better than other classes of men—was to deny his crudity altogether and portray him rather as the epitome of dignified behavior. He was seen as a true aristocrat, whose ideals, manners, ways of life, and standard of success the great mass of Americans strove to make their own.[35] He was viewed as a man "of discernment, of vision, and of ideals,"[36] a prophet who "must cultivate the habit of looking ahead, harden himself in the habit of thinking straight from cause to effect, the habit of thinking impersonally."[37] He was represented as the opposite of a roughneck, as an urbane gentleman, or, as one booster of business put it, "Courtesy is one of the finest products now being manufactured in the industries of the U.S.A."[38]

Numerous success stories were published underlining in particular the noble qualities of the men portrayed. For instance, Walter S. Gifford, had not reached his position through "pyrotechnics" and "fireworks," it was pointed out, but by means of sound judgment, hard work, and sober knowledge. He was delineated as a dependable, modest, sophisticated Harvard man.[39] Alfred P. Sloan was similarly held forth as a representative of the new school of corporation executives:

> These men of the newer type are a distinct contrast with the sledgehammer personalities of the earlier era. They do not lack force, but force is not their outstanding quality. They are doers, but perhaps even more conspicuously they are thinkers. Their task is to deal with human relationships upon a vast scale, to study economic principles, to lay out policies for the permanent direction of their prodigious companies. They combine in a most interesting way the qualities of the man of action and the philosopher. Mr. Sloan is characteristically of this type.[40]

It was often argued that business had reached a position where it should be accepted as a profession. This campaign to make business a profession had started before the war with the publication of Louis D. Brandeis's *Business—A Profession*.[41] Business had been self-seeking before the turn of the century, it was conceded, and thus not respectable. Then there had rightfully been a gulf between business and the professions. Now in the twenties, however, it was argued, the ethics of the businessman had improved so drastically that he had bridged the gulf. Business had adopted, according to one commentator, "one of the cardinal principles of the professions in considering the common good before the interests of its individual members."[42] Because of the "responsible attitude" of businessmen, Gifford assured his readers, "business is becoming a profession."[43] To convince the American people that the businessman was worthy of being called a "professional" man, many articles emphasized that he was of greater service to American society than most representatives of the professions:

> At the head of the list of all the professions is that of salesmanship. It is the salesman who keeps aglow the furnace-fires of the factory and the forge; it is the salesman who keeps on every sea, headed for every port, the laden ships of commerce; it is the salesman who makes possible the great cities, who builds the railroads, and gives employment to the myriads of workingmen throughout the land.[44]

The fact that the businessman's occupation was so much concerned with profit making seems to have been regarded as an obstacle to be overcome. The business advocates consequently tried to show that men like Gerard Swope, the President of General Electric, worked for something besides money. Swope and his fellow executives, it was pointed out, pursued their work with the

> disinterestedness with which a scientist follows a line of research. The interest of creating an entity out of a great corporation—something more than a mere money-making machine—guiding it in making industrial history with chemists and engineers as pilots, invoking advertising adding to the sum total of human comfort and even human happiness, as happiness goes in these days, offers more real thrills than any of the old-fashioned professions can offer.[45]

And besides, others argued, what was wrong with making money? The businessman *must* make money to be able to be of service. In his job as businessman, one critic said, "a man may have all the intellectual adventure and joy of service that come to the teacher or preacher, without the handicap of starvation wages. [Making money] gives a freedom and power, the lack of which so often hampers the 'professional' man."[46]

Some commentators even went so far in their accolades of the American businessman as to appoint him the romantic hero of the age. The work of making and selling things had formerly been looked upon as both "sordid and humdrum," one of them stated, but now it was acquiring a glamour of romance, and he continued:

> The type that once was a Ulysses, a Columbus, a Roland, a Sir Francis Drake, a Benvenuto Cellini, or a Balboa, is today a manufacturer whose business is really the charger or the galleon with which he sets forth to seek this modern version of adventure. ... Business is today *the* profession. It offers something of the glory that in the past was given to the crusader, the soldier, the courtier, the explorer, and sometimes the martyr—the test of wits, of brain, of quick thinking, the spirit of adventure, and especially the glory of personal achievement.... Business is today the Field of the Cloth of Gold.[47]

Another promoter of business ideals was convinced that if Carlyle had written his book on heroes and hero worship in the 1920s, the businessman would have been included as a matter of course. The "hero stuff" was now to be found in the world of business, whose spirit had changed to such an extent that "we are now living in an era when righteousness and not rapacity brings reward; when a stain on the trade mark causes as quick a challenge as once did a blot on the escutcheon."[48] Why seek romance in Arabia or on the moon, one admirer wrote, when we can find it here and now:

> Heroism is never the companion of idleness. The very essence of romance is *action*. American business is today creating enough material for a thousand Odysseys—sure to come. And epics of construction, not of destruction, they will be. Then why should not the heart beat high at the thought that we are the fortunate ones who are worthy players in the great event. Romance is here and now.[49]

BUSINESS THE CIVILIZER

A recurrent thought in the 1920s was that business and the capitalistic system were the foundation for all individual and social progress. In his article "Business the Civilizer," E. E. Calkins emphasized this ameliorative role of commerce and industry and came to the conclusion that the only sensible thing to do was to turn the administration of this planet over to the businessman, the only person capable of creating peace and harmony in the world.

Numerous general statements by business sympathizers were printed to the effect that industry was "the fundamental basis of civilization" or that business was one of "humanity's most promising instruments for its emancipation" or that the world "will have progressed magnificently when most of its activities have been truly 'commercialized'."[50] When they tried to be more specific, they explained that it was through capitalism—by obtaining and using capital—that humankind had risen "out of the cave and the wigwam." Through the natural motive of private selfishness on the part of the capitalist, this same writer felt, the world's surplus capital will be applied "where it will do the world the most good," thereby unwittingly paying homage to Adam Smith's theory of the "invisible hand."[51]

But commercialism was not only presented as the basis of modern social development; commerce had—from the time of the most primitive societies—always been dealing with "the fundamental necessities of life." "In its initial steps," Gerard Swope wrote, "it began before any of the arts or professions, before medicine or law or religion, and the very fact that it was a vital necessity for every human being made it something that everyone had of necessity to be engaged in at least to some extent."[52] And not only was business the most basic segment of social life, it was also the source of inspiration without which culture in general would wither, or as one critic preferred to phrase it: "No nation has ever been pre-eminent in art, science, literature, and general culture that did not first excel in commerce. Commerce leads the way, and all arts, all professions, all culture follow."[53]

As a consequence of this reasoning, the commercial spirit was seen as the foremost force in molding personality; "business is . . . a most successful manufacturer of character," as Glen Buck expressed it. On the one hand, business made a man truly moral; on the other, it made him well educated. If a man was to succeed in business, the argument went, such virtues as honesty, persistence, courage, thrift, courtesy, loyalty, and generosity were "almost imposed upon him." To attain his material purpose, he "must practice them all." The practice of business, it was held, consequently tends "to the development of the ethical nature and inculcates its own virtues in the businessman."[54] Similarly, Edward Bok expressed the idea that no other force was better fitted than industry to foster these moral qualities:

In fact the successful outcome of industry depends upon certain moral standards. Thrift, for instance, a higher standard of honor, the keeping of a man's word, steadiness, sobriety, a recognition of honorable dealings—all these Christian virtues have been brought directly into the life of civilized nations by Industrialism. The whole fabric of Business rests upon these moral forces."[55]

The business spirit also encourages a person to become educated, many writers pointed out, and to become truly civilized. One only had to look at the examples of successful businessmen to see the truth of this and to realize that what was needed was not a college education, but self-education. One book explained:

There is hardly a captain of industry, no matter how meager his schooling when a boy, who has not become an educated man, a man of wide knowledge, of keen judgement, a student of human nature. Most financial and business leaders have also contrived to steep themselves in history, particularly the biographies of the world's most famous achievers.

Financiers like Otto H. Kahn and industrial giants like Daniel Guggenheim had made it a "cast iron rule" to read for at least an hour every night.[56] Another book made clear that the "really cultured" men were businessmen. One of the foremost Greek scholars of the world was a successful American businessman. A dozen of Chicago's industrial leaders could earn good livings by the pictures they painted in spare moments. The musical compositions of one American man of commerce were played by symphony orchestras the world over. But this refinement did not only characterize the tycoons. Under the influence of business unnumbered thousands of "office slaves," the author explained, had become "discriminating collectors of first editions, fine etchings and the best of art's handiwork."[57]

If business made the individual improve in morals and learning, it also had a civilizing effect on the whole of society, according to many commentators. Commerce was the fountainhead of all culture, a conviction I have already touched upon previously. Society became more honest, more willing to serve because of its business spirit. Such organizations as the Standard Oil Company and the Steel Trust were held forth as "Christianized" corporations, which had "touched the hem of Christ's garment and felt the virtue that comes out of him." Science and education could not help being influenced by this commercial spirit, the author commented, "and one has good hope even for the ecclesiastical corporations. They cannot escape the spirit of which there is so much in the world and more coming."[58]

Business was also presented as a champion of beauty. One writer felt that there was little room for beauty in the twenties. There was no real appreciation of the artistic in newspapers, magazines, books or movies. Churchmen, schoolmen, doctors, lawyers, engineers, and politicians showed no understanding for the graceful and lovely. The shining exception, however, was business, which had come to realize the worth of beautiful design. As proof the article cited the new building of the Cunard Company on Broadway, which had become "a Mecca for lovers of beauty," and the Bowery Savings Bank on East 42nd Street, whose banking room was "a revelation of what our architects can accomplish when given the opportunity." Beauty was not only spiritually uplifting, it was pointed out, but offered additional advantages: "As the public will gladly pay more for beauty, whether it be found in a building, a garden, or in dress and house furnishings—the businessman with vision will do his utmost to foster art in the community, for he knows that 'beauty pays'."[59]

The cultural climate was intimately dependent on the world of commerce in at least two ways. First, business created the conditions necessary for a culture to develop. The more active business was in a community, the more "productive" was science, the more "flourishing" was art, the more "brilliant" was literature. Business had made it possible for the artist to give his time to his creation and had established a market for his products.[60] Secondly, the cultural life of America would have been infinitely less thriving without the numerous gifts and endowments given by businessmen. "There is no other country," explained one book, "in which rich men are so liberal in the endowment of all educational and benevolent enterprises as this country."[61] Booth Tarkington observed that countless seats of learning, institutions for scientific and hygienic research, hospitals, libraries, museums, art schools, and collections of masterpieces in art would not have existed without the generosity of the businessman, who was driven by "that passion of his for the enlarging and the bettering of everything—his business, his city and his country."[62]

BUSINESS AND GOVERNMENT

The improved economy, the publicity drive, and organized business pressure combined to let business exert a considerable authority over other institutions such as the professions, the schools, and the press. This influence was even more evident on government, labor, and the Protestant church.[63]

Shortly after the war, the American people elected a man who saw himself as a businessman, Warren G. Harding, and throughout the 1920s continued to elect as presidents men who were proud to identify with the business community: Calvin Coolidge and Herbert Hoover. These presidents chose as Cabinet members and administrators men with business experience. Andrew W. Mellon served in both the Harding and the Coolidge administrations. So did Herbert Hoover, before he became president. The ten members of Harding's cabinet, according to one estimate, were worth or could control, more than $600 million.[64] The business community had reason to feel that the right men were at the country's helm.

President Harding's personal view of business was friendly, to say the least. Shortly before he took office, he declared:

> American business is not a selfish privilege-seeking monster.... American business is a vast fabric woven through the upgoing years by the daily tasks of a faithful, virtuous

people. It is a blind idealist, indeed, who can find no thrill in that magnificent tapestry, and one blind indeed who recklessly pulls at its threads to unravel it.

Business must be helped to flourish, he maintained. Laws must be wiped out, the tariff and internal taxation readjusted to remove the burdens they impose upon "the will to create and produce, whether that will is the will of the big corporation or of the individual. . . . We must protect American business at home and we must aid and protect it abroad."[65] A few years later, at a business club convention in St. Louis, he expressed his faith in the American business spirit by stating that if this spirit could be planted throughout the world and turned to practical application "there would not be much wrong with the human procession."[66]

President Coolidge was no less appreciative of business than was President Harding. His often repeated utterances that "the business of America is business" and that "the man who builds a factory builds a temple; the man who works there worships there" made him into a favorite in business circles. And he remained a faithful champion of their ideals throughout his administration. He said:

True business represents the mutual organized effort of society to minister to the economic requirements of civilization. It rests squarely on the law of service. It has for its main reliance truth and faith and justice. In its larger sense it is one of the greatest contributing forces to the moral and spiritual advancement of the race.[67]

As his *Autobiography* reveals, Coolidge saw himself as the man who, by an active encouragement of business enterprise, had created the prosperity of the decade.[68]

As president, Herbert Hoover continued to uphold the unbroken fealty with business. As secretary of commerce between 1921 and 1929, his propagation of business values had endeared him to the world of commerce. More than once he saw it as his duty to defend business against its ill-informed critics, as he did, for instance, in 1924:

By some false analogy to the "survival of the fittest" many have conceived the whole of business to be a sort of "dog eat dog." We often lay too much emphasis upon its competitive features, too little upon the fact that it is in essence a great cooperative effort. And our home-made bolshevist-minded critics to the contrary, the whole economic structure of our nation and the survival of our high general levels of comfort are dependent upon the maintenance and development of leadership in the world of industry and commerce. It must be realized that any contribution to larger production, to wider diffusion of things consumable and enjoyable is a service to the community; and the men who honestly accomplish it deserve high public esteem.[69]

Such utterances as these were quoted again and again in various business publications to prove the merits and virtues of business.[70]

In the title of one of his articles, Harding coined one of the mottoes that came to characterize the business climate of the 1920s. He called his essay "Less Government in Business and More Business in Government (see illustration 2)." During the eight years preceding 1920, the year when the article was written, American government had been allowed on the one hand "to engage too much in enterprises which it has bungled and which American business can do better, safer, and cheaper, and on the other hand we have had too much ineffective tinkering with our economic structure." The result had been "a reckless governmental obstructing and harassing of business."[71] Coolidge was of the same opinion. He saw as one of his main duties as president to prevent government from interfering with business. The economy of the country should be run by the same men who had shown that they could handle money in industry and commerce.[72] Hoover felt that business should not be regulated but should be helped to become even more efficient. As secretary of commerce, he arranged over 200 conferences between 1921 and 1925 in which his department tried to convince various industries to become more efficient, to eliminate waste, and to reduce the varieties of manufactured articles. Hoover preferred not to see this as governmental regulation but described it as "putting government behind rather than in business."[73]

Business was grateful and had nothing but praise and support for its leaders in government. Samuel M. Vauclain wrote for instance about Coolidge: "Fortunately . . . we have a man at the wheel who won't be dominated. And in this man every sound, sensible business man in this country, regardless of party, has confidence. He feels that the United States is absolutely safe so long as this man sits in the President's chair."[74] Hoover was given the honorary epithet of "Super-Business Man" and was commended for the way he had cleared the road to free enterprise from many of its obstacles.[75]

Harding's article suggested not only less government in business but also more business in government, and this was a piece of advice that was gladly followed by himself and his successors. Harding stated that America was proud of her business methods:

> We have squeezed out of our method of doing business a good deal of inefficiency and waste. I think it would be a pretty fine piece of idealism to squeeze inefficiency and waste out of our administrative government. . . . Putting more American business methods into the government of the United States would save our resources, stop the drain upon the savings of our families, give us pride in doing something well, rather than saying something well.[76]

Shortly after Harding had been elected, he proceeded to organize the government on a business basis. He saw the Cabinet as a board of directors appointed to assist the chairman, that is, the president.[77] In May, 1921, the Budget and Accounting Act was passed, which was designed to bring business methods into government. Two years later Harding proudly announced: "Our govern-

Illustration 2

America wanted no interference with business prosperity. (*Commerce and Finance*, January 9, 1924.)

ment is the biggest business in the world.... I am rejoiced to speak to you as your President reporting on the state of affairs of the stockholders of this Republic."[78] Harding organized semiannual meetings on what he called "the Business Organization of the Government." At the second such meeting, Charles G. Dawes, then director of the Federal Budget System, spoke of the results achieved by the Harding administration: "The only reason we have gotten anywhere in this business reorganization of government is because we have not only completely absorbed, but I say completely demonstrated, the truth that the proper machinery with which to run governmental routine business must be similar to the machinery to run private routine business." The president, according to Dawes, should be looked upon "not as one engaged in carrying out great policies of State, or the members of the cabinet as his advisers upon these great policies, but as the head of a routine business organization and the members of the cabinet as nothing but the administrative vice presidents of this organization."[79]

One of the chief means of the business administrations of the twenties to help their colleagues in private industry was the reduction of taxes. Andrew W. Mellon, who embodied both the governmental and the private business spirit, saw to it that the surtax and the estate tax maximums were reduced from 40 to 20 percent each, that the inheritance levies were cut in half, and that the proposed gift tax was repealed. These tax reforms benefited the wealthy business community more than anyone else. According to one estimate, a man with a yearly income of one million dollars paid $200,000 in federal taxes after the tax reductions compared to the $600,000 he had paid before.[80] Mellon himself wrote in 1922: "Our very best thought... should be directed to seeing... that our system of taxation shall interfere to the least possible extent with the return of the country to normal industrial conditions."[81] To make up for the loss that these tax reductions meant, Mellon introduced license taxes, stamp taxes, and taxes on bank checks, all of which affected the public in general.

Business also received powerful help from the fact that such regulatory bodies as the Interstate Commerce Commission, the Federal Reserve Board, and the Federal Trade Commission were deprived of much of their power. The Sherman Antitrust Act and the Clayton Antitrust Act were still in existence, but they did not prevent a significant growth of business consolidation.[82] Instead of opposing mergers, the government rather welcomed combinations in the automobile industry, in the railroads, in the public utilities. The President of the Chamber of Commerce of the United States, John W. O'Leary, analyzed the shifting policy of the government in the following manner:

> The Sherman antitrust law, which at first was meant to prohibit any combination of any kind, however conducted, is now interpreted under the "rule of reason" to affect only such mergers as are shown to be hostile to the free play of competition and initiative. This is because freedom of individual enterprise is the keynote of our economic, industrial, and commercial system.[83]

BUSINESS AND LABOR

Business asked the government not only to smooth its path toward victory but also to roughen the road of its chief rival—labor. As a consequence, new labor laws were introduced and court decisions handed down that were detrimental to the cause of the workers.[84] One example is President Harding's successful quellings in 1922 of the strikes among the coal miners and the railroad shopmen. In the first instance, Harding simply ordered the mines to be opened; in the second, he asked the Federal Judge James Wilkerson to grant an injunction against the strikers. As Hicks puts it:

> Organized labor in general, if it had not known it before, knew now where the administration stood. It was clear enough, from the Wilkerson injunction and from the President's order to the state governors during the coal strike, that during industrial disputes the government would neither assist labor nor remain neutral; rather, it would throw its influence firmly on the employer's side. And it could trust the courts to rule accordingly.[85]

The unfriendly attitude of the government was not the only cause of the weakening of labor as a social force that took place during the twenties. Several other explanations can be found for the fact that the whole progressive movement suffered at this time. The labor unions did not work as zealously for their members as they had done, prosperity had made many workers content, and business had coaxed the workingman into believing that he should cooperate. Arthur S. Link points out that the common picture of the 1920s as "a period made almost unique by an extraordinary reaction against idealism and reform" is overdrawn; progressivism was not in decay but was "certainly on the downgrade."[86]

This decline in reform fervor was clearly noticeable in the labor unions, particularly in the fields of metal, machinery, and shipbuilding. The total union membership dropped from five million in 1920 to three-and-a-half million in 1923. During the same period of time, the American Federation of Labor lost 25 percent of its members, while the Industrial Workers of the World (IWW) was virtually wiped out. The Socialist Party, which in 1922 had 118,000 members, was reduced ten years later to one tenth of its former membership.[87]

The American Federation of Labor (AFL) wanted to have good relations with business. It shifted from a militant federation to an organization of respectability that often looked upon itself as a "necessary auxiliary of business," to use Bernstein's term. It saw itself as a bulwark against "radicalism" and as an upholder of the existing social order. Its president after 1925, William Green, both looked and acted like a businessman, earning the epithet of "the Calvin Coolidge of the labor movement." He was not unfavorable to the way in which business ran the country and saw it as his duty to come to its defense. He claimed that most businessmen wanted to maintain decent wage standards and humane conditions of employment, that they were not trying to exploit the workers, that they were inspired by a "keen sense of justice" and "a spirit of fair-dealing and fair-play." And Green was certainly not the only member of labor to commend the achievements of business. Many others sang the same song of praise, including the old muckraker Lincoln Steffens, who commented that "Big Business in America is producing what the Socialists held up for their goal: food, shelter, and clothing for all."[88]

Compared to their prewar predecessors, the leftist intellectuals of the twenties were less militant, more pessimistic, and more concerned with existential questions than with political matters. The intellectuals of the progressive era had shared an optimistic belief in the future and in man's ability to improve social conditions. From the prewar "Lyrical Left"—people like Mabel Dodge, Randolph Bourne, Floyd Dell, and John Reed—flowed an impressive creative energy and political commitment. Within a decade, however, this enthusiasm waned because of the business impact on American society, because of the disappointment over the war and the development of the Soviet experiment, because of inner strife, and because of oppression from the state. The careers of Walter Lippman and Max Eastman may be held forth as examples of the development from a position of social radicalism to one of a questioning and modification of the old ideology.[89]

There were still critical voices, it is true. But the longer the decade progressed, the more the expressions of social discontent were drowned by the encomiums offered up by government, labor, the church, and business itself, but it was also hushed up by the clink and rustle of money, the blaring of radios, the humming of household machines, the crackle of autos, and the rattle of stock-tickers. With a few glaring exceptions, the workingman was better off than before the war and found fewer reasons to complain about social injustices. He could not help being affected by the general optimism of the age. He worked fewer hours, had more time for leisure, and had more money in his pocket. He could buy a house and a car on the installment plan. Prosperity in the twenties became the great pacifier, a fact that the workingman himself may not have been aware of, but which his employer capitalized on. Businessmen realized that workingmen would not be willing to give up the good life—the house, the automobile, the radio, the telephone, the electric gadgets—that they had become used to. The automobile had become a "blessing to industrial relations," one business representative pointed out, and continued: "A man pays down a few dollars and then he can pay and pay and pay until he can't pay, but he has his machine, and believe me, one of these cheap automobiles will keep not only a man busy but his whole family busy, and we will have no trouble with them."[90]

A not uncommon argument at the time even held that the laborers were turning into capitalists. There was a rapid growth in labor's savings deposits. Laborers started to invest in the shares of corporations. Several labor banks came into existence. The first was established in 1920 in Washington, D.C., and by the end of 1924 the number had grown to about forty, located in several states. This argument about the laborer-turning-capitalist was usually propounded, not by labor, but by business.[91] What was not pointed out in the discussion, however, were certain facts. For instance, even though numerous workingmen owned shares, they owned so few each that their influence on the policy of the corporation was negligible.[92]

Business hastened to make use of the hesitancy and ambivalence that troubled the labor movement. It attempted, as we have seen above, to persuade the workingman that he was a capitalist only different in degree from his employer and that the traditional dissension between labor and capital had been based on a misunderstanding. We are all partners, these business advocates held, working for the same goal, or as Will H. Hays phrased it in his speech to the 1921 convention of the National Association of Letter Carriers:

> We must remember first that we are all one people; that we are all the workmanship of the same divine hand; that with our Creator there are neither kings nor subjects, masters nor servants, other than stewards of his appointment to serve each other according to our different opportunities and abilities.[93]

Business gained an influence over labor in other ways as well. Attractive but powerless company unions were organized in the corporations. The Open Shop system was introduced, which meant that an employer did not have to hire only union men and did not need to bargain collectively with the union. In the spirit of partnership, the great corporations also built living quarters, movie houses, clubs, and concert halls to be used by the workers. In doing so they hoped to kill two birds with one stone: to improve the lot of their employees, and to remove the threat of industrial discontent. In all honesty it must be said that a few industrialists—very few indeed—reacted against these "pacification" programs as the worst form of paternalism. Samuel M. Vauclain, who elsewhere spoke warmly for the partnership of business and labor, felt that the workingman had the right to his own leisure time:

> If, indeed, an organization is interested and sincere about this matter of industrial partnership, then let the gains come through on a real partnership basis. When two men are in business on a small scale and the profits are bigger than anticipated, the senior partner doesn't buy the junior partner a rocking horse. He increases his income. That's what men expect. Give them men's wages on men's jobs. If the profits of the company warrant it, increase those wages. Don't worry about how a worker spends his money. That's nobody's business but his own. Let him choose his own movie house, his own club, his own books, his own home. There's no need to uplift workers. They uplift themselves once they have the means.[94]

But most businessmen were not as enlightened as Mr. Vauclain; they felt that it was only natural that workers were dependent on them for most things in life.

That the business community in America harbored many unsolved problems and that it was leading the nation in some dubious directions became all too clear with the Crash of 1929 and the worldwide depression that hit its American bottom in 1933. While the 1920s lasted, however, businessmen rode a cresting wave of public esteem partly because of the new consumer goods they introduced in unprecedented number to a nation of eager consumers, and partly because their newfound art of public relations had created for them an exalted image. The image implied methods and values. The interaction of these methods and values with those of the Protestant church is the subject of the succeeding chapters.

NOTES

1. Arthur M. Schlesinger, Jr., *The Crisis of the Old Order, 1919–1933* (Boston: Houghton Mifflin Company, 1957), p. 71; Herman E. Krooss and Charles Gilbert, *American Business History* (Englewood Cliffs, N.J.: Prentice Hall, 1972) p. 10.
2. Thomas C. Cochran, *200 Years of American Business* (New York: Basic Books, Inc., 1977) p. 14; Thomas C. Cochran and William Miller, *The Age of Enterprise: A Social History of Industrial America* (New York: Harper & Row, 1961).
3. Schlesinger, *The Crisis*, p. 71.
4. Krooss and Gilbert, *American Business History*, p. 324.
5. Irving Bernstein, *The Lean Years: A History of the American Worker 1920–1933* (Boston: Houghton Mifflin Company, 1972), p. 88.
6. Alfred D. Chandler, Jr., *The Visible Hand: The Managerial Revolution in American Business* (Cambridge, Mass.: Harvard University Press, 1977), pp. 491–93.
7. Thomas C. Cochran, *Business in American Life: A History* (New York: McGraw-Hill Book Co., 1972) p. 248; Cochran, *200 Years of American Business*, p. 158.
8. Alan R. Raucher, *Public Relations and Business 1900–1929* (Baltimore, Md.: Johns Hopkins Press, 1968), p. 68.
9. Ibid., pp. 74, 93.
10. Morrell Heald, *The Social Responsibilities of Business: Company and Community, 1900–1960* (Cleveland: The Press of Case Western Reserve University, 1970), pp. 84–86; for the business reputation of the prewar period, see Thomas C. Cochran, *Basic History of American Business* (Princeton, N.J.: D. van Nostrand Company, 1959), p. 85; Robert H. Wiebe, *Businessmen and Reform: A Study of the Progressive Movement* (Cambridge, Mass.: Harvard University Press, 1962), pp. 207, 212–13; Louis Galambos, *The Public Image of Big Business in America 1880–1940* (Baltimore, Md.: Johns Hopkins University Press, 1975), Cochran, *Business in American Life*, pp. 240–41; Elisha P. Douglass, *The Coming of Age of American Business: Three Centuries of Enterprise, 1600–1900* (Chapel Hill, N.C.: University of North Carolina Press, 1971), pp. 520–22, 533.
11. Frederick Lewis Allen, *The Lords of Creation* (New York: Harper & Brothers, 1935), pp. 231–32.
12. Earnest Elmo Calkins, "Business the Civilizer," *The Atlantic Monthly* 141 (February 1928), pp. 146–50.
13. Alfred P. Sloan, Jr., "Modern Ideals of Big Business," *The World's Work* 52 (October 1926), pp. 695–99.
14. Walter S. Gifford, "The Changing Character of Big Business," *The World's Work* 52 (June 1926), pp. 166–68.

15. Walter Lippmann, *A Preface to Morals* (1929; New York: Time-Life Books, 1964), p. 240.

16. "The Golden Rule in Business," *The Saturday Evening Post* 201 (March 16, 1929), p. 24.

17. Arthur Train, *The Needle's Eye* (New York: Charles Scribner's Sons, 1924).

18. Harold E. Stearns, ed., *Civilization in the United States: An Enquiry by Thirty Americans* (London: Jonathan Cape, 1922), p. 413.

19. Stuart Chase, "New Outposts of Business and Industry," *The World Tomorrow* 11 (March 1928), pp. 107–11.

20. Charles A. Beard, "Is Babbitt's Case Hopeless?", *The Menorah Journal* 13 (January 1928), p. 22.

21. George S. Kaufman and Marc Connelly, *Beggar on Horseback* (New York: Boni and Liveright, 1924), p. 11.

22. Robert A. Long, "The Biggest Thing I Have Learned in Business," *The American Magazine* 89 (May 1920), pp. 60–61, 154–156.

23. Peter B. Kyne, *The Go-Getter: A Story That Tells You How to Be One* (New York: Cosmopolitan Book Corporation, 1922).

24. Sheldon Wills, "Graysons, Unlimited," *Munsey's Magazine* 72 (May 1921), pp. 686–94.

25. Booth Tarkington, *The Plutocrat* (Garden City, N.Y.: Doubleday, Page & Company, 1927), pp. 542–43.

26. Stuart Chase, *Prosperity, Fact or Myth* (New York: Charles Boni, 1929) p. 134. The new authority of the businessman has also been discussed in Herman E. Krooss, *Executive Opinion: What Business Leaders Said and Thought on Economic Issues 1920s–1960s* (Garden City, N.Y.: Doubleday & Company, 1970), pp. 17–18 and in James W. Prothro, *The Dollar Decade: Business Ideas in the 1920's* (Baton Rouge: Louisiana State University Press, 1954), pp. 30–34.

27. Beard, "Is Babbitt's Case Hopeless?", p. 21.

28. Winthrop S. Hudson, *American Protestantism* (Chicago: University of Chicago Press, 1961), p. 125. Miles H. Krumbine wrote in *The Rotarian* 21 (November 1922), p. 231:

> Time was when religion, through its prophets and priests, was the chief source of social authority. Whatever we did, both individually and socially, we sought to square with the standards set up by our religious teachings. Our social sanctions were all secured from religion. That time has passed. Commerce and business have usurped the place of religion as the source of social authority.

29. Quoted from Glenn Buck, *This American Ascendancy* (Chicago: A. Kroch & Company, 1927), p. 13.

30. Thomas Dreier, *The Silver Lining, or Sunshine on the Business Trail* (New York: B.C. Forbes Publishing Company, 1923), p. 74.

31. "And So I Left the Ministry to Go into Business!", *The American Magazine* 95 (June 1923), pp. 41, 122, 124, 127.

32. Edward A. Filene, *The Way Out: A Forecast of Coming Changes in American Business and Industry* (Garden City, N.Y.: Doubleday, Page & Company, 1924), pp. 44–45.

33. Calkins, "Business the Civilizer," p. 156.

34. Buck, *This American Ascendancy*, pp. 13–14; William Feather, *The Ideals and Follies of Business* (Cleveland: The William Feather Company, 1927), p. 176.

35. James Truslow Adams, *Our Business Civilization* (New York: Albert & Charles

Boni, 1929), pp. 14–15. This was not Adams's own view; he only reports how others felt.

36. Edward Bok, *Dollars Only* (New York: Charles Scribner's Sons, 1926), pp. 15–16.

37. Filene, *The Way Out*, pp. 14–15.

38. Buck, *This American Ascendancy*, p. 50.

39. French Strother, "Walter S. Gifford Typifies the New Leadership," *The World's Work* 52 (June 1926), pp. 164–65.

40. French Strother, "Alfred P. Sloan, Jr., a Leader of the New Type," *The World's Work* 52 (October 1926), p. 694.

41. See Heald, *The Social Responsibilities of Business*, pp. 62–65.

42. Calkins, "Business the Civilizer," p. 152.

43. Gifford, "The Changing Character of Big Business," pp. 166–68.

44. Orison Swett Marden, *Success Fundamentals* (New York: Thomas Y. Crowell Company, 1920), p. 267.

45. Calkins, "Business the Civilizer," p. 153.

46. Filene, *The Way Out*, pp. 9–10.

47. Earnest Elmo Calkins, "Business Has Wings," *The Atlantic Monthly* 139 (March 1927), pp. 306–16.

48. Everett W. Lord, *The Fundamentals of Business Ethics* (New York: The Ronald Press Company, 1926), p. 121.

49. Buck, *This American Ascendancy*, pp. 27–28.

50. See Krooss, *Executive Opinion*, p. 18; Jesse Rainsford Sprague, "Putting Business Before Life," *Harper's Monthly Magazine* 155 (November 1927), p. 707; Buck, *This American Ascendancy*, p. 18.

51. Henry S. McKee, *The ABC's of Business* (New York: The Macmillan Company, 1922), p. 41.

52. Owen D. Young and Gerard Swope, *Selected Addresses* (General Electric Company, 1930), p. 18.

53. John Candee Dean, "The Magic of Modern Industrialism," *The Forum* 67 (June 1922), pp. 507–9.

54. Buck, *This American Ascendancy*, p. 19; Lord, *Fundamentals of Business Ethics*, pp. 40, 47.

55. Bok, *Dollars Only*, pp. 8–9.

56. B. C. Forbes, *Keys to Success: Personal Efficiency* (New York: B. C. Forbes Publishing Co., 1926), p. 18.

57. Buck, *This American Ascendancy*, pp. 10–11.

58. Edward S. Martin, "Shall Business Run the World?", *Harper's Monthly Magazine* 150 (February 1925), p. 378.

59. Huger Elliott, "The Place of Beauty in the Business World," *The Annals of the American Academy of Political and Social Science* 115 (September 1924), pp. 52–56.

60. Lord, *The Fundamentals of Business Ethics*, pp. 51–52.

61. Thomas N. Carver, *The Present Economic Revolution in the United States* (Boston: Little, Brown and Company, 1925), p. 198.

62. Booth Tarkington, "Rotarian and Sophisticate," *The World's Work* 58 (January 1929), pp. 42–44.

63. For other descriptions of how in the twenties various social sectors willingly accepted the authority of business, see Cochran, *American Business in the Twentieth*

Century, p. 105 (government); Krooss and Gilbert, *American Business History*, pp. 320–22 (government); Galambos, *The Public Image of Big Business in America 1880–1940*, pp. 166–67, 201–3 (farmers); Cochran, *Business in American Life*, pp. 273, 278 (education); Heald, *The Social Responsibilities of Business*, p. 83.

64. John D. Hicks, *Republican Ascendancy*, 1921–1933 (New York: Harper & Brothers, 1960), p. 26.

65. Warren G. Harding, "Less Government in Business and More Business in Government," *The World's Work* 41 (November 1920), p. 26.

66. "President Harding Said——," *The Rotarian* 23 (July 1923), pp. 8–9.

67. Quoted from Lord, *The Fundamentals of Business Ethics*, p. iii.

68. *The Autobiography of Calvin Coolidge* (New York: Cosmopolitan Book Corporation, 1929), pp. 182–83.

69. Herbert Hoover, "If Business Doesn't, Government Will," *The Nation's Business* 12 (June 5, 1929), p. 7.

70. See, for instance, James Melvin Lee, *Business Ethics: A Manual of Modern Morals* (New York: The Ronald Press Company, 1926), pp. 52–53.

71. Harding, "Less Government in Business and More Business in Government," pp. 25–27.

72. See William E. Leuchtenburg, *The Perils of Prosperity, 1914–32*, (Chicago: University of Chicago Press, 1958), pp. 96–97, and Irving Stone, "Calvin Coolidge: A Study of Inertia," in Isabel Leighton, ed., *The Aspirin Age 1919–1941* (New York: Simon & Schuster, 1949), p. 147.

73. See, for instance, Hicks, *Republican Ascendancy*, p. 67.

74. Samuel M. Vauclain, *Optimism* (Philadelphia, 1924), p. 297.

75. George T. Odell, "Herbert Hoover—Super-Business Man," *The Nation* 121 (September 23, 1925), pp. 325–26.

76. Harding, "Less Government in Business and More Business in Government," pp. 26–27.

77. Bruce Minton and John Stuart, *The Fat Years and the Lean* (New York: International Publishers, 1940), pp. 56–59.

78. "The President of the United States to the Stockholders," *The Outlook* 134 (July 4, 1923), p. 306.

79. Charles G. Dawes, "Business Organization of the Government," in Basil Gordon Byron and Frederic René Coudert, eds., *America Speaks: A Library of Best Spoken Thought in Business and the Professions* (New York: Modern Eloquence Corporation, 1928), pp. 117–21.

80. Hicks, *Republican Ascendancy*, p. 106, see also pp. 50, 53. See further Minton and Stuart, *The Fat Years and the Lean*, pp. 109, 137.

81. Andrew W. Mellon, "Thrift and Progress," *The World's Work* 44 (May 1922), pp. 38–39.

82. See Harold U. Faulkner, *American Economic History* (New York: Harper & Row Publishers, 1960), pp. 609–14; Allen, *Lords of Creation*, p. 226; Hicks, *Republican Ascendancy*, pp. 64–66.

83. John W. O'Leary, "Twenty-five Years of American Prosperity," *Current History* 23 (February 1926), p. 703.

84. Elizabeth Stevenson, *The American 1920s: Babbitts and Bohemians* (New York: Macmillan Company, 1967), p. 131.

85. Hicks, *Republican Ascendancy*, pp. 72–73.

86. Arthur S. Link, "What Happened to the Progressive Movement in the 1920's," in Gerald N. Grob and George Athan Billias, eds., *Interpretations of American History: Patterns and Perspectives*, Vol. 2 (New York: The Free Press, 1967), pp. 309–14. On the question of labor's role in the 1920s, see also Mark Perlman, "Labor in Eclipse," in John Braeman, et al., *Change and Continuity in Twentieth-Century America: The 1920's* (Columbus: Ohio State University Press, 1968), pp. 103–45; Krooss and Gilbert, *American Business History*, pp. 289–91.

87. See George Soule, *Prosperity Decade* (New York: Rinehart & Company, 1947), p. 200; Eric F. Goldman, *Rendezvous with Destiny* (New York: Vintage Books, 1955), pp. 227–28; Bernstein, *The Lean Years*, pp. 84–85; Leuchtenburg, *Perils of Prosperity*, p. 128; William F. Ogburn, ed., *Recent Social Changes in the United States Since the War and Particularly in 1927* (Chicago: University of Chicago Press, 1929), pp. 80, 92.

88. Bernstein, *The Lean Years*, p. 97; Goldman, *Rendezvous with Destiny*, pp. 228–29; Minton and Stuart, *The Fat Years and the Lean*, pp. 167–68; George E. Mowry, *The Urban Nation, 1920–1960* (New York: Hill and Wang, 1965), p. 17.

89. See John P. Diggins, *The American Left in the Twentieth Century* (New York: Harcourt Brace Jovanovich, 1973), pp. 73–106.

90. Vauclain, *Optimism*, p. 302.

91. Carver, *The Present Economic Revolution*, pp. 11, 113.

92. Two independent studies in the 1920s came to similar results. One stated that, although the number of working class investors is large, these investors hold only 1.5 percent or 2 percent of the preferred issues in the companies studied. The other study investigated the employee stock ownership in twenty large companies and showed that only 4.26 percent of the outstanding issues were owned by the workers. See Chase, *Prosperity, Fact or Myth*, pp. 91–92.

93. Will H. Hays, "Teamwork," in Byron and Coudert, eds., *America Speaks*, p. 189.

94. Vauclain, *Optimism*, p. 290.

2

The Church and Business

The American Protestant churches in the 1920s underwent a period of what H. Richard Niebuhr calls "institutionalization," that is, a period when they lacked vitality and spontaneity and when they were willing to adjust to the predominant social environment of the time.[1] The churches were held back by timidity and circumspection.

Protestantism in the twenties did not lose the bodies of its members as much as it lost their hearts. Church membership continued to grow, while church attendance decreased and commitment cooled. This decline was apparent in two ways: first, the individual members grew less spiritually committed to their Christian faith, and, secondly, the Protestant faith and church did not enjoy the authority it had been used to. Many Protestants were satisfied with an affirmation of faith merely in words but not in acts. This inconsistency was not as surprising as it might seem at first, according to Clifton E. Olmstead: "At no time in American history had formal religious connections been more socially admired and dynamic religious living more casually ignored than in that morbidly gay and effervescent period known as the Jazz Age."[2] Religious life also suffered from compartmentalization; it was isolated from other social activities to such an extent that it was not allowed to have a real impact on them. Walter Lippmann complained in 1929 that while in the past all things were phases of a single destiny—the church, the state, the family, the school were means to the same end—now this unity had been shattered:

In the modern world institutions are more or less independent, each serving its own proximate purpose, and our culture is really a collection of separate interests each sovereign within its own realm. We do not put shrines in our workshops, and we think it unseemly to talk business in the vestibule of a church. We dislike politics in the pulpit and preaching from politicians. We do not look upon our scholars as priests or upon our priests as learned men. We do not expect science to sustain theology, not religion to dominate art. On the contrary we insist with much fervor on the separation of church and state, of religion and science, of politics and historical research, of morality and art, of business and love.[3]

This lack of religious authority, Lippmann meant, was only a reflection of a similar separation of selves, of one man from another, and so was the loss of spiritual fervor.

In spite of the bustling activity and the growing membership of the Protestant churches, many signs pointed to a vanishing devotionalism, that is, personal communion with God. In the Lynds' Middletown, many believers ceased having family prayers and reading the Bible. To growing numbers of Americans, prayer became a mechanical formula rattled off as Jimmy, the spoiled rich boy, does in Dos Passos' *Manhattan Transfer*: "Nowilaymedowntosleep Iprаythelordmy-soultokeep If ishoulddiebeforeiwake Iprаythelordmysoultotake." As Protestant church services became more businesslike, reverence and worship were often replaced by discussions and theoretical analyses, one observer complained.[4]

Besides the increasing unwillingness to live in obedience to the faith they professed, and besides their dwindling devotionalism, the Protestants of the twenties were reluctant to commit themselves to evangelization and missionary work. They did not hesitate to devote their power and their money to introducing elaborate liturgy or erecting attractive church buildings and gymnasiums, but when it came to giving themselves and their possessions to missionary work they were less enthusiastic. In 1920, 2,700 students had volunteered for missionary work abroad; eight years later only 252 volunteered. Contributions to foreign missions also took a downward course during the decade, and there was an increasing emphasis on the dissemination of technological, agricultural, medical, and educational knowledge at the missions rather than on evangelism. In a parallel development, the city missions in the United States that had been established as primarily evangelistic centers were transformed during the 1920s into social agencies.[5]

This lack of dynamic commitment caused American Protestanism to lose its authority and become a subordinate institution. The disintegration of authority was noticeable on all levels: faith and doctrine were disregarded; the church more and more lost control over its members; the minister no longer played the key role he had played earlier. In many American minds, religion had been crowded to the wall, because people had such confidence in the scientific control of life, as Harry Emerson Fosdick pointed out:

Why should we trust God or concern ourselves with the deep secrets of religious faith, if all our need is met by learning laws, blowing upon our hands, and going to work? So even Christians come secretly to look upon their Christianity as a frill, something gracious but not indispensable, pleasant to live with but not impossible to live without.[6]

The loss of authority led to a willingness on the part of the Protestant church to adapt to the values of another social sector in an attempt to retain its members and to reach a new audience. The threshold for what was permissible in the change of doctrine had gradually been lowered; the safeguards and the bulwarks against doctrinal innovations were suffering more and more from corrosion. But the accommodation to the human-centered philosophy of the time did not attract hosts of new believers, but rather contributed to a further undermining of the authority of the church. Reinhold Niebuhr wrote:

> The temper of Western civilization has made the modern church quite ashamed of the other-worldly character of traditional religion, and intent upon discarding it as much as possible. Everything is done to impress the generation with the mundane interests of religious idealism and to secularize religion itself so that it may survive in a secular age as a kind of harmless adornment of the moral life.[7]

The desire to adjust also caused the great religious controversy of the 1920s, the clash between the fundamentalists and the modernists, which led to dissension and discord not only between but also within denominations. The ultimate effect of this protracted internal strife was that the Protestant church lost even more of its credibility.

In the business-dominated cultural climate of the 1920s, the zeal for reform was largely forgotten. The Social Gospel movement underwent a decline during the "Dollar Decade."[8] However, the twenty-five years of reform preceding the Great War had a definite effect on the attitude of the churches toward business. Compared to the post–Civil War era, the Protestant churches in the twenties were much less ostentatious in their support of economic conservatism. Church leaders were much more cautious in stating explicitly whether they accepted or rejected the business ideals that dominated the age. Fewer Christians unashamedly ran to the defense of rugged business individualism. Simultaneously, the impact of business on church organization and methods was more extensive than ever before.

The churches had certainly not dissociated themselves from business. Their relationship was still very friendly, but they were no longer speaking so loudly about it; their support had become more sophisticated. What was characteristic of the twenties was that the majority of the churches did not engage in doctrinal discussions of the business ideals. Looking into the Protestant journals and magazines of the period, one finds occasional evidence of support for business values and occasional evidence of a critical attitude. But many Protestant journals, such as *The Nashville Christian Advocate*, *The Presbyterian Survey*, *The Religious Herald*, *Southern Churchman* or *The American Lutheran*, say hardly anything about business, materialism, money, wealth, or stewardship. They are concerned mostly with other doctrinal or denominational questions, and when they concern themselves with social issues, they limit the discussion to Prohibition, war, education, and immigration. Such subjects as the danger of materialism, industrial relations, business ethics, and the distribution of wealth do not seem to have been regarded as central enough to demand discussion.

Consequently, by leaving such problems alone, most churches contributed to a tacit support of the political and economic *status quo*.

In addition, when churchmen did address economic issues, they were often ambivalent and confused. One may take an article on "Wages," written by Arthur P. Gray, a social gospel minister from southern Virginia, as a case in point. He started by saying that workers were now better off than ever before, but that the state of affairs was only comparatively good, not absolutely so. He reported in a favorable light how forty-one "representative" churchmen had written to industrial leaders of the South asking them to improve the conditions of the workers. Gray then reported how John E. Edgerton, president of the National Association of Manufacturers, refuted point by point the criticism of the ministers, after which Gray surprisingly concluded his article:

> Mr. Edgerton is a splendid type of man, who has shown himself to be genuinely interested in the welfare of his employees and he is a power in the manufacturing world. It is gratifying to hear from him, that, in spite of the assertion that wages "never can be determined by the necessities of man, nor by moral requirements," yet they "will be advanced on the whole as rapidly as economic conditions permit."[9]

Gray's conclusion would have been easier to understand if it had been ironic, which does not seem to be the case; Reverend Gray rather seems to have suffered from a divided heart.

Multiple causes may be seen for the relative silence of the churches. Many churches were financially dependent on their wealthy members, and it would take a courageous minister indeed to question their economic values. Furthermore, in most churches where economic conservatism was influential one may assume that the pastor did not even in his heart disagree with his congregation. In most congregations the pastor believes as the majority of his flock believes, or as one critic complained in the twenties: "If Babbittry has triumphed in the churches, it is only because Babbittry really embodies the attitude of those who there worship."[10] In certain instances churches were more or less "owned" by industry. In Southern mill towns, the mill provided the land for the church, met construction costs, paid the minister's salary. As a result, Irving Bernstein says, "religion was a branch of the textile industry" in the South.[11] One of the ministers in Gastonia confessed that they never took the initiative on economic questions. They were "opposed only to things downright evil, such as pool rooms." Many American ministers consequently regarded it as impossible to even try to change the economic structure of the country. They agreed with Miles H. Krumbine's description of the situation:

> To attempt to interpret, in terms of modern industrial enterprise, the self-renouncing, non-acquisitive, simple way of life of Jesus in our self-assertive, aggressive, acquisitive industrial and commercial world would be like tampering with the foundations of an enormous building at the very moment when ten new stories are being added at the top.[12]

Another reason for church reticence on economic matters was that the churches were often devoted to the moral regeneration of individuals to such an extent that there was little room for instruction in Christian social ethics. Responsible Christians turned against the "personal" sin that abounded in the lost generation: drinking, necking, dancing, smoking, improper clothing, profane language, and cardplaying. Social sins were not as highly visible and were therefore neglected.

One may find still further causes for the cautious attitude of the churches. Many Christians, particularly Fundamentalists, were worn out from the long controversy about evolution and welcomed a withdrawal from the turmoil of the world.[13] One may finally mention a cause of the greatest importance, namely that social injustice was no longer as glaring as it had been. The business culture of the 1920s had improved the working conditions for the average workingman, and the need for protest was not felt by the churches to be particularly great. This also made the churches assume a friendly attitude toward business.

In Europe, in the latter part of the 1920s, business became an increasingly influential institution. Efficiency and rationalization became key concepts in the reconstruction of Europe. As in the United States, the European Protestant churches went through a crisis, in which their members not only grew indifferent but even left the church in hundreds of thousands. This general weakening of the European Protestant churches might have made them susceptible to the growing influence of business. However, the situation in Europe differs widely from the one that developed in America. The European churches never let themselves be molded as their sister churches in America by the predominant business spirit. There are mainly two explanations for this resistance to business ideology. First, as I have pointed out above, business in Europe never gained the same social role or prestige as in America. Secondly, many of the European Protestant churches were supported financially by the state; if they were not state churches, as in Sweden or England, they received financial help, as in Germany. They were consequently not dependent to the same degree as the churches in the United States on the resources of the business community. They did not feel the same need, at any cost and with any method, to keep the members within the church. And so, they did not have to resort to the latest ideas and methods to continue their work.

THE CHURCHES ENDORSE BUSINESS VALUES

Even though the Protestant churches in America did not enter into doctrinal discussions of business-related questions or openly sanction the business ideology, they nevertheless contributed to the general adoration of commercial values that characterized the decade. Many Christian publications and individuals expressed friendly attitudes toward business and businessmen, toward prosperity and success, toward investments and the accumulation of wealth.

This sympathetic attitude was noticeable in the treatment of business theories and practices in general. Under the title of "Business—Maker of Morals," Shailer Mathews, the well-known dean of the Chicago Divinity School, wrote that people who do not know business have no right to criticize it, after which he presented an encomium, high-flown even for the business-adoring twenties:

> Business does more than wait for others to make its moralities. It evolves its own, for it is not a machine, but a social operation. What else than trade could have taught men to be honest? How else have women standardized their right to be treated as persons? How else would men have been taught self-control and foresight which spring from thrift and the desire to produce new wealth.... Business cannot continue to be successful where human welfare is ignored. Every great change in the ways of producing and using wealth has evolved a new appreciation of the human element. Advertising is psychology converted into the art of creating and directing human wants. When business men talk of rendering service they are not hypocrites, for they do serve their day.... For business does more than make money.—It makes morals.[14]

Shailer Mathews's piece was published in *System*, the leading business magazine of the time.

This benevolent attitude was characteristic of numerous Protestant representatives, even though they were less excessive in their statements than Mathews. The sanctioning of business values ranged from letting businessmen propagate their views in Christian magazines to publishing Christian novels about businessmen. I will mention a few representative examples. Roger W. Babson, a key figure in the business establishment, had an article published in *The Presbyterian Survey* on the "six *I*'s" of success: by means of Industry, Integrity, Intelligence, Initiative, Intensity, and Inspiration one was bound to succeed in life.[15] *The Christian Herald* let Dr. Arthur Holmes, president of Drake University, explain to its readers that modern business was founded on the Golden Rule: "No man can stay in business who does not at least live up to the standard of probity set by honest dealing in the open and by keeping one's word under ordinary circumstances. Modern business recognizes the Golden Rule in all this realm."[16]

Owen D. Young, Chairman of the Board of Directors of General Electric, was invited to deliver, from the pulpit of the Riverside Church in New York, an address on "What Is Right in Business," in which he carefully explained to the congregation that big business was honest since its moral standards had improved tremendously. He concluded his speech in the following manner:

> As time goes on, I feel that the right in business will more and more prevail. The larger business becomes, the more scrupulously careful the administrators of it will be.... Somehow, as responsibility increases, men are found big enough to meet adequately

the great questions of right and wrong which come to them. So I welcome big business and big responsibility, not in the fear that it will make business wrong, but in the hope and belief that it will make business right.[17]

In several instances the Christian journals made statements of their own in favor of business. An article in *The Nashville Christian Advocate* stated that Christianity certainly could combine with business, that chicanery and dishonesty did not form the basis for success in business, but that "it is God that giveth power to get wealth," and most frequently that "this power is manifested in an endowment of good sense, sound judgment, and upright living."[18] *The Methodist Quarterly Review* wanted to elevate business to the level of profession together with law, medicine, teaching, and preaching, because "business is more and more accepting its obligations to the community and working for the improvement of the community without ulterior motive."[19] Without referring to the distress of thousands of workers, *The Presbyterian Survey* wrote in glowing terms of the "abounding prosperity" of the South, drawing the conclusion that "in this abounding prosperity the members of the Southern Presbyterian Church have a large part, and it is a matter of pardonable pride that in the great economic development of the South many of our members are constructive leaders."[20] *Church Management* recommended that all Christians read Peter B. Kyne's *The Go-Getter*, because it expressed a spirit of efficiency that should be emulated in Christian work.[21] *The Christian Herald* printed a full-page picture of the 792-feet-high Woolworth Tower with the subtitle "a Cathedral of Commerce" followed by the text: "In such skyscrapers, our country has developed a form of architecture which does not suffer by comparison with the cathedrals which Europe built in that marvelous burst of energy which ushered in the modern era."[22]

These expressions of good will to business were often visible in Christian novels as well. It will suffice to refer to Harold Bell Wright's *God and the Groceryman* (1927), in which a group of local businessmen under the direction of industrialist Dan Matthews, called Big Dan, correct the mistakes that ministers and laymen have made and restore to the churches of the town the unity that has been missing for so long. Wright depicts the businessman, and particularly Big Dan, as a person to be greatly revered, as the peacemaker of the new age. Big Dan fights courageously against the greatest enemy of the church, denominationalism, and wins a glorious victory which brings harmony to all sections of the community.

Protestant publications not only sanctioned business in general but also devoted space to success stories of individual businessmen. Most of these articles follow the rags-to-riches pattern. These men—whether their names were John Wanamaker, John G. Shedd (the President of Marshall Field & Co), James Schermerhorn (the man behind the "Truth in Advertising" campaign), or James M. Speers (the President of James McCutcheon and Company)—had worked their way up from the lowest rung of the social ladder to prominence and leadership. And they had all done so with the help of thrift, diligence, patience, self-reliance, and a Christian upbringing.[23] R. A. Long, the president of the world's largest lumber company, had during his phenomenal rise been driven by a vision to "build a city of God on earth." He hoped to be able to make use of his business acumen even after death: "If there is a saw-mill up there in heaven—when I get there—and I hope to get there—I am going to ask the Lord to let me run it. Then, if He'll give me plenty of lumber, plenty of orders, and all the transportation I want, I'll be happy, no matter what else I have to do, or do not get to do."[24]

In certain instances the Christian support of particular businessmen was disputable. Henry Ford, who often had been depicted as an infidel, was made into a Christian gentleman, who belonged to a church, who read his Bible regularly, and who above all had applied his Christian faith to industry. The author of the article solemnly declared: "For the first time on the face of the earth Henry Ford is really putting the social gospel to work in industry," and he found support for his view in Edwin Markham, who was known to have said that "I put the social gospel into words. Mr. Ford puts it into works."[25]

Other phenomena also show that Christians were affected by the commercial spirit of the twenties. Protestant magazines carried articles advising believers how best to invest their money. *The Christian Herald* had a weekly investment column, which treated the most varied economic topics. Here the readers could find out how fellow-believers had planned their budgets, saved part of their salaries or invested their surpluses. Only in one of the Christian investment articles I have studied was there a reference to what the Bible says in money matters, and that reference said that both the Old and New Testaments often speak about interest and that this "testifies to the antiquity of money earning money."[26] The author of the article forgot to say, however, what the Bible says about the taking of interest, information which would not have served his purposes.

These investment articles exuded an optimistic belief in the power of money to improve the lot of both individual and society. Increasing one's wealth was generally portrayed as a worthy and exciting enterprise: "There is a thrill about investing the first $1,000 which will be shared by all concerned. It's like Lindbergh's first flight to Paris."[27] If you invest wisely, was the message, it is within your power as well to build that long-desired fortune. The wise way was to start by saving. Sententious sayings like the following drummed home the message:

"As service is at the foundation of all money making, so thrift is at the foundation of all investment"

"Saving is the price we pay for independence"

"The man who has no savings reserve is little better than a slave, financially speaking"

"The habit of thrift and the accumulation of a competency result in a species of self-respect that is wholesome and helpful"

"If you want to know whether you are destined to be a success or a failure in life you can easily find out. The test is simple and it is infallible. Are you able to save money? If not, drop out.... The seed of success is not in you."[28]

Having accumulated at least $1,000 in that "dependable friend," the savings passbook, a person was ready to invest. But it was important to have the right attitude toward the saved-up money since it represented "postponed vacations, years of hard labor, refraining from buying unnecessary luxuries, long periods of careful planning."[29] Do not speculate, all the columns warned, but be careful and expect only a modest return. "Safety first" was the principle generally advocated. The Protestant readers were informed in detail about which investments were the safest—apparently the first mortgage real estate bond—and how to go about buying it. Nor did they have to have a bad conscience about investing their money in bonds, because, while they were building their own fortunes, they were simultaneously performing a great service to both city and country: "The purchase of these bonds has done much to build up the cities of the country, and as the cities have been upbuilt, the whole country has benefited, for there has been created a better and more stable market for the products of the farm."[30]

The advertising sections of the Protestant magazines, particularly the non-denominational ones, show that the Christian readers were regarded as prospective investors and consumers of wealth. Every issue of *The Christian Herald*, for instance, contained a surprising number of advertisements from banks, trust companies, and investment houses, urging believers to invest their money. To mention a few randomly chosen issues: *The Christian Herald* of December 15, 1923 printed eight advertisements from investment companies; the January 27, 1923 issue of the same magazine contained one advertisement from Columbia Mortgage Company on investing in mortgage bonds; one from G. L. Miller, Bond & Mortgage Company urging the same; one entitled "What Rich Men Know" from American Bond & Mortgage Company; one from Caldwell & Company on investing in first mortgage real estate bonds; one from the Miami Mortgage & Guaranty Company promising 8 percent on an investment; one from The Atlantic Trust Co. for "high-grade bonds with BANK SAFETY"; and one from A. H. Brickmore & Co. offering securities in well-managed companies in the "prosperous electric light and power industry" (see illustration 3).

On certain occasions the advertisers made use of captions they felt would be particularly enticing to Christian readers. Under the title of "What Shall It Profit a Man?" the Trust Company of Florida wrote: "What profit is there in keeping money safety invested, but without an adequate interest return? The only value in having money is to make it earn more, and all it is capable of earning."[31] S. W. Straus & Co. had a full-page advertisement printed headed

"Big Cash Dividends
while we live
A Blessing on Humanity
after we are gone"

YOU can confer the greatest blessing on humanity —and at the same time safeguard your financial interests as long as you live, by investing your money in tax exempt Bible Annuity Bonds.

Bible Annuity Bonds
Yield as High as 9% Interest

You may invest any amount from $100.00 up.

No Anxiety—No Fluctuations

Endorsed by business men and churches; may be issued on two lives, husband and wife, mother and daughter. A record of all bonds is kept so that income continues in event bonds are lost.

Illustration 3

Advertising in the Protestant press. (*The Christian Herald*, October 31, 1925. Used with permission.)

by the word "FAITH" in big block letters, under which the text ran: "Faith and confidence should govern everything in life. The greatest asset a man or an institution can have is the faith and confidence of fellow-men. S. W. Straus & Co. take a not unworthy pride in the faith reposed in us by tens of thousands of investors who have bought Straus First Mortgage Bonds."[32] Most of these investment houses printed their own booklets on investing. *The Christian Herald* listed them all and distributed them free of charge; above the list it wrote: "If you will write and indicate which subjects or types of securities are of interest to you we will be glad to have them forwarded or if you wish you may write direct to the Investment House. In writing the concerns listed below be sure to mention Christian Herald. It will insure a prompt and courteous reply."[33]

Protestant journals also carried advertisements on how to make money in other ways, by selling ladies' clothes or by writing stories for the screen. Such magazines as *Success* and *The Business Woman* evidently believed that they would find ready subscribers among the readers of *The Christian Herald* since they advertised there. *The Business Woman* and *The Christian Herald* even made a deal that anyone who subscribed to *The Business Woman* would get a reduced subscription rate for *The Christian Herald.* In accepting this deal, a reader would be highly rewarded:

> Then read each month in *The Business Woman* stories of the women who have reached their goals and you will be inspired to go on, step by step, toward your own. Never before has the business and professional woman had a publication devoted exclusively to her interests and stories of remarkable successes which many women have made have gone untold.[34]

WINNING BUSINESSMEN FOR CHRIST

One can easily detect in the Protestant publications a sincere desire to win the American businessman for Christ. The representatives of the churches were primarily concerned about his spiritual well-being as an individual, not merely as a powerful force to be incorporated in the church. In certain instances, however, one gets the impression that businessmen are being wooed more than other groups in society. Articles dealing with businessmen and their possible salvation are occasionally leavened with a reverence that is never present when the salvation of the workingman is discussed.

Many articles were devoted to why it was so important to reach the businessmen with the gospel and how one could evangelize among them. The businessman needs to be a Christian, one author stated, first of all because no business achievement could satisfy his soul. It was also important for him to accept Christ "because of the vast opportunities for representing his Lord in a manly and robust way." For every one, it was pointed out, who was saved through reading the Bible, hundreds of people would be saved when observing the life of a Christian businessman.[35] "Businessmen are naturally religious,"

Roger W. Babson explained, and the churches should seize the opportunity to influence this "great, latent spiritual power." The church should emphasize, he felt, that it exists for sinners and not for saints, because businessmen know that they are sinners and will welcome an institution that can help them keep to "the straight road."[36] Some Christians also felt a calling to witness exclusively to businessmen, and prayer groups were formed "to pray and to plan to win other business men for Christ."[37]

The success stories mentioned previously, depicting the lives of Schermerhorn, Wanamaker, Ford and others, also served the purpose of attracting other businessmen to Christianity. If such undeniably successful men had seen anything of value in the Protestant faith, the ordinary businessman may have thought, then why shouldn't I? The argument was made even more powerful since almost all the industrialists portrayed deliberately stressed the importance of their Christian background for their success. Ford's remarkable achievement had its origin in the fact that the Bible was regularly read to him as a child. And Wanamaker's success was based on his possession of firm Christian principles. Oliver M. Fisher, the Christian President of the M. A. Packard Company, a shoe producer, used fitting imagery to express his conviction:

> As we have always considered a good lining to be the strength and support of all our shoes, we are equally sure that the background of a religious life is the heart of the covenant of all good business to make it ring true, and the very foundation of continued business prosperity. We talk about prosperity, but real prosperity can not exist or long continue without a fine sense of honor, and a respect for obligations—in other words, the maintenance of good faith with each other.[38]

To some businessmen the most powerful argument to join a church would be that religion pays in dollars and cents. The churches did not intend to put forth such a message, but this may have been the way some businessmen understood it. One minister interviewed by the Lynds in *Middletown* stated: "The church is the 'reason why' of America. . . . The church has made America prosperous. . . . It is no mere happening that church people become well to do."[39] Roger Babson wrote in *The Presbyterian Survey* that, according to his investigation, in the success of American businessmen only 6 percent was due to "instinct or environment or inheritance," a bare 10 percent could be accredited to intellect, while religion, to his amazement, accounted for "not less than thirty per cent of the results of every truly successful business career!"[40] In Lloyd C. Douglas's *Magnificent Obsession* (1929), Bobby Merrick discovers the "mysterious potentiality" of the Bible, which leads to success in every walk in life. There is particularly one page in the Bible—which one Douglas never reveals—that describes "the exact process of achieving power to do, be, and have what you want." It later turns out that the Biblical success formula is "personality projection," which means that by helping others you enlarge yourself, and the success of the people you have helped will in turn affect your success.

The Nashville Christian Advocate expressed the success message in the following words:

For the truth is that were it not for the saving salt of the Church in the world nothing would be safe, nor would there be any sure basis for success in any business, so that the Church gives value of a most substantial kind to all property and business in our country, and neither would be worth much without the good influence of the Church in a community.[41]

This kind of argument was even used, according to Luccock, as an appeal to the wealthy to contribute money to the church, even if they were not church members. A prominent churchman instructed canvassers for funds for building a cathedral thus:

Go to the men who command great wealth either in their own right or in the trust funds which they administer. Tell them that the Cathedral and the presence of the religion which it symbolizes is the guarantee of the continuance of the social order on which their prosperity depends. Tell them that religion is the insurance of their prosperity and ask them whether they think they are paying enough for their insurance.[42]

Behind the particular concern that the Protestant churches felt for the businessman and his spiritual well-being was also the hope that Christian principles might be worked into business and industry. The stories of the successful Christian businessmen very often tried to show how these men had applied faith to their industries or firms, thus serving as examples for other men to follow. James M. Speers, one of the interviewed industrialists, was even characterized as the man who "built religion into business."

Other articles and books underlined the importance of letting Christian ethics, and in particular the Golden Rule, become the foundation on which to build American business. One article asked businessmen to evaluate their situation—how they treated their employees, whether they hired labor spies, whether they were honest in advertising—and finally asked them if they felt practicing the Golden Rule was good business. The author gave the answer himself: "The principles of Jesus work in the world of business, because they unite all in the interest of each."[43] Another author pointed out that the business world "only haltingly and doubtfully" had discerned that it needed the Golden Rule. "Whose task is it," he continued, "but the Church's to stabilize this faith and to establish consciously and regnantly the supreme law of Christ once and forever as the acknowledged principle of business? This opportunity lies now before the Church."[44] Roger Babson also felt, as a representative of the churches of America, that religion was the only solution to America's industrial problems, for the following reasons:

(1) Labor must get back its desire to produce.

(2) This desire is intangible and can be brought about only by winning the confidence of the workers.

> (3) To win the confidence of the workers, we must realize that the interests of labor are paramount to the interests of capital, and that the real purpose of industry shall be not to produce material things, but to develop human souls.
> (4) To so develop the workers, we must permit them to organize, must recognize their leaders, and must give them full knowledge regarding the business, consulting them when they desire to be consulted.
> (5) We should strive to apply the same principles in dealing with our employees as we apply in dealing with our families. This is in accordance with the teachings of religion and the meaning of the Golden Rule.[45]

Babson here showed greater sensitivity than most other advocates for the application of religion to business; to him the introduction of the Golden Rule obviously meant more than mere pacification of the workers.

WHAT THE CHURCHES TAUGHT

The churches offered little doctrinal teaching on property, wealth, and stewardship. What was written about business matters and economic questions often revealed a desire to remain on good terms with the reigning commercial institution. However, occasional articles and books were devoted to doctrinal explications of what the Bible taught on social and economic issues.

In general, these writings are more orthodox than one would have reason to expect, judging from the friendly attitude of the churches toward business culture that characterized the twenties. More or less explicitly, they all stated the nonacquisitive philosophy of the Bible and did not try to make a case for righteousness-through-riches or Christianity-as-a-good-business-proposition.

There seems to be a discrepancy between the attitude of Biblical teachings and the widespread admiration in the churches of the business spirit of the decade. If the churches knew what Christ taught in economic matters and even forwarded their Master's views without much adulteration, why did not the churches take the consequences of their own doctrinal teachings? Why did they not become prophetic voices that refused to pay homage to the materialistic spirit of success? The discrepancy was one between theory and practice. Many Christians believed that what Christ taught about a sacrificial life was true. They believed that the Sermon on the Mount should be the norm for Christian living—as an ideal. But to try to live according to these maxims, and to let one's faith find an expression in works, would be impractical and would cost too much.

This discrepancy may of course only be apparent. Some denominational journals and books speak more openly on economic matters, because the denomination sees it as important to propagate a social gospel. This is certainly true of the Methodists, whose journals devote proportionately more space to such issues than, for instance, the publications of the Episcopal church. But this is not the whole truth. As we have seen, such Methodist journals as *The Nashville Christian Advocate* and *The Methodist Quarterly Review* often express admiration for the commercial spirit, but when they analyze what the Bible says about stewardship, the attitude toward the acquisition and spending of money changes considerably. The same phenomenon is noticeable in other denominational and nondenominational publications. Even *The Christian Herald*, which had a business-oriented image, taught a much more radical message of economic altruism in its stewardship articles.

Property

The consensus in the Protestant churches was that all property belonged to God, and to Him only, and had been given to men in trust. Men were responsible before God for the use of the property entrusted them. Property in itself was neither good nor evil. "Jesus certainly taught that riches are not an evil thing in themselves," one writer stated. "Indeed, to accept any other view is to rebuke the Almighty for having placed the gold and silver in the mountains, and the cattle upon a thousand hills."[46] Property was seen merely as a nonmoral tool which should be put to work for the good of mankind; wealth was recognized as "one of the mightiest agencies in the world for bringing in and establishing and building up the kingdom of righteousness in the earth."[47] The all-important thing was the individual's attitude toward property; it was "absolutely wicked" to love the tool: "Indeed, love of money distorts the whole vision of life, and leads not only to wicked practices but to certain alienation from God."[48] And the man who makes and spends money justly and for "high and holy purposes" was seen as "one of the finest and noblest types of character that Christianity can produce."[49] Christ had put no limit to how much property a Christian may possess. Under the law of Christ, every believer might be safely trusted with as great wealth as he would "ethicize," that is, as he would use "in ministering to the physical, social, intellectual, and moral needs of his fellow men."[50]

A few commentators said that property has no value in itself. It only represents the degree of service a person has done or expresses his character. Jesus taught, according to one writer, that anyone who works only to get money is living on a low plane of service. The service extended through work is as sacred as prayer, and its values are "beyond all monetary computation."[51] Another explicator held that money measures a man. It is "coined personality," but the personality of brain is superior to that of brawn, an idea that Jesus presumably would not have sanctioned:

> The laborer who gets $4.00 a day puts $4.00 worth of muscle, of physical effort, into his pocket, or $4.00 worth of himself. When a clerk gets $30.00 a week, he puts $30.00 of himself in his pocket on pay-day. The merchant with a higher brain power, a higher grade of intelligence, has a greater worth in dollars and cents. Whatever we are or whatever we do, we are getting the result of our labor in the shape of cash. The point is this: when you get money into your pocket, it is not merely silver and gold, but it is something human, something with power, because it represents power expended.[52]

The writer above was not on firm biblical ground in his assumptions; other commentators similarly ascribed to Jesus ideas that He may have been hesitant to endorse. Several writers state that Jesus recognized the character-making power of property. According to one of them, Jesus taught

> that one of the most potential ways by which personality can express itself and minister to life is through the use of material substance. . . . In the processes of acquiring, saving, spending, and giving, men develop qualities that cannot be developed in any other way. When the Christian motive is central in these processes, they become mighty factors in making character Christian.[53]

Another writer stated that the New Testament agrees with the Old "in esteeming highly the value of wealth and in commending the virtues that lead to its possession."[54]

Even if one could find a certain biblical basis for such arguments as the ones above, they could, if not properly understood, lead writers and readers further away from a true understanding of the teachings of Christ. A few explicators drew the conclusion that it was a Christian duty to earn money and accumulate wealth. One of them held that it seemed to be the logical inference, from what Jesus said in the Sermon on the Mount about laying up treasures in heaven,

> that he considered it not only legitimate to acquire property, but an obligation to do so both from the point of view of the Christian acquirer's own welfare and the opportunity acquisition affords for Christian beneficence. . . . It is God who gives the talent for making money. To neglect to use this talent is sin.[55]

The same author was fully convinced that private property was "more conducive to the higher life" than any form of common ownership, because

> (a) it tends more to real unity of sentiment than communism; (b) it is economically superior to communism, for people bestow more attention upon the management of private than of public property; (c) ownership is a source of pleasure; (d) it is more conducive to the growth of character, since communism makes impossible the exercise of the virtues of self-control and liberality.[56]

It would be utterly vain and visionary, several churchmen concluded, to advocate an equal distribution of wealth. "If all the property of the race," Mr. Tillett said, "could be equally distributed among men, in less than a week thousands would be penniless and hundreds would be well on their way to wealth."[57] Reverend Price was convinced that equality would not remain even for an hour. "It is often a catastrophe," he continued, "to give to people money which they did not earn. The most important $100 that anyone ever had was the first $100 that he saved, both by working hard to get it, and then by denying himself to keep it."[58]

In another article, however, the same Reverend Price explained that we are not allowed to assume that wealth necessarily is a sign that the owner is blessed by God. From the text about Dives and Lazarus we may learn "that earthly riches are not necessarily rewards of righteousness, nor earthly suffering an indication of sin."[59] The linking of righteousness to riches, which had not been uncommon at other times in American church history, was denounced by other critics as well. Drawing attention to the facts that Jesus was without sin, that he had nowhere to lay his head, that he walked the way of opposition and misunderstanding, that he died "in the flower of young manhood" upon a cross between two thieves, one commentator concluded: "With the life of Christ before us we should be careful ere we give the impression that righteousness surely leads to worldly prosperity, or that the lack of such prosperity is an indication of faithlessness and sin."[60]

Most of the doctrinal articles not only agreed that property is God-given but also that the misuse of property is a sin against the giver. Jesus taught, these commentators stated, that a selfish accumulation of wealth is evil. He rebuked with scorn the motive to use one's God-given ability, position, and resources chiefly to improve one's own advantage, or as one theologian exemplified it, "The motive to pile up profits, the motive to get luxuries, the desire to be able to enjoy extravagances, the passion for possessing things—this is what he called serving Mammon. 'Ye cannot serve God and Mammon'."[61] Anyone who believes that wealth in itself will bring happiness is a fool, another pastor explained: "The successful man of the world works like a slave until he makes his fortune, and then watches it like a detective the rest of his life; and all this he does for his board and clothes."[62] And if one has earned his wealth in an ungodly way, no degree of liberal giving will make up for the evil motive in acquiring it. Men who act in such a way should, as happened in the early Church, be excluded from church membership.[63]

Hoarding wealth is dangerous, most Protestants agreed. Sherwood Eddy summarized the argument when he said that "accumulated treasure *is perishable, it is absorbing*, it is *enslaving*." It gives no security, it commands your whole attention, it becomes your sole master.[64] Fosdick even held that Mammon had been the preeminent enemy of the Gospel of Jesus Christ. Jesus saw then, as Fosdick and others saw in the twenties,

> rich young men not far from the Kingdom, held back from whole-hearted service by the love of money (March 10:17f). He, too, saw Dives lulled into selfish indolence by great possessions (Luke 16:19f); saw brotherhood cut asunder by covetous desires (Luke 12:13f);... saw grafters even in the temple courts (March 11:15). He, too, found his message met by the sneers of "Pharisees, who were lovers of money" (Luke 16:14), and in the circle of his friends he was betrayed by a man with an itching palm.[65]

A few churchmen of the decade also taught that, according to Christ, wealth was a danger and a grave temptation to the believer as well. They pointed out that the Bible contains only one hint of the peril of poverty—the prayer of

Agur, where poverty is seen as a possible source of bitterness—while it abounds in warnings against the peril of riches.[66] Jesus himself had held himself free from the entanglements of worldly possessions. The early Christians as well had recognized the danger that "*things* might easily take the place of more important considerations." But Jesus and the apostles saw the insidious character of the desire for wealth, and they warned against it again and again. What might easily happen to the believer who desires property is that gradually "conscience is narcotized, judgment is clouded, sympathy chilled, and the will to do the will of God is atrophied." Wealth also gives power over the lives of others and may as such turn into a source of corruption. The man of great riches is more sorely tempted, but no one goes free:

> Let no one of us delude himself. We are all tempted and at all times desperately tempted to fall into the error of the rich man and some of us with far less excuse than he had. We must all fight against covetousness; against falling into the wrong attitude toward physical things and sensual. Don't be the slave of things! Be the master.[67]

Stewardship

God was seen as the owner of all property; He was also regarded as the giver of all life. Protestant churchmen repeatedly made clear that stewardship was not limited to the question of money; we owe everything to the Lord. Our life, our health, our time, our energy, our ability—and our property—rightfully belong to God and should be used according to His will.[68]

At the basis for stewardship, it was pointed out, lay redemption. Only the redeemed Christian could serve the Lord properly, since his old self had died and Christ now lived in him instead. One writer stated: "My life, my health, my intelligence, my character, my truth, my children, my time, my property,—all these have been redeemed in the precious blood of Jesus, and they are mine only as a trust from God, and are to be administered in His will for the benefit of every member of the race."[69] To be a Christian steward meant complete submission to Christ. One author held that church membership had been made too easy: "It has become a polite gesture, when it ought to be a fervent surrender. It is regarded as a soft cushion for tired souls, when it ought to be the West Point and the Annapolis for Christian warfare."[70] We must never forget, another critic said, that Jesus is not only our Savior but also our Lord: "He, and he alone, is the true and ultimate basis for Christian stewardship. His centrality and the primacy of his kingdom demand loyalty to him and identification with his spirit and purpose."[71]

As Christian stewards, the argument went, we become active partners of God, participating in His plans regarding the world. His dominant idea is "the everlasting salvation of souls through the proclamation of His Gospel." Helping one's neighbors in various needs is also important, but is secondary to "His great prime object of eternal blessedness for His redeemed children."[72] And the foundation for helping others and for giving money is a consecrated life. Money is an extension of our own personality and power, and "only as the whole life is committed to the Kingdom will it be possible for giving to be consistent."[73] The giving of money was not necessarily a sign of good stewardship; one could even tithe and still be an unfaithful steward.[74]

The character of stewardship varied from one profession or position to another. If you were a teacher you had been given a particular responsibility in teaching, and the same was true if you were engaged in law, politics, journalism or the ministry. There was a special stewardship for women, one article explained, listing such fields as the stewardship of hospitality, influence, cooking, testimony, needlework, training children and—somewhat surprisingly—the stewardship of business ability.[75] Businessmen had been called to be stewards in their field. Suggesting the "spirit and attitude" of John D. Rockefeller, Jr. as an ideal, one author stated that the kind of stewardship needed in the modern business world was "the stewardship of brains and managerial ability that concerns itself about providing opportunities for reasonable acquisition of wealth by others instead of the common practice of making profit for self the main motive."[76]

Articles and books on stewardship in general, and business stewardship in particular, taught that alongside the sin of loving money came the sin of thriftlessness and waste. When Jesus, having fed the five thousand, told his disciples to "gather up the broken pieces which remain over, that nothing be lost," he was issuing a "warning against a careless use of anything which a needy humanity can use." The bases of all great fortunes, it was pointed out, were laid by men of thrift, for instance George Eastman of Kodak who saved $37.50 the first year on a weekly wage of $3. "Out of fifty of America's foremost business and financial leaders today," this writer continued, "twenty-four were born poor and seventeen were born in moderate circumstances. Every one of them started with habits of thrift."[77] Even though many writers on stewardship commended industry and thrift, few went as far in their exhortations as H. R. Calkins:

> A faithful steward is required in honor to increase his possessions, for he is thus enlarging his Lord's estate. The cowardly steward who hid his master's talent was justly rebuked. God gave the earth into the hands of men, and said, "Subdue it." He commanded them to take possession of earth's mighty values and hold them in domination. The sluggard and the dullard are exhorted to "be wise." Poverty is a calamity that came with sin. The godly man, under normal conditions, should expect to be prosperous. He has a right to be rich, as that perfect servant of the Lord, Job, was rich. But he is not to be a rich fool withal. He is to know the meaning of wealth. Stewardship can alone defend a man against "the deceitfulness of riches" and curb the wickedness that would increase its possessions by evil devices.[78]

The common practice among these writers was not to put such a heavy emphasis on the Christian's right to be rich, as Calkins did, but rather on the danger of becoming entrapped in commercialism, "which is another name for covetousness, 'which is idolatry.' That evil spirit tries truthfulness and hinders honesty," as one explicator expressed it.[79]

Even though the churches were aware, as we have seen above, that stewardship concerned all aspects of life, many articles limited it to a matter of money, and particularly to the giving of money to the church. Under the title of "Stewardship," one Lutheran churchman asked why Lutherans gave so little to the Lutheran church.

> The cheapest thing we have today is our religion. There is hardly a hobby, certainly not a habit, which does cost us far more than our church connection. All too frequently the church gets the nickels and the dimes, whilst gas and oil, theatres and movies, the superfluities and relaxations of life, get the lion's share without a murmur.[80]

The Presbyterian church asked similarly why its members were so tightfisted and asked them to consider that eleven times as much money was spent on crime and its punishment as on church and religious interests and that people squandered $29 on luxuries to every dollar given to the church.[81]

Not seldom, stewardship articles boiled down to an argument for tithing. Referring to verses in the Old Testament, and occasionally also in the New, writers tried to show that it was a Christian duty to give 10 percent of one's earnings to the denomination one belonged to. When the Presbyterian church set apart the month of November 1924 as "Christian Stewardship Study Month," its suggestions on what to study concerned mostly tithing and proportionate giving.[82] A few voices reacted against this practice and charged that the stewardship idea had been corrupted within the churches.

Since the Great War, the stewardship departments of various Protestant denominations had been allied to money-raising campaigns. These stewardship departments had been expected "so to emphasize stewardship principles that massive amounts could be raised." Only those phases of stewardship were stressed, the critics said, that were sure to accelerate giving to the church. "Hence the tithe was exalted out of all proportion to the subject itself." But the church must teach stewardship, not to protect itself, but to save the world: "the doctrine of stewardship must not be drawn for ecclesiastical profit. *It must be drawn for economic righteousness*."[83]

Several Protestant churchmen, however, saw the stewardship of money in a wider context than denominational tithing. Giving should not be restricted by a legalistic interpretation of the Old Testament, some felt; money should be given with true generosity from the heart. Men like Chester Ward Kingsley, the Boston banker, and William Earl Dodge, the railroad magnate, who had given much more than 10 percent every year and who in everything else had been "exemplary Christians," were held forth as ideals.[84] John Wesley's well-known phrase "Get all you can, save all you can, give all you can" was repeated by many with a special emphasis on his third advice. The conclusion these writers all drew was that a Christian should not be compelled to give; he should only give out of gratitude for what Christ had done for him. The attitude of the giver should be one of sacrifice, as Christ had sacrificed himself, and he should not expect his gift to be paid back to him, as some churchmen taught.[85]

The motive and object for Christian giving, these critics felt, should not only be the church and its work. The needs of the world were equally important. "Hunger, ignorance, disease, and unsocial attitudes curse many hundreds of millions of inhabitants of the earth," one writer pointed out. "And no person can turn a deaf ear to these needs and still remain in the fellowship of Christ."[86] Jesus and the apostles had consistently preached and practiced a liberality toward the less fortunate in society, an attitude that Protestants of the twenties were urged to adopt as well: "The great concern of Jesus for the underprivileged, his tender compassion for the poor and needy, could lead to no other conclusion than that the fortunate should be joyously extravagant in giving to lift the burdens of the needy."[87]

The Social and Economic Order

Even though many appeals were made to Christians to live sacrificial lives free from materialism, the American economic order of the twenties was never questioned. In most cases it was taken for granted and not even commented upon. Not even the most extreme of the advocates for the social gospel seem to have considered an alternative economic system. On the other hand, I have found only one or two examples of a writer trying to find biblical sanction for the system predominant in the 1920s. One explicator pointed out that in Christ's day "capitalism was the unquestioned method," and that Christ at no point condemns such an economic order but rather "that his counsels assume not only the righteousness of capitalism, but its values as a means of moral discipline."[88] But, as I said, such pronouncements are extremely rare.

Rather than wanting to exchange the reigning economic system for a new one, a few commentators argued that there was a need to change the already existing system from within. Business and industry needed to be "Christianized." John the Baptist had demanded that people face the "ungodly social order" of their day, one writer pointed out and continued: "We need a new generation of John the Baptists who shall help us to see the ramifications of our sins. The first step to the solution of the industrial problem is an honest facing of the fact that industry is not deeply and thoroughly Christian; that it must be Christianized."[89] The basis for such a social change, it was felt, was a change of the heart of the individual. No improvement of the industrial order was possible before people in industry experienced a personal rebirth in Christ. This regeneration would lead to a "pentecost of property," an "outpouring of the Spirit of God" upon the economic order.[90]

What was primarily needed in industry and business was cooperation, or the application of the Golden Rule, these writers asserted. The industrialist could not go on exploiting his employee and still remain a Christian. The employer who forgets "the value of persons in his quest for material gain, is likely to be a very well-matured pagan in his general outlook on life."[91] Labor must not be looked upon as a mere commodity to be bought in the market; the laborer is "your fellow human being, your brother, and has social and moral rights which you are bound by the moral law to respect."[92] The employer should constantly put himself in the workingman's position and do unto him as he would be done by. Similarly, the laborer who "interprets his job as an opportunity to get the highest possible wage for the least amount of service" exploits his employer and denies his Christian faith. Such selfish behavior, both in employee and employer, is sinful: "the man who pays low wages for the sake of high profits is immoral. The laborer who fails to do an honest day's work is likewise immoral."[93] The goal that both employer and employee should strive for together is industrial peace. Strife, in the forms of strikes and lockouts, is a social disease and should be cured by the obedience of all to the Golden Rule. An industry or a business "cannot be Christian so long as it divides men into warring groups."[94] The spiritual, moral, and physical welfare of both workers and their masters is dependent on mutual understanding and the will to obey the maxims of the Sermon on the Mount.

As we have seen in this chapter, the impact business had on the Protestant churches was neither universal nor uniform. The churches were affected in their general attitude toward the business culture. They endorsed the business spirit, they expressed admiration for the American businessman, they gave advice on how to become investors and fortune builders, and they strove to win the businessman for their cause and to make him join their fellowship. However, the Protestant doctrine was, on the whole, not affected by the dominant business ideology. The churches hesitated to make doctrinal statements on business-related issues, but when they did, their views were conservative and traditional. This leads us to investigate, in the next chapter, how the friendly attitude of the churches affected their operational methods and how business thus came to serve as a model for their activities.

NOTES

1. H. Richard Niebuhr, *The Kingdom of God in America* (New York: Harper & Row, 1959), pp. 168–69.

2. Clifton E. Olmstead, *History of Religion in the United States* (Englewood Cliffs, N.J.: Prentice-Hall, 1960), p. 556.

3. Walter Lippman, *A Preface to Morals* (1929; reprint, New York: Time-Life Books, 1964), pp. 105–6.

4. John Dos Passos, *Manhattan Transfer* (1925; reprint, Boston: Houghton Mifflin Company; 1953), p. 86; W. J. Dawson, "Vulgarizing Religion," *The Century Magazine* 86 (September 1924), p. 636.

5. Winthrop S. Hudson, *Religion in America* (New York: Charles Scribner's Sons, 1965), pp. 372–73; Sydney E. Ahlstrom, *A Religious History of the American People,*

(Garden City, N.Y.: Doubleday & Company, 1975) Vol. 2, pp. 384–85; Winthrop S. Hudson, *American Protestantism* (Chicago: University of Chicago Press, 1961), p. 152.

6. Harry Emerson Fosdick, *Christianity and Progress* (New York: Fleming H. Revell Company, 1922), p. 53. See also *Recent Social Trends in the United States* (New York: McGraw-Hill Book Company, 1933), Vol. 1, pp. 397–414.

7. Reinhold Niebuhr, *Does Civilization Need Religion?* (New York: Macmillan Company, 1927), pp. 176–77.

8. See Paul A. Carter, *The Decline and the Revival of the Social Gospel: Social and Political Liberalism in American Protestant Churches, 1920–1940* (Ithaca, N.Y.: Cornell University Press, 1956).

9. Arthur P. Gray, "Wages," *Southern Churchman*, July 30, 1927, p. 10.

10. John Herman Randall, *Religion and the Modern World* (New York: Frederick A. Stokes Co., 1929), p. 96. See also Olmstead, *History of Religion in the United States*, p. 561.

11. Irving Bernstein, *The Lean Years: A History of the American Worker, 1920–1933* (Boston: Houghton Mifflin Company, 1972), p. 8.

12. Miles H. Krumbine, "Are We to Have a Non-moral Religion?", *The Atlantic Monthly* 144 (December 1929), p. 823.

13. See Paul A. Carter, *The Twenties in America* (New York: Thomas Y. Crowell Company, 1968), p. 82; Robert Moats Miller, *American Protestantism and Social Issues, 1919–1939*, (Chapel Hill: University of North Carolina Press, 1958), pp. 18–22.

14. Shailer Mathews, "Business—Maker of Morals," *System, the Magazine of Business* 51 (March 1927), pp. 291, 398.

15. Roger W. Babson, "The Church's Greatest Asset—Its Young People," *The Presbyterian Survey* 16 (September 1926), pp. 519–521.

16. Arthur Holmes, "Business Must Have the Golden Rule," *The Christian Herald* 45 (February 11, 1922), p. 101.

17. Owen D. Young and Gerard Swope, *Selected Addresses* (General Electric Company, 1930), pp. 249–65.

18. John R. Pepper, "The Christian Man in Business," *The Nashville Christian Advocate* 95 (January 21, 1927), p. 70.

19. John W. Barton, "Business as a Profession," *The Methodist Quarterly Review* 74 (October 1925), pp. 640–55.

20. R. E. Magill, "Abounding Prosperity," *The Presbyterian Survey* 16 (April 1926), p. 202.

21. W. Edward Raffety, "The Go-Getter Adult Class: Its Areas and Aims," *Church Management* 5 (May 1929), p. 569.

22. *The Christian Herald* 45 (November 25, 1922), p. 2.

23. See "A Life of Real Service," *The Christian Herald* 45 (December 30, 1922), p. 926; "One Man's Road to Success," *The Christian Herald* 45 (September 16, 1922), p. 646; William L. Stidger, "The Man Behind Truth in Advertising," *The Christian Herald* 52 (September 28, 1929), p. 9; William Armstrong, "He Built Religion into Business," *The Christian Herald* 46 (June 16, 1923), p. 477.

24. Jack Mackenzie, "If There's a Saw-Mill in Heaven I Want to Run It," *The Christian Herald* 52 (July 27, 1929), pp. 4, 16.

25. Cameron Wilkie, "If You Could Talk for an Hour with Henry Ford," *The Christian Herald* 52 (July 20, 1929), pp. 4–5.

26. W. J. Moore, "Value of Real Estate Bonds: They Provide a Sound Investment and One Yielding High Returns," *The Christian Herald* 45 (March 4, 1922), p. 175.
27. John C. Madden, "Investing the First $1,000," *The Christian Herald* 50 (July 2, 1927), p. 589.
28. R. W. McNeel, "Wise Men and Their Money," *The Christian Herald* 46 (January 3, 1923), p. 15; Cary A. Rowland, "Bonds That End Bondage; Systematic Saving Leads Directly to Independence and Promotes Happiness," *The Christian Herald* 48 (November 7, 1925), p. 20; John C. Madden, "A Minister's Plan: By Systematic Thrift, He Succeeds in 'Buying an Income'," *The Christian Herald* 50 (March 5, 1927), p. 203.
29. John C. Madden, "Building a Fortune," *The Christian Herald* 48 (December 5, 1925), p. 16.
30. W. J. Moore, "Value of Real Estate Bonds," p. 175.
31. *The Christian Herald* 48 (December 5, 1925).
32. *The Christian Herald* 46 (February 24, 1923).
33. *The Christian Herald* 48 (November 7, 1925).
34. *The Christian Herald* 46 (August 18, 1923), p. 646.
35. John R. Pepper, "The Christian Man in Business," pp. 70–71.
36. Roger W. Babson, "Business Men and the Church," *Southern Churchman* (August 29, 1925), p. 9.
37. John R. Ewers, "The Conversion of a Business Man," *The Christian Century* 48 (April 30, 1925), p. 579.
38. Oliver M. Fisher, "The Golden Rule and Prosperity," *The Christian Herald* 45 (February 18, 1922), p. 118.
39. Robert S. and Helen M. Lynd, *Middletown: A Study in American Culture* (New York: Harcourt, Brace and Company, 1929), p. 403.
40. Roger W. Babson, "The Church's Greatest Asset", p. 520.
41. Pepper, "The Christian Man in Business," p. 71.
42. Halford E. Luccock, *Jesus and the American Mind* (New York: Abingdon Press, 1930), p. 195.
43. H. H. Horne, "A Moral Inventory for a Business Man," *The Christian Herald* 52 (February 23, 1929), p. 21.
44. Holmes, "Business Must Have the Golden Rule," p. 101.
45. Roger W. Babson, *Religion and Business* (New York: Macmillan Co., 1920), pp. 38–39.
46. Ralph S. Cushman, *The Message of Stewardship* (New York: Abingdon-Cokesbury Press, 1922), p. 158. See also Richard Braunstein, "Spending God's Money," *The Christian Herald* 50 (September 3, 1927), p. 768.
47. Wilbur Fisk Tillett, "The Golden Rule Versus the Rule of Gold," *The Methodist Quarterly Review* 74 (January 1925), p. 5.
48. Cushman, *The Message of Stewardship*, p. 161.
49. Tillett, "The Golden Rule Versus the Rule of Gold," p. 5.
50. Ibid., p. 8.
51. Peter Ainslie, "A Man with a Pitcher of Water," *The Christian Herald* 50 (July 23, 1927), p. 642.
52. "What Is Money?", *American Lutheran* 10 (October 1927), p. 8.
53. Julius Earl Crawford, *The Stewardship Life* (Nashville, Tenn.: Cokesbury Press, 1929), pp. 74–75.

54. Henry Burton Trimble, *The Christian Motive and Method in Stewardship* (Nashville, Tenn.: Cokesbury Press, 1929), p. 119.
55. Crawford, *The Stewardship Life*, p. 109.
56. Ibid., p. 107.
57. Tillett, "The Golden Rule Versus the Rule of Gold,", p. 7.
58. Samuel D. Price, "The Parable of the Pounds," *The Christian Herald* 46 (February 17, 1923), p. 143.
59. Samuel D. Price, "The Rich Man and Lazarus," *The Christian Herald* 46 (January 20, 1923), p. 61.
60. Edwin Holt Hughes, *Christianity and Success* (Nashville, Tenn.: Cokesbury Press, 1928), p. 29.
61. J. Marvin Culbreth, "Christianizing Property," *The Methodist Quarterly Review* 74 (October 1925), p. 635. See also, for instance, Sherwood Eddy, *Facing the Crisis: A Study in Present Day Social and Religious Problems* (New York: George H. Doran Company, 1922), p. 213.
62. Jesse T. Whitley, *Filled with Messages from Thee* (Richmond, Va.: Whittet & Shepperson, 1923), p. 22.
63. Trimble, *Christian Motive and Method*, p. 149.
64. Sherwood Eddy, *Religion and Social Justice* (New York: George H. Doran Company, 1927), pp. 64–65.
65. Harry Emerson Fosdick, *The Meaning of Service* (New York: Association Press, 1921), pp. 176.
66. Hughes, *Christianity and Success*, pp. 104–5.
67. Culbreth, "Christianizing Property," pp. 628–32; Dorr Frank Diefendorf, *The Christian in Social Relationships* (New York: The Methodist Book Concern, 1922), p. 10; Crawford, *The Stewardship Life*, pp. 114–15; Trimble, *Christian Motive and Method*, pp. 116–17; Daniel A. Poling, *An Adventure in Evangelism* (New York: Fleming H. Revell Company, 1925), pp. 186–87.
68. See for instance Samuel D. Price, "Christian Stewardship," *The Christian Herald* 50 (January 29, 1927), p. 96; "Do We Owe or Own?", *American Lutheran* 10 (October 1927), pp. 6–8; Crawford, *The Stewardship Life*, p. 8; Ernest Fremont Tittle, "The Why and How of Service," *The Christian Herald* 52 (July 27, 1929), p. 13.
69. Edwin M. Poteat, "Stewardship and Redemption," *The Missionary Review of the World* 43 (February 1920), pp. 113–16.
70. George Koenig, "Stewardship," *American Lutheran* 10 (October 1927), p. 10.
71. Crawford, *The Stewardship Life*, p. 39.
72. "The Principles of Stewardship," *American Lutheran* 10 (October 1927), p. 9.
73. Trimble, *Christian Motive and Method*, p. 155.
74. See, for instance, Joseph M. M. Gray, "Stewardship of the Whole Life," *The New York Christian Advocate* 102 (July 14, 1927), pp. 866–67, and Koenig, "Stewardship," p. 10.
75. Eva M. Cavers, "A Study in Stewardship," *The Presbyterian Survey* 16 (July 1926), pp. 436–38.
76. Crawford, *The Stewardship Life*, p. 115.
77. Cushman, *The Message of Stewardship*, pp. 165–66.
78. Quotation from H. R. Calkins reprinted in "Nuggets of Gold," *American Lutheran* 10 (October 1927), p. 17.

79. Warren A. Chandler, *Current Comments on Timely Topics* (Nashville, Tenn.: Cokesbury Press, 1926), p. 22.

80. E. J. Gallmeyer, "Stewardship," *American Lutheran* 9 (December 1926), pp. 11, 14. See also Theodore Graebner, "Who Is to Be Blamed for These Deficits?", *American Lutheran* 10 (October 1927), pp. 4–5; "Proportionate Giving," *American Lutheran* 10 (November 1927), pp. 1–2.

81. "The Lord's Business," *The Presbyterian Survey* 16 (June 1926), p. 383.

82. Mrs. Wilson W. Keyser, "Stewardship of Money," *The Presbyterian Survey* 16 (August 1926), pp. 461–62; "Is Tithing God's Plan?", *The Christian Century* 44 (December 1, 1927), pp. 1414–16; Roswell C. Long, "Getting Ready for Stewardship Study in November," *The Presbyterian Survey* 14 (October 1924), pp. 682–83.

83. John M. Versteeg, "Rescuing Stewardship from Materialism," *The New York Christian Advocate* 102 (October 6, 1927), pp. 1202–3.

84. Crawford, *The Stewardship Life*, p. 35.

85. Trimble, *Christian Motive and Method*, p. 166; Tillett, "The Golden Rule Versus the Rule of Gold," p. 6; Cushman, *The Message of Stewardship*, pp. 163–64.

86. Trimble, *Christian Motive and Method*, pp. 156–57.

87. Ibid., p. 158.

88. W. M. Clow, "The Gateway to Industrial Peace," *The Homiletic Review* 84 (November 1922), p. 396.

89. Cushman, *The Message of Stewardship*, pp. 176–77. See also Harvey Reeves Calkins, "The New Stewardship Methods," *The Missionary Review of the World* 52 (September 1929), pp. 705–7.

90. J. C. Venable, "Pentecost and Property," *The Presbyterian Survey* 101 (January 1926), p. 79. See also W. M. Clow, "The Gateway to Industrial Peace," *The Homiletic Review* 84 (November 1922), p. 397.

91. Trimble, *Christian Motive and Method*, pp. 138–39.

92. Tillett, "The Golden Rule Versus the Rule of Gold," pp. 10–11.

93. Trimble, *Christian Motive and Method*, p. 139.

94. Cushman, *The Message of Stewardship*, p. 183.

3

Religion as Business

The sympathetic attitude of many churches toward business produced a desire to organize ecclesiastical work according to commercial principles. Business was set up as a model worthy of being imitated both for the formation of church bodies and in the methods of evangelism. As Ben Primer has shown, American Protestant churches had already started to adopt business methods before World War I, but it was not until after the war that the religious agencies fully understood the value of a businesslike mode of operation.[1] There was a general feeling during the twenties that the churches must be made more efficient; they should be run on the same basis as a factory or a business corporation.

To American Protestantism the twenties was a period of compromise and adjustment. Many churches were leaning over backwards to fit into the pattern set by the commercial interests. They were convinced, as *The American Lutheran* said, that to be able to survive the church had to regain the appeal it had once had: "Today she must adjust her appeals and her methods to a complex social organism which is completely absorbed in countless temporal interests. In order to meet present-day difficulties and solve present-day problems the Church must meet present-day needs by an intelligent readjustment and gearing up of its machinery."[2] The church should, as *The Christian Herald* put it, "be thoroughly modern, making use of all modern devices to attract, competing, but in a more dignified manner, with those commercialized entertainments that are said to be keeping many away from church."[3]

Many churches were so taken in by the business spirit that they soon wished to become successful enterprises. Achievement was no longer measured in spiritual terms but in the size and numbers of salaries, budgets, members, and church buildings. Still the spiritual language was kept, creating in many churches a secular foundation with a religious superstructure. Visitors from Europe were puzzled by this development. André Siegfried noticed how the American churches had become "partially materialized," how, "although the vocabulary of the mystic still survived," money and efficiency were worshiped. Christ was no longer the "mystic of tradition" but the "perfect type of useful citizen, an efficient producer, almost . . . a successful and honest businessman."[4]

Like Siegfried, a few American churchmen were disconcerted by the tendency to equate membership drives with the work of the Holy Ghost and church attendance with submission to God. These critics deplored the development that had led to the fact that the church was only interested in people "as prospective customers and supporters of the institution." The old solemnity of worship was fast disappearing, they felt, and in its place there was a

general tendency to resort to popular lectures, moving pictures, Rotarian methods, church suppers, wild advertising, . . . follow-up letters, a paid official to detect the arrival of any new-comer to town and sign him up, programmes of sensational sermon courses, cartoonists, whistlers, comedians, enormous signs at the church porch, dwarfs, Indians, Negro Jubilee singers, freaks of all sorts, free ginger ale, services conducted exclusively by children, and a thousand other Chautauqua devices, in the hope of drawing a crowd.

Instead of trying, by any means, merely to get the people into the church building, the church should devote its time to getting "the spirit of Christ into the hearts of men."[5] R. A. Torrey, the well-known evangelist, was one of the most explicit critics:

I think it would be perfectly safe to say, that the church of Christ was never in all its history so fully and so skillfully and so thoroughly and so perfectly organized as it is today. Our machinery is wonderful, it is just perfect; but alas it is machinery without power; and when things do not go right, instead of going to the real source of the failure, our neglect to depend upon God and to look to God for power, we look around to see if there is not some new organization we can set up, some new wheel that we can add to our machinery. We have altogether too many wheels already. What we need is not so much some new organization, some new wheel, but "the Spirit of the living creature in the wheels" whom we already possess.[6]

THE CHURCH—THE GREATEST INDUSTRY IN THE WORLD

The tendency toward scientific management that Torrey deplored in the church was pervasive indeed. The business spirit was so infectious as to permeate much thinking and many activities of the Protestant churches. Both churchmen and laymen started to see the church in a new light. Charles M. Sheldon, author of the bestseller *In His Steps* and editor of *The Christian Herald*, wrote that "the biggest business in the world is not banking, railroading, journalism, manufacturing, or the machinery of science. The biggest business of the world is making Christian disciples of all nations."[7] This was not mere rhetoric, but a reflection of a not uncommon attitude. Roger Babson called the church "the greatest industry in the world today, as well as the oldest." However, he also held that it was "the most inefficiently operated of any industry in the world," a deficiency that should quickly be remedied. Babson imagined a future when churches would not operate independently but would be "linked up together under a general manager who will not be a parson, but who will be a business man."[8]

Babson's call for increased efficiency in the church was echoed by many. The church should turn to business and industry in order to learn not only efficiency, but also honesty, faith, and perseverance. The virtues of business leaders and the ideals of the industrial world were held forth as the norm after which the churches should model their work. As one editorial pointed out, the churches should adopt the policy of Henry Ford, who when asked what he would do if he were to take over a defunct auto industry answered that he would "tidy it up," and the editor continued: "No church, any more than a business, can go forward happily and helpfully in which there are dark passages, neglected committee corners, unhappy personal relationships."[9] *The Presbyterian Survey* pointed out that the modern industrial world had arrived at its high state of development after long years of study and efforts. The chief lesson it had learned was the one of efficiency. Only those "daring souls" who had sacrificed and persevered in order to make their business truly efficient had managed to get their names into "the "Who's Who' of high finance." The church should follow in the footsteps of business, the writer pleaded, and adopt its formula for success: "Let not our Southern Presbyterian Church retreat one step from the stand she has taken, viz., that the business of the Lord is worthy of the same business efficiency as any other organization."[10]

One of the most fervent advocates for the introduction of business acumen into the work of the church was Bruce Barton, famous as the author of *The Man Nobody Knows*, which portrayed Jesus as the most successful businessman of all times. Barton preached again and again that the church had much to learn from business. It could, for instance, learn honesty. Unlike business, he meant, the church tried to fool itself by including into its membership statistics people who were no longer active. Like business, the church should instead dare to start an objective investigation into its weaknesses. The church could also learn faith from business. As an example Barton mentioned how the General Electric company spent millions every year in its laboratories, "knowing that any day a scientist may come down with a discovery that may necessitate a complete change of method, and the discarding of millions of dollar's worth of machinery." The church did not have the same faith and courage. It rather feared every change. "Stated in another way," Barton wrote, "business is endlessly flexible and adaptable; the church is too often rigid and unadaptable." From business the church could also learn to make regular checkups to be sure that it was still headed to its original goals. By neglecting this, Barton felt, the church had changed the joyous, fun-loving Christ into a moralistic spoilsport. Finally, Barton argued that "any business is terrifically concerned if there be the slightest depreciation in the quality of the men who enter its ranks." Business was willing to make any effort and expense to get the right leaders. The church must likewise take great pains to find the men around whom the organization could be built.[11]

If many churchmen could not agree that the church had to go to business for faith, they still said amen to suggestions that would increase the efficiency of their own organization. Numerous articles and editorials tried to change the hesitant attitude of some Protestants toward the introduction of a more efficient mode of operation. They ridiculed the present ineptitude of the church by, for instance, quoting what a successful businessman had said: "If I were to conduct my business as most churches do, the sheriff would very soon close it up. The greatest proof to me of the divine origin of the church is its survival in spite of its unbusinesslike finance methods."[12] Churchmen argued persuasively to convince those who feared that the introduction of business efficiency "might detrimentally affect the spiritual life of the church," pointing out that the present confusion and slovenliness was a "very thorough way of keeping the manifestations of spiritual life throttled." And so they pleaded: "Let us stop speaking contemptuously of business efficiency in the Church. It has its place and it is an extremely important one."[13] They also found scriptural support for running the churches on business principles. Referring to such "excellent illustrations of business efficiency" as Moses and Nehemiah, they stated: "The Old Testament is a business document through and through—order, everywhere, the result of planning and preparation, day and night." The New Testament was no different; it was a "manual of business conducted on a big scale." And the first disciples continued in their turn the same work: "Church effectiveness in Paul's eyes was but a form of associated holiness."[14]

It was no coincidence that the twenties saw the appearance of such a journal as *Church Management*, which from 1923 on served the churches by giving advice on how to become more efficient organizing Sunday school classes, or drawing crowds to the midweek prayer meeting, or paying church debts, or advertising the activities of a new parish house. In the advertising section of the magazine, pastors could get useful information on the latest bulletin boards that would "pep up" their church and that would attract "attention at least two blocks away at night." Or they could study advertisements for typewriters, stencil duplicators, film projectors, screens, and invitation cards "that are sure to get attention."

THE BUSINESSMAN IN THE CHURCH

As the propagators of business efficiency gained an increased hearing within the churches, the position of the businessman became even more central than before. Businessmen were invited to take larger responsibility, both as volunteers and as hired professionals. Many churches employed business managers on a permanent basis; other churches hired an efficiency expert temporarily to get the rundown church on its feet. Strong voices argued that each church should have a fulltime business executive "to manage money matters and superintend details of the organization." Such a man should have "an aptitude for business, and a business education." This special commercial training would equip him "to talk with business men of the church in the language of everyday business" and would make it "much easier for him to raise money." The duties of the business manager were to sell the church to the community, to develop sociability and friendliness, and to "manage the activities in such a way that there will be a steady growth in membership."[15] The need for personal conversion as a basis for church membership was seldom emphasized in these articles.

Respectful articles were written about the new business managers in the church. One of these new men was Walter J. Bailey, who, starting out with a business education, made an impressive career within the church. While working for the Lakewood Church in Cleveland, for instance, he added 750 new members and developed the finances so that the church was able to pay all bills promptly. This was certainly a man worthy of being admired: "Mr. Bailey is primarily an organizer. He knows how to enlist, direct and enthuse a congregation of hundreds of people, and induce them to work for a common object. He is young, enthusiastic, a wonderful mixer, a good talker and very likable. He has blazed a new trail for capable young men who feel that they should find service in the church, but are not qualified to preach."[16]

If churches could not afford a permanent business manager, they often hired men who made it their job to turn failures into successes. Such a miracle worker was Harvey C. Miller, who used the same methods, he said, to put both businesses and churches on their feet. He had, for instance, made the Messiah Lutheran Church of Philadelphia into a "conspicuous success." What was wrong with many churches, Miller said, was that they used the "canal boat while business use[d] the airplane." When fishing for new members they did not get "the right bait." By adopting business methods, he claimed, the church could be made more attractive than the Sunday paper and the movie. Together with the pastor of the Messiah Lutheran Church, who "had enjoyed a business training," Miller had managed to defeat these mighty rivals. "Our first move," he explained, "was to secure the Philadelphia Orchestra for a Sunday evening service. The church was packed."[17]

A more common and cheaper way of reorganizing the church was to ask the businessmen in the congregation to put their abilities at the disposal of the church. Businessmen in the twenties were often exhorted to give to the church their wisdom and acumen. There was a great need for "our practical, successful Christian businessmen" to assist in solving the many complex problems that confront the church, a Methodist journal wrote, and continued: "The hour has struck in the Kingdom of God when a man who really desires to be a factor in promoting the success of God's Church must as surely commit himself to it as he would to any business from which he might fairly expect to gain his livelihood."[18] Lewis B. Franklin, Vice President and Treasurer of the National Council of the Episcopal Church, issued a call for 4,000 volunteers to assist him "as business managers in installing business methods in the Episcopal parishes of the country." Commenting upon this, *The American Lutheran* wrote: "Business needs more Christianity and Christianity needs more business. There is less excuse for doing God's work in a slip-shod way than there is for doing our own work in that manner."[19] The Presbyterian Church made a similar appeal: "Financing the Church is a great Kingdom Enterprise and deserves the best thought, prayer and energy of our business men.... No class of business men anywhere excell the Presbyterian group in capacity for leadership, business acumen or wealth."[20]

As the Christian businessmen answered the calls of their churches, they were often asked to take prominent positions and were elected elders or members of the church board. And the churches were proud to hand over much of the authority to their businessmen. *The Presbyterian Survey* boasted: "The Northern Presbyterian has among its members some of New York's foremost financiers. ...The historic American Board (Congregational) has for members some of Boston's best business men.... The Southern Methodist and Southern Baptist Boards have in their membership some of the South's ablest business men."[21] In the local congregation the man of commerce was also elevated into high positions and much admired by the other church members. When Roger Babson visited an Episcopal church, the collection was taken by four finely dressed gentlemen. The vestryman whispered to him: "Those are our four leading business men. One is the attorney who has just been fighting the prohibition law before the Supreme Court; another is the head of our steel company, who succeeded in crushing the late strike; the third is our leading banker; and the fourth is the owner of our largest department store."[22]

One of the businessmen who answered the call to service was Alonzo C. Monagle. When he became a board member of the Williams Avenue Church in Brooklyn, the congregation had dwindled and its finances were in a poor state. Monagle immediately presented a plan for a "bigger, better Williams Avenue." He approached the problem with the attitude that "religious affairs are exactly like business in the character and abilities required in handling them....A church problem has a different content from a business one, but in solving it a man needs the same sort of equipment he uses in facing business challenges." The old pastor of the Williams Avenue Church was asked to leave, and a new, young and enthusiastic minister was employed. Another man was also hired, a salesman who was to sell the church to the neighborhood through the method of door knocking. The message he was asked to give to the community was the following:

> Have you been in this Williams Avenue Church down at the corner? Great place. Shouldn't miss it. Brightest spot in the neighborhood. Wonderful man there. Preaches; tells you how to be happier and better. Great entertainments, too. Man preaching is a Billy Sunday, a three-ring circus, Saturday afternoon at Coney Island and Dwight L. Moody all in one. Don't miss it![23]

Under the guidance of Alonzo C. Monagle, the Williams Avenue Church soon became a "bigger" church, but whether it also became "better" remains a matter of definition.

In order to activate the businessmen within the church and to attract new businessmen, churches arranged special groups, clubs, and Sunday school classes whose program and organization were geared toward men and women from the commercial class. The goals and set-ups of these fellowships varied. Some were meant as Christian counterparts to such civic clubs as Rotary and Kiwanis; others were characterized by a heavier emphasis on Bible study. In one Business Women's Circle that Julia Lake Skinner described, members made up and sang their own "circle songs," had contests and games, and presented music programs, but they also found time for Bible study and prayer.[24] The "Business Bible Class" of a Protestant church in St. Louis met every Sunday to study the Bible from a particular point of view. The leader of the class, Donley D. Lukens, explained his intentions:

> Taking the Bible all the way through, there are plenty of passages which have a direct bearing upon business today, and if these passages are studied and applied they will be found to be practical business sense. They will make for success in business—looking at the question from the material side only—and they certainly will make business a better and cleaner thing for all of us who are in it.[25]

One churchman wrote an article arguing for the introduction of what he called "Go-Getter" Adult Classes in Sunday school. He had been so impressed by the indomitable spirit that characterized Peter B. Kyne's *The Go-Getter*, a "fascinating little story" with a "big, unforgettable message," that he felt the church could profit from: "The joyous optimistic message of Kyne's book will put iron in the blood and the glow of success on the cheek of discouraged adult class leaders, or ought to if they once catch the spirit of it." This spirit of success should also form the basis for a new kind of adult class, which would be characterized by aggressive Christianity that "keeps going from success to success, turning difficulties and defeats into glorious triumphs." Organized according to business principles, divided into efficient subgroups and headed by an executive committee, the go-getter class should not, however, study business ethics or solve the financial problems of the church, but should release its dynamic energy into spiritual growth and "personal evangelism."[26]

THE PASTOR AS EXECUTIVE

Not only was the church willing to pattern itself after business and to hand over authority to the businessmen; the pastor was expected, and often willing, to model his work on that of the businessman, to become an executive of a firm or a supervisor of a plant. The businessman was often held forth as a paragon for the minister, whether it concerned the organization of his work, his relations to the community, or his personal conduct. The following comment by Robert Cashman is only one in a host of similar comments:

> Just as a salesman is rewarded in business by his ability to adopt his personality to those with whom he comes in contact, so the minister's success in the work of his parish may depend upon his ability to so conduct himself that in his daily living, he will win the respect, confidence and co-operation of his people.[27]

Those pastors who felt at a loss about how to become more businesslike had access to numerous courses, handbooks, and articles giving practical advice. Many divinity schools started offering courses in business administration for pastors. The one offered by the Chicago Theological Seminary included such subjects as

> the minister's office, its organization and equipment; his correspondence, files and records, his use of time, his personal conduct, appointments, bills, investments; his staff, paid or volunteer, and how to secure their cooperation; conventions, conferences and special meetings, care of church property, financial campaigns, church advertising and publicity; building a new church; the minister and his young people; the minister and his men; the minister and the women's groups; pastoral calls; church officials; clerical habits and manners; weddings and funerals, the conduct and the follow-up; community relationships, lodges, politics, outside interests; dealing with misfits; the minister's home life.[28]

Reporting upon this, *The Christian Century* felt that such courses were sorely needed in the church. Roger Babson wished that the seminaries would go even further: "The church will never come to its own until the theological schools give the best course in economics procurable, and until the preachers are the best informed economists in their communities."[29] If the pastor did not have the time nor the money to attend a business course, he could read one of the many business manuals published especially for pastors, such as Clausen's *The Technique of a Minister*, Day's *Business Methods for the Clergy*, or Leach's two books, *How to Make the Church Go* and *Church Administration*.

Or the minister could consult the many articles dealing with various aspects of business efficiency. Even though most Protestant journals published articles of this kind, *Church Management* took it as its special duty to inform and enthuse its readers, usually pastors, concerning ways and means to ministerial success. It published articles on how to organize the minister's office so as to save the minister's "precious time" and give it a "more businesslike appearance." The author gave detailed advice on everything from desks and filing cases down to statistical charts on the wall showing "church growth as related to the community." He also made clear that this was the basis for all future work: "If the minister is to be an executive, and is to control the forces at his command, he must first organize his own office."[30] Other articles discussed the minister as executive and as salesman. Quoting as norm the advice of E. P. Ripley, president of the Santa Fe Railroad: "The executive's chief business is to organize, deputize, and supervise," the author of one article stated that it was the pastor's duty "to multiply himself." He should put natural leaders to work, should discover and train the latent leaders, and should replace the inefficient helpers "just as a business house might do."[31] "The minister is a salesman," another article stated. He is constantly selling his wares to the public, and "his success or failure depend upon the skill with which he persuades people to accept that which he has to offer." To succeed, the minister should study the salesmanship of the businessman, which always starts with the buyer's interests: "This higher type of salesmanship is greatly needed in the ministry."[32]

From October 1926 to April 1927, *Church Management* published a series of seven articles by J. W. G. Ward on "Factors in Ministerial Success." The seven topics dealt with were "Be Ambitious," "Concentrate," "System," "The Will to Power," "Enthusiasm," "Perseverance," and "Optimism." These titles read like the chapter headings in one of the common secular success manuals, and the contents are not much different. Although Ward states occasionally that the motive of the pastor must be that Christ should be glorified, the reader is left with the impression that ministerial success is the equivalent of self-aggrandizement. The message of positive thinking and the sententious sayings that truffle these articles sound like echoes from the handbooks for business success. There is nothing here of obedience and submission to Christ, but rather there is the asserting of the will and the ambition that are already within you. Ward asks in "The Will to Power":

> How can spineless consent to bafflement be supplanted by an aggressive faith which spells success? The answer is in himself. None can tell what heights are possible if only there be the will to power.... Visualize courage and fortitude. Inhale deeply, brace the shoulders, hold both head and chest high. Then you can affirm ... "I am magnetic in influence, and I radiate strength and good-will. I am happy, and increase happiness everywhere. I am conqueror of my circumstances, and victor over environment. I am ambitious, determined, sure that success will eventually crown my efforts because Christ shall be magnified in all I do."

Again the businessman was set up as the guiding light to the minister. When speaking of the need for systematization, for instance, Ward commented: "No merchant would achieve anything if he neglected the elemental principles of punctuality and industry. Can the minister dare to disregard them?" Discussing the virtue of perseverance, he pointed out that, in times of adversity, many a businessman had discovered the Moses within him: "Dismissed from his post as a young man, or confronted by ruin, a new self emerged. Powers of determination and resourcefulness undreamt of before, gushed forth like water from the smitten rock. And he never looked back from that hour." A few ministers, he pointed out, have followed this example set by the businessman and have succeeded through perseverance: "Through long years, they have kept on keeping on. Refusing either to abandon their work or to slacken speed, they have outdistanced many a competitor, and are a living commentary on the legendary hare and tortoise."[33] By openly declaring fellow-ministers to be competitors who were to be outdistanced, Ward here went further than most authors in the twenties, even though the idea as such was not foreign to the ecclesiastical climate of the time.

Those ministers who had made "successful" careers were written up as exemplars whose thinking and actions were worthy of being copied. In most of these ministerial success stories, it was pointed out that the pastor in question had a background of commercial training or experience. John Timothy Stone, for instance, was presented as a "business man in religion." Already in college he had proved to be a business genius, and all his professors advised him to pursue a commercial career. Stone chose the ministry, but into it he took "his talents of organization and business and an energy that clicks twenty-four hours a day." As a matter of course he rose swiftly and accomplished much, because he had never "deserted the tenets of business." When the interviewer met Stone, at the peak of the latter's career, he was not sure whether he met a minister or a businessman: "You are speaking with a man of handsome physical aspect, clear-eyed, firm-lipped, hard-headed and outspoken. Coming across him in the business world, in Wall Street, in New York, in the grain exchanges in Chicago or in the shipping business in California, you would know you had encountered a superior businessman who was making a success of his life, who was master of his environment and who took leadership when it was not readily granted him."[34]

Rev. E. J. Unruh of Macomb, Illinois, also had a commercial background, associating freely with "business executives, salesmen, promoters." He had also taken his efficiency expertise into the ministry and was still applying it to all he did. He had systematized sermon writing, constantly adding thoughts and quotations on index cards. In this way he had twenty-five sermons taking form at the same time. The minister must "carefully budget his time," Unruh advised his fellow ministers, and he must be efficient: "Any procedures that do not make for reasonable efficiency must be replaced at once." As an example he mentioned that pastoral calls can easily be cut down from 20–30 minutes to 10–15 minutes, if one abandons the alphabetical list system and makes the calls according to geographical location.[35] One may also mention Dr. Burris A. Jenkins, pastor of the Linwood Christian Church in Kansas City, Missouri, who was depicted as a "prophet of a new day and the new way," and who used movies, "sermonettes," Open Forums, discussion dinners to attract a crowd, and who ran a "regular psychiatric clinic" on Mondays and Fridays.[36]

Not all ministers felt at ease in their role as business executives. James Brett Kenna, heading a "successful" church, was not alone in feeling that this role had been forced upon him much against his will. The church and the minister had been caught in the American obsession, so characteristic of business, of organizing everything "from the production of toothpicks to the educational system," Kenna stated, and in the American habit of "gauging success by the spectacular." A successful church, he held, "like a successful furniture shop, is the one which has the biggest assortment of wares, and affords the biggest income." Kenna deplored the influence this business climate had on him as a pastor: "I see myself inevitably becoming little more than the well-paid executive of a large business organization, and that my dreams of spiritual influence are not coming true and, apparently, have small chance of ever coming true under existing circumstances." He complained that he had no time for Bible study, no time to grow spiritually, because he was always expected to be "efficient" and to "hustle." One third of his energy was devoted to the job of "coaxing money out of men's pockets," and most of what was left went into planning visitation campaigns and surveys and into "selling" his institution "just as surely and skillfully as the man hired by the local Chamber of Commerce 'sells' his organization." And the final judgment of him was based on his abilities and accomplishments as an administrator and hustler: "I am a successful minister if at the end of the church year I can show an imposing number of new members. If under my direction the membership doubles in three years, I am a wonder and certain to be asked to a new and bigger parish where the salary is more, the publicity better, and the advertising problem stiffer."[37]

Sinclair Lewis also made fun of the willingness of certain ministers to adopt business attitudes and practices. In *Babbitt*, he satirized both the evangelist Mike Monday, "the world's greatest salesman of salvation," and John Jennison Drew, the pastor of Babbitt's church. The "eloquent, efficient, and versatile," Drew was "proud to be known primarily as a business man" and was often heard to say that he certainly was not going to "permit the old Satan to monopolize all the pep and punch." From his lowly origin as a newspaper boy, he had risen to the top to head one of the largest and richest churches of Zenith. He had made his church into a true community center, which "contained everything but a bar." He wrote much-admired editorials on "The Dollars and Sense Value of Christianity" and decorated his office with a wall-placard reading "This is the Lord's Busy Day."[38]

Lewis drew his most cruel—and scandalously injust, many said at the time—portrait of the businessman-pastor in *Elmer Gantry*. The picture of Elmer Gantry was partially based on weekly "Sunday School classes," in which Lewis met Kansas City pastors for discussions. During these sittings he met an attitude of success-thinking and unbelief, which he included in his novel and which made him accuse the ministers present of hypocrisy. "Don't you see," he charged, "that no man can be a successful preacher unless he is a fundamentalist, because dogmatic denunciation is the intellectual gait of the people in your pews?"[39] However, the portrait of Elmer Gantry came out much more extreme than all his models combined, and the satire would have been more convincing if it had been more low-keyed. Elmer is an infidel, a charlatan, a wolf in sheep's clothes, which most "success pastors" obviously were not. But otherwise Lewis perceptively draws attention to many of the phenomena that characterized the situation of the modern pastor. Gantry worked alternatingly as pastor and businessman, and to him there was no real difference between the two professions. When he worked as a salesman he used the oratory of the preacher, and when he served as a minister he employed the technique of the salesman; necessary for success in both jobs were "buttery words and an important manner" (Gantry, p. 116). After a successful time in Sharon Falconer's money-making evangelistic "circus" and a period of teaching students how to become prosperous, Gantry becomes a Methodist minister and starts climbing the ecclesiastical ladder. Making use of all imaginable methods of the commercial world, he manages to draw attention to his church and himself, to build an everspreading reputation, with the consequence that he is called to larger and larger churches. After a few years he is called to the Wellspring Methodist Church, Zenith, and he enters it "like the new general manager of a factory"; his first comment is: "The plant's run down—have to buck it up." And this he certainly does. Soon the church is bustling with activities. There are groups and committees for everything. The attendance rises from a hundred to a thousand. Elmer dresses and behaves more and more like an executive, becomes a Rotarian, meets weekly with the other Methodist ministers of Zenith who look like a "group of prosperous and active business men." At these meetings they listen to

> papers on trade subjects—the sort of pews most soothing to the black; the value of sending postcards reading "Where were you last Sunday, old scout? We sure did miss you at the men's Bible Class"; the comparative values of a giant imitation thermometer, a giant clock, and a giant automobile speedometer, as a register of the money coming in during special drives; the question of gold and silver stars as rewards for Sunday School attendance; the effectiveness of giving the children savings-banks in the likeness of a jolly little church to encourage them to save their pennies for Christian work; and the morality of violin solos.[40]

In the end Elmer Gantry reaches his ultimate goal, which gives him national attention. He becomes pastor of a New York church and in addition is appointed executive secretary of the National Association for the Purification of Art and the Press. And during his rise to power and glory, he is always aware that he is a whited sepulcher.

BUSINESS METHODS IN THE CHURCH

Reverend John Jennison Drew in *Babbitt* made use of the latest techniques, plans, and tools to make his church "progressive." The Chatham Road Presbyterian Church had a nursery, a Thursday evening supper, a gymnasium, a fortnightly motion picture–show, a library of technical books for young workmen—"though, unfortunately, no young workman ever entered the church except to wash the windows or repair the furnace"—and a sewing circle, which made pants for the children of the poor. In another part of Zenith, however, Elmer Gantry was even more deft at pepping up his Wellspring methodist Church and drawing a curious crowd. The methods he used were more vulgar, and Dr. Drew presumably considered it beneath him to resort to such uncouth gimmicks. Gantry started his "Lively Sunday Evenings," which made him famous and which really appealed to the masses. Each Sunday night the church was crowded with people eager to be entertained and to take part in the singing of such songs as "Swanee River" and "Tipperary." Gantry was in his right element, goading the crowd into feeling that they were all "happy boys and girls together":

> He made the women sing in contest against the men; the young people against the old; and the sinners against the Christians. That was lots of fun, because some of the most firmly saved brethren, like Elmer himself, pretended for a moment to be sinners. He made them whistle the chorus and hum it and speak it; he made them sing it while they waved handkerchiefs, waved one hand, waved both hands.
> Other attractive features he provided. There was a ukulele solo by the champion uke-player from the University of Winnemac. There was a song rendered by a sweet little girl of three, perched up on the pulpit. There was a mouth organ contest, between the celebrated Harmonica Quartette from the Higginbotham Casket Factory and the best four harmonicists from the B. & K.C. railroad shops.[41]

Gantry's reputation grew, and he continued to use increasingly extreme methods to put himself and his church in the limelight. He illustrated his sermons with live frogs and wrecked cars. He started the "only class in show-window dressing in any church in the United States."

Lewis's pictures of the business methods used by clergymen Drew and Gantry are not particularly overdrawn. They present tendencies and attitudes fairly representative of numerous Protestant churches in the twenties. Obviously, not all churches went to such extremes as that of Elmer Gantry. But some went even further. And few were completely unaffected by the new methods. There is little difference between Lewis's portrait of Dr. Drew's church and the *Homiletic Review*'s description of the City Temple (Presbyterian U.S.A.) in Dallas, which carried

> as institutional features monthly motion pictures, gymnasium classes for both sexes, auditorium to be let for community purposes, daily vacation Bible-school, clubs for boys and girls, employment bureau, gallery of sacred art, hospital for babies, clinic, school for nurses, kindergarten for unprivileged children, open house for young people on Thursday nights, physician and free service on demand, reading-room for boys, afternoon Sunday-school, twenty-seven languages for foreign-speaking people, organized charities, cemetery lot.[42]

In the twenties many Protestant churches became community-oriented service institutions, which deliberately employed secular methods to become acceptable to as many people as possible. Gymnasiums, clinics, and kindergartens were included in the church program partly because church authorities thereby hoped to reach the unchurched and partly because these activities gave the church an appearance of being a dynamic and necessary force in society. Size and variety became fundamental to church life. The more activities a church could offer, the more progressive it was regarded; the more people that could be lured to put their feet within the church premises each week, the more successful the church and its minister were considered. The establishment of more or less secular groups within the church was a method in itself to attract people. In order to convince prospective attendants of their need for such activities, sales methods were introduced: the use of newspapers, parish papers, advertising, rally days, and house-to-house canvassing, all of which were "signs of progress," according to *The American Lutheran*, which witnessed of "a spirit of new aggressiveness"[43] (see illustration 4). Again the church could learn from business to employ the "aptest tools." God is no friend of fools, Harry Emerson Fosdick declared, and continued: "We can no more successfully serve him with obsolete ecclesiastical machinery and methods long outgrown than we can carry on modern commerce with dugout canoes or clothe the world from family spinning wheels."[44]

Many people responded favorably to this frantic, seven-day-a-week activity of the churches. After playing basketball in the church gymnasium or attending the Thursday night discussion dinner on "the Significance of Eugene V. Debs," many people left with the conviction that they had taken part in something "churchly" or "religious," which may have been a soothing thought. As one minister, critical of the system, pointed out: "To be active is far less taxing than to pay attention to spiritual matters." The same clergyman held that many outsiders saw the hollowness that existed behind the screen of activity: "When the church begins to stress athletics, entertainments, and social clubs, the outsider wonders if it has failed to make a go of religion. To his eyes these things are evidence of spiritual bankruptcy."[45] Even if some outsiders were as perspicacious as this, many more were not; they participated gladly in the many nonspiritual activities. The churches may have emphasized social activities to such an extent also because it was easier to ask for money for something tangible and socially "useful." It was much more difficult, one minister explained, to make people contribute economically in gratitude for "that most intimate and intangible value which Jesus called 'abundant life'."[46]

To provide quarters for these numerous functions, many churches built what they called "church houses," "parish houses," or "community houses." These buildings were usually separated from the church edifice, because this would make it easier for the unchurched to feel at home. The community house and its surrounding area offered sites for tennis, baseball, basketball, billiards, bowling, swimming, and occasionally boxing. Here the visitor could also eat, read, listen to lectures, see movies, meet his friends and make new social contacts. As an example I may mention the Methodist Church of Second Avenue, New York, where "the church and community building have elevators and provide

Illustration 4

A parish paper as a tool to make the church more efficient. (*The American Lutheran*, November 1925. Used with permission.)

a small but attractive chapel, offices, pool room, bowling alleys, the largest swimming pool in Manhattan, assembly hall with stage and motion-picture outfit, gymnasium, dining room, class rooms, parlors and club rooms, roof garden, and quarters for residents."[47] As may be seen from this description, the community house was often organized to attract men, since so few men felt drawn to the church in the 1920s. The parish house of St. Bartholomew's Church, New York, offered, for instance, "informal Tuesday evening one-hour talks, regular social events such as ladies' night, pool and billiard contests and card tournaments, an annual smoker which is a tremendous success, business men's classes in the gymnasium three times a week, athletic teams, and boxing classes."[48] The manager of the parish house reported that it was so filled with men that larger space was needed.

But the needs of men were not the only ones to be satisfied. Nurseries and kindergartens were opened. The services of physicians and psychiatrists were offered. Employment agencies were operated.[49] St. James Episcopal Church, New York, ran a cafeteria for girls, serving 200–250 girls a day. This cafeteria was really a club with "restroom, writing facilities, piano, periodicals, lavatory, and showers." After the girls had had their lunch they turned on "a phonograph and danced in the gymnasium." To underline the nonspiritual atmosphere, the church had decided that "no announcements of services or proselyting" would be permitted.[50] And if a church did not feel confident about how to establish its community house, it could get advice from firms specializing in precisely this, such as the Brunswick-Balke-Collender Company of Milwaukee, which had helped "hundreds of progressive churches" to install "highly successful recreational centers."[51]

It may be argued that such activities as those described here were not necessarily the result of a business influence but were merely social activities that have always been arranged by American churches in order to reach a larger audience. This claim is partially true, but then one must remember two things. First, in comparison to European churches, for instance, churches in America have always been more prone to arrange secular activities to sell their message, which may certainly be a result of the continuous business influence on the Protestant churches. Secondly, the increase in secular activities in the American churches that undoubtedly took place in the 1920s runs parallel to the increase in business authority and the spreading of business methods that characterized the age.

One of the most favored methods of drawing an audience, particularly a male audience, to the community house or the church was to arrange discussions, lectures, open forums, "men's nights," and club meetings noncommittal enough to be palatable to most nonbelievers. If we only get them within the church walls, ministers and church boards argued, we can make people feel at home and we can influence them by our genial fellowship; then they might want to join the church. The policy was to make the visitors gradually accustomed to the Christian message by first introducing in secular discussions and lectures a few comments of a religious nature, later making these comments more specific. The danger with this method was that the minister never felt that the audience was ready for a full presentation of the Gospel. Instead, the "spiritual" message was often limited to an appeal to join the church.

These lectures and discussion meetings were more or less secular. Every Sunday over a period of two years, Dr. Percy Stickney Grant, the liberal minister of the Church of the Ascension in New York, gave lectures entirely restricted to social and economic problems. "I have treated my congregation as though they were members of the Century Club," he said of his 800 regular attendants, "and the Century Club considers itself a pretty highbrow club."[52] Other gatherings of this type were more Christian, at least in name. The Bible Discussion Class of Brick Presbyterian Church, New York, used biblical texts as a starting point for discussions on such topics as "Peace; the Washington Arms Conference; The Significance of Eugene V. Debs; Jazz—Its Manifestations in Fashions, Manners, and Character; The Cynic; Socialism—New and Old; Prohibition; The Soldier Bonus; Women in Public Life; Demagogs and Prodigals; The Complications of the Simple Life."[53]

As step-by-step introductions to the Gospel, most of these discussion and lecture events were failures. In a few instances, however, the underlying policy seems to have worked. The Central Presbyterian Church of Buffalo, New York, organized "The Brotherhood," a club where men met for lectures, discussions, entertainments, bowling, and billiards. Here lifelong friendships were formed, character was "well-built," and manhood was "uplifted in the wholesome atmosphere," as in so many other clubs. But this club also had a spiritual dimension to it; out of the Brotherhood grew a Bible-study class of about 200 men.[54] Rev. William L. Stidger could report similar results from his "Chautauqua Church" meetings in Detroit. Modeling his Sunday night services on the format of the Chautauqua lectures, he devoted the first half of the service to secular entertainment such as trumpet solos, "dramatic book talks," and art pictures on a silver screen, after which he introduced a spiritual message. "As for us," Reverend Stidger wrote, "we have not had a single service of this kind winter or summer in which the end has not been the giving of an invitation to men and women to give their hearts to Christ and that somebody has not done it." During the summer of 1923 alone, he pointed out, more than fifty had responded to that invitation.[55]

Many articles were written on how to make such discussion clubs and men's classes successful. The techniques and methods suggested were almost invariably inspired by those used in business. The men's class of the Allegheny Baptist Church in Philadelphia had more than doubled in a year. This had been achieved not by a change of teacher or officers, but through a change of methods: "Running a Bible Class successfully requires the same methods as running a factory or running a grocery store." Many new men had joined the group after they had experienced its "modern spirit of 'get up and go do it'."[56] Rev. Arthur Talmadge Abernathy from Ashville, North Carolina, proudly boasted that he had built up the largest community Bible school in America. In order to increase the number of students from 75 to 2,000, he had shown films, invited local and national celebrities to sing and give addresses, and employed all publicity methods possible.[57] Another article told of how a young men's class had become a success. A bright young man—a sales and efficiency engineer—had been engaged in organizing the class. He had promptly organized it "as though it were a manufacturing plant," establishing such business positions for the boys as president, sales manager, works manager, floor superintendent, efficiency engineer, and shipping clerk. Every boy got a position and a duty to fulfill. At the end of each month, judging from the performance of the boys, promotions and bonuses were distributed. The first part of the meetings were devoted to "management business," and the latter half usually to the study of a Bible hero, where it was shown, for instance, "how Paul was one of the greatest salesmen the world has ever known."[58] When Babbitt is turning the Sunday school of the Chatham Road Presbyterian into his "Christianity Incorporated," he is working very much in the same spirit.

To "compel" the unwilling in the highways to come to the house of worship, the American churches in the twenties also employed the method of showing films, and to a lesser extent plays,[59] in their evening services. The tremendous growth of the film industry in the 1920s had made the movie a dangerous rival to the church. In an attempt to neutralize this mighty competitor, the church incorporated it into its own program. In addition, it was soon discovered what undreamed-of possibilities the movie offered for presenting the Gospel.

Films were employed in the most varied ways, as evangelistic appeals, as dramatizations of Bible stories, as a basis for religious interpretation, and as secular attractions to the unchurched. The medium became so popular that it was reported as early as 1923 that 15,000 church schools and clubs were using motion pictures in their work.[60] Some churches used secular films to present a religious message. The First Congregational Church in Rockport, Massachusetts, had managed to increase its attendance on Sunday night from 12 to 500 by showing films based on such popular stories as Channing Pollock's *The Enemy* and Warrick Deeping's *Sorrell and Son*. These films were then made the starting point for a Christian message.[61] Charles M. Sheldon tells of another church where the attendance had grown from 300 to more than a thousand. In this church the pastor always commented on the film and finished by making a "plain, straightforward evangelistic appeal . . . for those present to make their definite promise to God to serve Him." Sheldon warned that a movie must never be used to "make a show of it.": "A church is not organized to entertain people. It is not in the amusement business."[62] And there was evidently a cause for Sheldon's warning. Some churches believed themselves to be in the amusement business. They showed secular films without comments or ulterior motives, and managed to draw large crowds. To mention only one example, Rev. Claude S. Hanby of Rolla, Missouri, was proud to have shown such films as *Anne of Green Gables*, *The Courtship of Miles Standish*, *Daddy Long Legs*, *Pollyanna*,

Bunty Pulls the Strings, *The Little Lord Fauntleroy*, and *The Three Musketeers*. To make the showings even more popular, Hanby gave prizes to the boys who did the best impersonations of characters in the films and to those who wrote the best essays on the subject treated in the films. When he showed *The Colonial Girl*, "an award was made to the girl wearing the best colonial costume." To justify his showing of secular films, Hanby explained that "the aims of the Church are cultural and social as well as religious."[63]

Hanby's use of contests and prizes, like Elmer Gantry's exhibitions of frogs and wrecked cars, was part of a predilection among certain American preachers to resort to ever increasingly spectacular and eye-catching methods. Many historians, such as Frederick Lewis Allen, Herman Krooss, Paul Carter and Robert Moats Miller,[64] have made fun of how pastors made an usher blow a whistle every time a dollar bill was dropped in the collection plate or of how the Swedish Immanuel Congregational Church in New York offered an engraved certificate of preferred stock in the Kingdom of God to all who would contribute $100 to its building fund. The list of such extreme gimmicks can be made much longer. A "conspicuous protestant church, of a regular denomination" in Los Angeles planned a "pugilistic exhibition," starring Jack Dempsey. The proceeds, expected to be $20,000, were to pay the church debt.[65] Another example of aggressive Christianity could be found in the First Presbyterian Church of Tulsa, Oklahoma, which organized a team of thirty "Minute Men" whose task it was to recruit new members to the church.[66] Or one could mention Paul F. Boller's church, which had a special "stunt committee" to organize the "funs and thrills," particularly for Men's Night. Basing its activity on that of Rotary and Kiwanis, the church made the men feel at home by letting them participate in contests in which they ate crackers and whistled Yankee Doodle or ran relay races by pulling toy trains on the end of strings.[67] Finally one may point to the businesslike methods used on the annual Rally Day to "wake up the community and tag up the town," as W. Edward Raffety phrased it. Churches used special bulletin boards, posters, ads, banners, auto stickers, pennants, buttons, hat bands and armbands to draw attention to themselves. Raffety wrote: "Ingenious committees use balloons, kites, bands, radios, and everything under the sun to get the Rally Day message to the eyes and ears of the people." They also used specially composed songs and poems, one of which Raffety reprinted because it had "pep in it." The poem made no reference at all to either God or Christ, but sounded rather like a theme song for Peter B. Kyne's *Go-Getter*. Its first verse ran as follows:

> If you strike a thorn or rose—
> Keep a-goin'!
> If it hails or if it snows—
> Keep a-goin'!
> 'Tain't no use to set and whine
> When the fish ain't on your line;

Bait your hook and keep a-tryin'—
Keep a-goin'![68]

The most extreme gimmicks were criticized and ridiculed by many believers as well as nonbelievers. In its anticlericalism, *The American Mercury* welcomed every stunt that put the church into a ludicrous light, as when the Baptist Temple in Brooklyn gave a free Bible to the father and son who looked most alike or when Reverend Brougher, after a baptismal service, gave a talk on "Are Scotch People Stingy, and Would a Scotchman Make a Good Husband?"[69] But many sensible Christians as well took exception to the ballyhoo methods. The means by which we try to attract the unchurched, *The American Lutheran* held, must always be in conformity with the dignity of the church message:

The enticing of people to church by means of all sorts of strange allurements, with the underlying purpose of giving them an unexpected little Gospel dose, smacks of dishonesty and is so recognized by all honest men. The crowds that the modern sensational preacher draws are not seekers after truth but seekers after amusement, after a thrill. . . . May the Lutheran Church never prostitute its God-given commission to the restless desires of emotional sensation seekers.[70]

CHURCH ADVERTISING

The most significant business method adopted by the church in its struggle for survival was advertising. Commercial advertising was well established after the war, but its growth during the twenties was astounding. Although this development has not been fully recorded, it has been estimated that the sums spent on advertising probably tripled during the decade. It has further been computed that in 1927 the volume of advertising was about a billion-and-a-half dollars, a figure that by 1929 had grown by another 300 million. The number of national advertisers grew from around 5,000 in 1925, to 8,500 at the end of the decade. Through this expansion the advertising industry became a force that helped transform American society, as President Coolidge explained in 1926: "It makes new thoughts, new desires and new actions. . . . It is the most potent influence in adopting and changing the habits and modes of life, affecting what we eat, what we wear, and the work and play of the whole nation."[71]

At an early stage, the Protestant churches were made aware of the new possibilities that the publicity industry offered. In the spring of 1920, the Episcopal Church and the Northern Baptists launched very successful advertising campaigns. These campaigns, as so many others later in the decade, were inspired and carried out with ideals and methods from the business world. The Episcopal Church explained the basis for its new policy in the following manner: "If cigarets, breakfast foods, life insurance, and motor-cars are susceptible of successful advertising campaigns, why not the greatest thing in the world—

religion?"[72] Most of the other denominations expressed the same dependence on business methods. *The American Lutheran* held that church advertising should learn from the methods of the department stores, which managed to put "such an urge into the consciousness of the people that if my wife or your wife has a dollar in her pocketbook it burns a hole to get out and be exchanged for something one of these stores has to sell."[73] In a book published by the Southern Baptist Convention, Richard Beall Niese wrote:

> If nations are molded through publicity, wars are fought and won through publicity, great industries grow greater through the use of advertisements, the moving picture business was born and bred on "blaring hokum" spread through the press, and great cities are built by the use of newspapers, then is it not feasible to believe that the greatest business in the world, the winning of lost souls to Jesus, can be made to sweep the world through the use of the great newspapers?[74]

New organizations and positions were created by the church to handle publicity questions. Most denominations hired their own publicity secretaries. Together with the Associated Advertising Clubs of the World and local advertising clubs, they established special church advertising departments. Propaganda organizations like the Gospel Advertising League of New York came into existence. In addition, churches often paid professional publicity agents to place news items, to rewrite sermons so that they would become more "newsy." The national councils of the denominations used well-known experts in the field: the National Lutheran Council hired the acumen of Winifred Elson; the National Council of the Congregational Churches paid Herbert D. Rugg to sell its message; and W. E. Compson performed the same duties for the Reformed Church of America. The best known of the experts, however, was Dr. Charles Stelzle, who worked for several Christian organizations, one of which was the Federal Council of Churches of Christ. A few professional agents, such as Edward L. Wertheim, Mary A. Dunn, and Julia Seton, even specialized in publicity for religious organizations, regardless of faith; for pay they sold the message of Protestants, sufis, and many obscure sects.[75]

Numerous courses and conventions were arranged, and equally numerous books were written, on how to advertise one's church, its message and activities. Courses arranged by the churches and local advertising clubs were well attended. One source calculated that during 1919–1920 two hundred ministers in New York had taken courses in publicity.[76] The Advertising Club of Kansas City regularly instructed the ministers and laymen of that city in "the application of modern advertising science to their attendance and financial problems."[77] The Department of Church Advertising in the Associated Advertising Clubs of the World arranged conventions. At the 1923 convention in Atlantic City, Frederick E. Potter, pastor and advertising man, gave detailed advice on everything from bill-posting, producing magazines, and wooing the press to arranging processions on Mother's Day.[78]

The advice was even more particularized in the many publicity handbooks that appeared on the market. In such books as Christian F. Reisner's *Church Publicity* (The Methodist Press), Charles Stelzle's *Principles of Church Advertising* (Revell), Ernest E. Elliott's *How to Fill the Pews* (The Standard Publishing Company) or Roy L. Smith's *Capturing Crowds* (The Abingdon Press),[79] the minister could inform himself about all the intricacies of how to disseminate the message of his church. These books preached that the pastor must not have any hesitation about advertising. "The desire for publicity is not a wicked one," one expert explained. "No Christian worker will succeed in 'putting over' his work in a great way without the aid of some publicity."[80] Advertising should rather, as Francis H. Case put it in his *Handbook of Church Advertising*, be looked upon as "a weapon of the Church militant."

The even more numerous articles on publicity in denominational and non-denominational magazines also led their readers into the mysteries of advertising. Here one could read about the need for a survey before one started selling the church: "You need to know just what goods you have to advertise, just how they are packaged, just how you propose to deliver them, and a good many more things of like nature. Then too, you need to unprejudicedly look at your market, the community around you, to see in what esteem it holds your church, its plant, its people, its pastor."[81] One could read simple stories of how advertising had established a Lutheran church in a town where no such church had existed before.[82] One could learn how to reach the heart of the local newspaper editor, not to convert him, but to place an item about "a service at 2 in the afternoon to accommodate the milkwagon drivers." The same writer also strongly advocated the use of photos: "For some reason or other the art editors prefer pictures of women, the prettier the better, and it is well to comply with this in as far as one can."[83]

Even though many forms of publicity were employed, such as posters, billboards, placards, cards, and letters,[84] the most common form was newspaper advertising. The spirit and modes of expression of all these forms were clearly derived from the commercial world. Most of the advertising was dignified and low-key, but occasionally "progressive" publicity agents were given too free rein. The message was most often an appeal to attend a local church of one's choice, because religion, as one of these advertising campaigns proclaimed, "is not merely the moral force that protects the community but is also the vital force that makes it."[85] This was the information that the churches of Reading, Pennsylvania, wanted to get across in their ad in the *Eagle*:

Think what is offered! Reading has about seventy churches. There is an investment of possibly $5,000,000, all for your benefit—and it is a benefit indeed. There are over 100 soloists, choirs that number 500 trained voices, scores of organists; there are orchestras, chimes and everything in melody that can bring peace and contentment to a troubled mind after a week of business cares. Over threescore pastors, educated men, have put in hours of study preparing sermons covering a wide range of themes. If you get but a single new thought, you will be amply repaid for attending some service on Sunday.... There is clear reasoning, splendid delivery, excellent composition, all bound to inspire you. And the Sunday schools; your parents sent you—are you giving your children the same opportunity to lay the foundation for correct living, right thinking and reverence?[86]

To give an example of an even more extreme and business-inspired ad, I will reproduce one printed in the *Bolivar Democrat*:

WE ARE REPRESENTATIVES FOR THE FOLLOWING ARTICLES:

CLOTHING	Stays Clean—Tailor Made-Guaranteed to Fit—The Robe of Righteousness.
FOOD	One Loaf will last a life-time—Thoroughly Seasoned—Never gets Stale—The Bread of Eternal Life.
DRINKS	Fresh from the FOUNTAIN—the only DRINK that lasts a LIFE-TIME.

The oldest business in the world. Organized in the year 0. MILLIONS of satisfied customers vouch for the integrity of this BUSINESS. You are cordially invited to look over our stock of goods. Every article and package bears the trademark—JESUS. One price to all. Local office—BAPTIST CHURCH.

—B. W. WALKER, PASTOR[87]

An advertising campaign that met severe disapproval and ridicule was launched by the businessmen of Kansas City, Missouri, who had the following ad printed in *The Star*:

FLAMING YOUTH! GET THIS NEW THRILL!

What is that something toward which you are groping? Could it be God? Could it be that these physical pleasures are but the shadow, the mirrored reflection of a capacity for spiritual enjoyment whose depths you have never sounded? You say you are after "big-time stuff." Then why don't you come into the main tent? The real thing is better than any tawdry imitation. There are thrills galore in Christian life, thrills that will last to the grave—and beyond. They are all pure gold—the gilt does not wear off.
Christ typifies youth. He lived intensely. He died a young man. Maybe He knows your problems.
Be a sport and give Him a chance. He will not take the fun out of life. He will add to it. He is a Builder. He does not destroy. He helps, inspires, enriches. He leads the way to the higher hills and the brighter flowers.[88]

As part of this "peppy" sort of publicity may be seen the increased use of slogans to advertise denominational drives, rally days, and Sunday sermons. Publicity-minded pastors advertised their sermons with captivating captions. They either thought up slogans themselves, such as "How to Wash without Soap," "Two in a Bed,"[89] "Christ: From Manger to Throne," or "Business

Success and Religion Go Together."[90] Or they did what Rev. Harold Sugden Metcalfe, Methodist minister of North Adams, Massachusetts, did; they picked up slogans for well-known products and applied them to their sermons. In 1922 Reverend Metcalfe held a series of sermons under such headings as "His Master's Voice," "Ask Dad, He Knows," "Eventually, Why Not Now," and "The Flavor Lasts."[91] This novel approach drew large crowds to his church and was consequently considered a great success.

SKYSCRAPERS FOR SKYPILOTS

One of the most successful advertisers of the church was Christian F. Reisner, mentioned above as the author of *Church Publicity*. As pastor of Grace Methodist Episcopal Church in New York, he had made the acquaintance of O. J. Gude, the billboard man, and soon there were four large electric signs on top of Grace Church and billboard slogans around the city, one of which read "Why Do Ministers' Sons Go Wrong?" Because of his ministerial success, Reverend Reisner was called to become head of the new Church Advertising Department of the Associated Advertising Clubs of the World. No clergyman in America was more high-powered than Christian F. Reisner.

In the mid-twenties, Dr. Reisner was called into another business-oriented church project. He was asked to pastor one of the new skyscraper churches, the Broadway Temple, which was being built in Washington Heights, New York City. The skyscraper, like the Woolworth tower, had fast become the chief symbol for the soaring business spirit of the twenties. Some denominations, particularly the Methodists, soon saw the possibilities of this new form of edifice. The skyscraper was visible from afar, it was impressive in structure, it emanated solidity and progressiveness, and it was a very good business proposition. The idea behind the skyscraper church was to devote, say, the three lower stories to the church, and let the rest of the building be used for offices and apartments. The rent from the latter would then finance the church, an arrangement which *The Christian Century* felt would be appealing to many: "We may confidently expect that, for at least the next half-dozen years, the efforts of any committee to plan for the needs of a downtown church will lead to the proposal of an income-producing skyscraper. As a business proposition, the church that is part fane and much larger part office or apartment space will have little difficulty in securing the approval of business men."[92]

Of the skyscraper churches being erected in cities all over America, the most publicized was Dr. Reisner's Broadway Temple (see illustration 5). According to the prospectuses and advertisements, this temple was to cover a whole block with a 24-story apartment tower and 26 million feet of floor space. The structure would be surmounted by a 34-foot cross. The building was financed through a two-million-dollar loan and through the sale of second mortgage, 5 percent, cumulative interest bonds, which raised another $2,000,000. These mortgage bonds were sold with the help of a slogan worthy of Dr. Reisner's acumen:

Illustration 5

"Altitudinous Christianity": Christian F. Reisner's skyscraper church. (*Forum*, July 1930.)

"Buy a Bond and Let God Have an Office Building on Broadway—a Bond between You and God!" The annual income of the building was expected to be $300,000, which was to be used for "social and religious work in New York under the direction of the Methodist Episcopal Church."

In the words of one prospectus, the Broadway Temple would represent "big business practically applied to religion," a phrase which was meant to be the highest form of recommendation. The prospectus continued: "The commercial, income-producing side will be in the hands of some of the keenest, shrewdest and most successful business men of New York City." This was the best guarantee possible that the church would be a success. This "Twentieth Century Cathedral" would sell Christianity to New York and to the world; through its impressive structure and its many progressive activities it would become a beacon in a dark world. One advertisement described the Broadway Temple as a "Methodist Church lifting the light-flooded Cross into the skyline of America's greatest city, so prone to *forget the Church*, God's visible body on earth. A flashlight at the foot of the Cross will send a stream of light 150 miles out to sea, and so prove to thousands seeking these shores that New York appreciates religion." Hearing about the building plans, Daniel A. Poling saw a similar vision: "A supreme modern cathedral dream will rise into a reality of marble and steel in the very heart of New York City. Then every inquirer who enters the 'Narrows' with the question, 'What is the genius of America?' will receive an answer: 'The Christian Church'." When interviewed by *Collier's*, Dr. Reisner himself enumerated all the aspects that would make his church into a financial, social, and spiritual success:

> Broadway Temple will be impressive in architecture, serviceful in arrangement, and effective in financial returns. It will contain modern elevator apartments for five hundred people, with playgrounds on the roof. It will also have dormitories, all furnished, for five hundred young men in the twenty-four-story tower, with windows overlooking the Hudson River and Long Island Sound. The street level will be occupied by stores and a church auditorium seating twenty-two hundred. The basement will have a social hall for one thousand, swimming pool, gymnasium, game rooms, cafeteria, and full equipment for social work to be enjoyed by the whole neighborhood. A high-class day nursery will offer relief for weary mothers.[93]

Another much-admired example of this "altitudinous Christianity," as one critic called it at the time, was the Chicago Temple of the First Methodist Episcopal Church. At its completion in 1924, this four-million-dollar, 568-feet-high skyscraper church was the tallest church building in the world as well as the highest building of any sort in Chicago. Its motto was "Coming Up to God out of the Earth." The first five stories housed the church, with its auditorium seating 2,000, gymnasium, club rooms, and educational facilities. The rest of the building had been let to various kinds of offices, "all revenue-producing." The rentals of the stores and the offices were eventually expected not only to support the church activities but also to "yield a very large annual income which may be applied to the assistance of other churches in the city." On top of the Temple's Gothic spire, there was an illuminated, revolving cross, visible in four states, "keeping the light of God aglow in the heart of Chicago's loop." The minister of this aspiring enterprise was Rev. John F. Thomson, who had earned his nickname "the prophet of profit."[94]

In the last two chapters, we have seen how the Protestant churches were influenced by the ideology and methods of the business world. The churches, confused and insecure, looked to business for guidance; business came to serve as a model for the reconstruction of the churches. However, one must be cautious not to misinterpret the development that took place. The original motive for building skyscraper churches and community houses, for turning the churches into industrial plants and the pastors into business executives, for using gimmicks and slogans, films and contests, was to draw more people into the church and thereby within hearing of the word of God. We must believe that most churches intended to use business methods as a means to an end, namely to save souls. However, in many cases the business methods started living their own life and became an end in themselves. Or rather, the activity of the churches became the goal, irrespective of the content of that activity. The church as a cultural institution became more important than the church as a living body of believers. Consequently one may sum up by saying that many Protestant churches in the 1920s set out to make use of the values and methods of business in order to regain their popularity and authority but ended up accommodating themselves to such a degree that they lost much of the authority they had left and often came to look like a poor copy of the business world they tried to imitate.

NOTES

1. Ben Primer, *Protestants and American Business Methods* (UMI Research Press, 1979), pp. 94, 132. Concerning the prewar interest of the churches in business methods, see also Clifton E. Olmstead, *History of Religion in the United States* (Englewood Cliffs, N.J.: Prentice-Hall, 1960), p. 479; William Warren Sweet, *The Story of Religions in America* (New York: Harper & Brothers, 1930), pp. 496–97; Gaius Glenn Atkins, *Religion in Our Times* (New York: Round Table Press, 1932), pp. 160–62.

2. "Necessary Systematization," *The American Lutheran* 9 (May 1926), p. 3.

3. Rae D. Henkle, "The Sixty-Four Per Cent," *The Christian Herald* 46 (September 29, 1923), p. 752.

4. André Siegfried, *America Comes of Age* (London: Jonathan Cape, 1927), pp. 37, 45–46.

5. John A. McAfee, "Religious Restaurants," *The Christian Century* 42 (June 4, 1925), pp. 732–33; Herbert Parrish, "The Break-Up of Protestantism," *Atlantic Monthly* 139 (March 1927), p. 301.

6. R. A. Torrey, *The Power of Prayer* (New York: Fleming H. Revell Company, 1924; reprint; Grand Rapids, Mich.: Zondervan Publishing House, 1971), p. 16.

7. Charles M. Sheldon, "The Biggest Business in the World," *The Christian Herald* 46 (January 20, 1923), p. 52.

8. Roger W. Babson, *Religion and Business* (New York: MacMillan Co., 1920), pp. 4–6; Roger W. Babson, *Fundamentals of Prosperity* (New York: Fleming H. Revell Company, 1920), pp. 90–92.

9. "Editorial Comment: Tidy Up," *Homiletic Review* 86 (October 1923), pp. 287–88.

10. L. T. Newland, "Efficiency," *The Presbyterian Survey* 16 (July 1926), pp. 424–25.

11. Bruce Barton, *What Can a Man Believe?* (Indianapolis: Bobbs-Merrill Company, 1927), pp. 188–207. See also "Publicity for Virtue, Too," *The Literary Digest* 91 (November 13, 1926), p. 36, which reports on one of Barton's speeches.

12. "Nuggets of Gold," *The American Lutheran* 10 (October 1927), p. 19.

13. "Necessary Systematization," pp. 2–3; see also Charles Merz, *The Great American Band Wagon* (New York: The John Day Company, 1928), p. 191.

14. Richard Braunstein, "Business Efficiency in Church Work," *Church Management* 4 (October 1927), pp. 54–56.

15. Albert Sidney Gregg, "A Church Business Manager," *The Christian Herald* 48 (October 3, 1925), p. 11; "Business Men as Church Trustees," *The Christian Century* 43 (July 29, 1926), p. 932.

16. Gregg, "A Church Business Manager," p. 11.

17. George T. Wood, "He Turns Failures into Successes," *The Christian Herald* 50 (December 10, 1927), p. 1097.

18. John R. Pepper, "The Christian Man in Business," *The Nashville Christian Advocate* 95 (January 21, 1927), p. 71.

19. "Church Business Managers," *The American Lutheran* 7 (March 1924), p. 5.

20. M. E. Melvin, "A Message to the Business Men of Our Church," *The Presbyterian Survey* 16 (March 1926), p. 190.

21. "Why Does Not the Foreign Mission Committee Use Business Sense and Keep Its Expenses With Its Income?" *The Presbyterian Survey* 16 (February 1926), p. 97.

22. Babson, *Religion and Business*, p. 12.

23. George L. Moore, "A Salesman in Religion," *The Christian Herald* 46 (October 13, 1923), p. 808.

24. Julia Lake Skinner, "The Parable of the Business Girl," *The Presbyterian Survey* 14 (May 1924), pp. 351–53.

25. V. A. L. Jones, "A Business Bible Class," *The Christian Herald* 46 (March 31, 1923), p. 265.

26. W. Edward Raffety, "The Go-Getter Adult Class: Its Areas and Aims," *Church Management* 5 (May 1929), pp. 569–71; "The Technic of the Go-Getter Adult Class," *Church Management* 5 (June 1929), pp. 667–68, 684.

27. Robert Cashman, "The Minister's Personal Conduct," *Church Management* 3 (April 1927), p. 376.

28. "Business Training for Ministers," *The Christian Century* 43 (June 17, 1926), pp. 765–66.

29. Babson, *Religion and Business*, p. 19.

30. Robert Cashman, "The Minister's Office," *Church Management* 3 (January 1927), pp. 197–98.

31. Robert Cashman, "The Minister as an Executive," *Church Management* 4 (November 1927), pp. 87–88, 90.
32. John R. Scotford, "The Minister as a Salesman," *Church Management* 4 (October 1927), pp. 7–8.
33. J. W. G. Ward's articles under the title of "Factors in Ministerial Success" appeared in *Church Management* in the following order: "Be Ambitious," October 1926, pp. 7–8; "Concentrate," November 1926, pp. 71–72; "System," December 1926, pp. 131, 134; "The Will to Power," January 1927, pp. 205–6; "Enthusiasm," February 1927, pp. 267, 272–73; "Perseverance," March 1927, pp. 319–20; "Optimism," April 1927, pp. 397–98.
34. William G. Shepherd, "John Timothy Stone: A Business Man in Religion," *The Christian Herald* 46 (January 27, 1923), pp. 67, 79.
35. E. J. Unruh, "Sure, A Minister Can Speed Up," *Church Management* 5 (May 1929), p. 578.
36. William L. Stidger, "Prophets of a New Day and the New Way—Dr. Burris A. Jenkins," *Church Management* 3 (November 1926), pp. 69–70. For descriptions of such successful Christian workers, see also Allison Grey, "Miss Schooley Isn't *Called* a 'Salesman', But She *Is* One," *The American Magazine* 94 (October 1922), pp. 54–55, 150–54; and Carey McWilliams, "Aimee Semple McPherson: 'Sunlight in My Soul'," in *The Aspirin Age*, ed. by Isabel Leighton (New York: Simon and Schuster, 1949), p. 60.
37. James Brett Kenna, "Minister or Business Executive?" *Harper's Monthly Magazine* 157 (June 1928), pp. 38–44.
38. Sinclair Lewis, *Babbitt* (1922; reprint; London: Jonathan Cape, 1929), pp. 200–202. In a passage dealing with the 1920s in *The Folks*, Ruth Suckow describes one of the modern business pastors as "kind of a Rotarian": "He was one of the modern-style ministers, heartily secular, wearing business men's glasses, brought here at an increased salary in a last attempt to build up the dwindling Presbyterian flock, in this spurt of prosperity that followed the war." *The Folks* (New York: Farrar & Rinehart, 1934), pp. 273–74.
39. Samuel Harkness, "Sinclair Lewis' Sunday School Class," *The Christian Century* 43 (July 29, 1926), pp. 938–39.
40. Sinclair Lewis, *Elmer Gantry* (New York: Harcourt, Brace and Company, 1927), p. 324.
41. Lewis, *Babbitt*, p. 200, and *Elmer Gantry*, pp. 341, 367. For another literary description of business methods in the church, but from a supposedly Christian point of view, see Harold Bell Wright's *God and the Groceryman* (New York: D. Appleton and Company, 1927), pp. 171–74, 279, where Wright shows how more or less unrefined stunts, slogans, lectures, and advertisements are used to draw attention to the "Go-Getter" church depicted in the book.
42. "The Church at Work," *Homiletic Review* 85 (June 1923), p. 463. For a survey of Protestant business methods, see also Robert Moats Miller, *American Protestantism and Social Issues 1919–1939* (Chapel Hill: University of North Carolina Press, 1958), pp. 22–29.
43. "Signs of Progress," *The American Lutheran* 8 (January 1925), pp. 2–3. In an issue later the same year, *The American Lutheran* carried an advertisement that promised that a parish paper would successfully compete with "the movies, the automobile, the Sunday newspaper, with golf," and would bring out the congregation, fill the Sunday School and keep it filled, bring new members in, activate the members and fill the

treasury. The parish paper would help the minister "knit /his/ congregation into a live, happy, working unit." (November 1925).

44. Harry Emerson Fosdick, *The Meaning of Service* (New York: Association Press, 1921) p. 158.

45. John R. Scotford, "Do We Want a Seven Day Church?" *The Christian Century* 42 (March 5, 1925), pp. 315–17.

46. Kenna, "Minister or Business Executive?" p. 41.

47. "The Church at Work," *Homiletic Review* 85 (July 1923), p. 35. Other community houses were described in *Homiletic Review* 85 (March 1923), p. 206, and vol. 86 (September 1923), p. 210. For an article describing bowling as the "great church game," see William H. Leach, "The Pins Are Falling," *Church Management* 3 (February 1927), pp. 251–52.

48. "The Church at Work at Home and Abroad," *Homiletic Review* 86 (September 1923), pp. 210–11.

49. As an example may be mentioned the West End Presbyterian Church, New York, which ran a Vocational and Social Service Office. See "The Church at Work," *Homiletic Review* 85 (April 1923), p. 304. This was very much in line with what the famous Fifth Avenue minister, Dr. Daniel A. Poling, did in his National Radio Conference, in which he gave vocational guidance according to Christian principles.

50. "The Church at Work," *Homiletic Review* 85 (April 1923), p. 303.

51. Advertisement under the title of "A Sure Way to Rally the Young People to Church," *Church Management* 3 (March 1927), p. 347.

52. Percy Stickney Grant, *The Religion of Main Street* (New York: American Library Service, 1923), pp. 12, 98.

53. "The Church at Work," *Homiletic Review* 86 (November 1923), p. 381.

54. "A Great Brotherhood in Action," *Church Management* 3 (February 1927), p. 257.

55. William L. Stidger, "Sunday Night Chautauqua Church," *Homiletic Review* 86 (December 1923), pp. 463–65.

56. Richard S. Bond, "Business 'Pep' for the Men's Class," *The Christian Herald* 46 (January 6, 1923), p. 5.

57. Arthur Talmadge Abernathy, "How I Built Up the Largest Community Bible School in America," *Homiletic Review* 86 (November 1923), pp. 385–88.

58. Arthur H. Van Voris, "That Class for the Boys," *The Christian Herald* 46 (February 3, 1923), p. 99.

59. In 1923, Mrs. A. Best ran a course in religious drama under the auspices of the Drama League of America. She commented: "Instead of shunning the drama, as in the past, churches of all denominations are to-day beginning to look upon it as an opportunity to impress truth, interpret life, and powerfully influence emotions." "The Church at Work," *Homiletic Review* 86 (November 1923), p. 381.

60. "The Church at Work," *Homiletic Review* 85 (March 1923), p. 205.

61. James Myers, "Lights and Shadows in Church Pictures," *The Christian Herald* 52 (July 13, 1929), p. 7.

62. Charles M. Sheldon, "How to Use Pictures in the Church," *The Christian Herald* 45 (October 14, 1922), p. 719.

63. Claude S. Hanby, "Seconding the Motion Pictures in Church," *Homiletic Review* 86 (October 1923), pp. 311–16.

64. Frederick Lewis Allen, *Only Yesterday* (New York: Harper & Brothers, 1931), p. 177; Herman E. Krooss, *Executive Opinion: What Business Leaders Said and Thought*

on Economic Issues, 1920s–1960s (Garden City, N.Y.: Doubleday & Company, 1970), p. 3; Paul A. Carter, *The Twenties in America* (New York: Thomas Y. Crowell Company, 1968), pp. 53–54.

65. Lewis Thurber Guild, "The Church on Main Street," *The Methodist Quarterly Review* 78 (April 1929), p. 202.

66. "The Church at Work," *Homiletic Review* 86 (November 1923), p. 380.

67. Paul F. Boller, "Funs and Thrills for Men's Night," *Church Management* 3 (February 1927), pp. 249–50.

68. W. Edward Raffety, "Onward and Upward on Rally Day," *Church Management* 5 (September 1929), pp. 809–10.

69. G. Edward Pendray, "Publicists of the Ghostly Faculty," *The American Mercury* 18 (November 1929), p. 362.

70. " 'Popularizing' the Service," *The American Lutheran* 8 (March 1925), pp. 2–3.

71. See George E. Mowry, *The Urban Nation 1920–1960* (New York: Hill and Wang, 1965), p. 6; Preston William Slosson, *The Great Crusade and After 1914–1928* (New York: Macmillan, 1930), pp. 363–367; George Soule, *Prosperity Decade* (New York: Rinehart & Company, 1947), p. 149; Thomas C. Cochran and William Miller, *The Age of Enterprise: A Social History of Industrial America* (New York: Harper & Row, 1961), p. 311.

72. Quoted from " 'Selling' Religion," *The Literary Digest* 70 (August 20, 1921), pp. 28–29. A committee of the Chicago Church Federation came to the conclusion in 1923 that it "pays in dollars to advertise" and suggested that the churches use the methods of selling soap and toothpaste. "The Church as Advertiser," *The Literary Digest* 76 (February 17, 1923), p. 35.

73. "Church Advertising," *The American Lutheran* 7 (March 1924), p. 9; see also Edwin P. Beebe, "Bringing in the Sheep," *The Christian Herald* 52 (May 4, 1929), p. 13.

74. Richard Beall Niese, *The Newspaper and Religious Publicity* (Nashville, Tenn.: Sunday School Board of the Southern Baptist Convention, 1925), pp. 38–39.

75. "How to Advertise Religion," *The Literary Digest* 67 (November 20, 1920), pp. 37–38; G. Edward Pendray, "Publicists of the Ghostly Faculty," pp. 359–62.

76. "How to Advertise Religion," *The Literary Digest* 67 (November 28, 1920), p. 37.

77. William H. Besack, "Church Publicity from the Standpoint of an Expert," *Church Management* 3 (October 1926), p. 13.

78. "Live 'Copy' for the Church," *The Literary Digest* 78 (July 28, 1923), p. 32.

79. Other books may be mentioned as well: William L. Stidger, *That God's House May Be Filled* (Doran); W. B. Ashley, *Church Advertising* (Lippincott); Herbert H. Smith, *Church and Sunday School Publicity* (The Westminister Press).

80. Niese, *The Newspaper and Religious Publicity*, p. vii.

81. Joseph A. Richards, "Spirituality in Church Advertising," *Church Management* 3 (July-August 1927), pp. 575–76.

82. F. W. Korbitz, "Does Church Advertising Pay?" *The American Lutheran* 7 (May 1924), p. 3.

83. William H. Leach, "Getting Publicity for Your Church," *Church Management* 4 (October 1927), pp. 15–16.

84. See for instance Hubert Cowley-Carroll, "The Church and Poster Advertising," *The American Lutheran* 6 (August 1923), pp. 4–5; R. N. Fellows, "Selling Your Church by Mail," *Church Management* 3 (March 1927), pp. 352, 355. "The Church at Work," *Homiletic Review* 86 (November 1923), p. 381 tells of how the churches of Cape Gir-

ardeau, Missouri, put up huge billboards, changing such legends as "The Church is the Foundation of the Home Life in the Community" and "The Church has Contributed Creative Power for all Business and Social Prosperity" every three weeks. In New York, one church advertised itself by putting the following message on the billboard: "Come to Church. Public Worship Increases Your Efficiency." See Jesse Rainsford Sprague, "Religion in Business," *Harper's Monthly Magazine* 155 (September 1927), p. 438.

85. Rhys G. Thackwell, "Church Advertising 'Pays'," *The Christian Herald* 45 (December 23, 1922), p. 916.

86. Quoted from "The Church in the Newshopper," *The Literary Digest* 86 (October 31, 1925), p. 30.

87. Quoted from "Americana," *The American Mercury* 7 (October 1926), p. 172.

88. Quoted from "A Jazz Appeal to 'Flaming Youth'," *The Literary Digest* 89 (April 24, 1926), p. 32.

89. W. J. Dawson, "Vulgarizing Religion," *The Century Magazine* 86 (September 1924), pp. 638–39.

90. Robert S. Lynd and Helen Merrell Lynd, *Middletown: A Study in American Culture* (New York: Harcourt, Brace and Company, 1929), p. 373.

91. "Sermons in Slogans," *The Literary Digest* 73 (April 29, 1922), pp. 31–32.

92. "The Skyscraper Church," *The Christian Century* 42 (January 22, 1925), pp. 112–13.

93. The information on the Broadway Temple from: Advertisement in *The New York Christian Advocate* 101 (September 9, 1926), p. 1247; Byron Dexter, "Wanted: A New Messiah," *The American Mercury* 7 (October 1926), pp. 238–39; Daniel A. Poling, *An Adventure in Evangelism* (New York: Fleming H. Revell Company, 1925), pp. 93–94; Frederick L. Collins, "Upward, Christian Soldiers!" *Collier's Weekly* 74 (October 18, 1924), p. 17.

94. For information on the Chicago Temple, see advertisement in *The New York Christian Advocate* 101 (September 9, 1926), p. 1245; "The Church at Work," *Homiletic Review* 85 (March 1923), p. 205; "The First Skyscraper Church," *The Christian Herald* 46 (May 5, 1923), p. 360; "Skyscrapers for Skypilots," *The Literary Digest* (November 1, 1924), pp. 32–33. Such churches were erected not only in New York and Chicago, but in many other cities including San Francisco, Minneapolis, and Detroit. In San Francisco the revenue-producing part of the twenty-five-story structure consisted of a five-hundred-room hotel. The Northwest Methodist Temple in Minneapolis had a similar arrangement, where one wing and the 300-feet-high tower were occupied by a hotel. The Boulevard Temple in Detroit was not exactly a skyscraper church, since it was only nine stories high, but the basic idea was the same, to let office, stores, and apartments pay the church expenses. The office/apartment section of the church was calculated to yield a net income of $50,000 per year. See "To Scrape California's Sky," *The New York Christian Advocate* 102 (June 2, 1927), p. 677; "The Northwest Methodist Temple," *The New York Christian Advocate* 102 (April 7, 1927), p. 421; "Boulevard Temple, Detroit," *The New York Christian Advocate* 102 (February 3, 1927), p. 151.

4

Business Adapts and Benefits

As we have seen, business in the 1920s had a wide-ranging impact on American Protestantism. However, a dominant institution can seldom remain completely unaffected by subordinate social sectors. To a greater or lesser degree, the leading social group must adapt to the rest of society and must take its values and wishes into consideration. To continue to enjoy its authority, the dominant sector must make its ideology acceptable to the majority of the people. Labor in the United States, for instance, would never attack the concept of "free enterprise," because of the sanctity of this concept to the average American. A racist organization would never use the term "racial discrimination" because that would limit its chances of persuading the public to accept its racist views.[1] Such adaptation is not merely a matter of vocabulary but also one of actively including concepts that can be embraced by the general public.

It was essential for business in the 1920s to keep the authority it had gained, and it was consequently important to create a profile that did not deviate drastically from the Protestant values subscribed to by so many Americans. The adaptation of business took different forms. Business leaders made clear their view that Protestantism was the foundation for material success. They pointed to the Bible as a guide in economic matters and were convinced that it expressed basically the same views as those advocated by business.

Many representatives of business spoke warmly in favor of the Protestant faith. Some did so from sincere conviction. Others did so with the deliberate intention of gaining economic advantages. The great mass of businessmen parroted their leaders without reflecting too much over their own motives. Even though the adaptation to Protestantism may have meant a certain limitation and modification of the business ideology, it also meant that business benefited, and even profited, from the sanction and justification that the inclusion of Protestant concepts brought with it. Business paid homage to Christian beliefs and made use, wittingly or unwittingly, of the situation. To be able to make the business spirit tally with the Christian message, business often, again consciously or unconsciously, modified the latter.

In the twenties business became, as I have pointed out, more sensitive to the views of the consumer. Such a statement as William Vanderbilt's "The public be damned," uttered in 1882, might have wrecked an economic empire in the 1920s. Samuel Insull knew this when he said: "It matters not how much capital you may have, how fair the rates may be, how favorable the conditions of service, if you haven't behind you a sympathetic public opinion, you are bound to fail."[2] This new development may then also explain why so many business leaders, advisers, and ordinary businessmen kept insisting during the decade that business was based on Christian principles, and that in many instances it was even fulfilling biblical prophecies.

To succeed, businesses and corporations needed an impeccable front. To choose only one example of this new attitude, one may mention the fact that most of the 15,000 business conventions held annually in the twenties included sessions for religious inspiration, a feature that had not been common before the war. For instance, the 1927 conventions of the National Association of Credit Men and of the Associated Advertising Clubs, held in New York and Philadelphia respectively, had on their programs religious services, prayer sessions, song services, and speeches by well-known preachers. In the evenings, the usual drinking parties, cabaret entertainments, and beauty pageants were offered to the convention delegates. One commentator on this new religious activity among businessmen, Jesse Rainsford Sprague, was convinced that this was a sophisticated way of creating a good impression on consumers. He felt that the convention organizers probably argued something like this: "These things will make a good impression when our convention proceedings are reported in the newspapers. Church people everywhere will get the idea that the Aluminum Ash Tray industry stands for morality, and they will be that much more inclined to buy aluminum trays instead of brass, china or silver trays."[3]

It would be utterly false, of course, to imply, as may have been done here, that all businessmen were hypocrites who adopted an air of religiosity in order to make more money. Many businessmen in the twenties, we must believe, were sincere believers who conscientiously tried to apply their Christian faith to their business practices. One may, for instance, point to such men as J. C. Penney, John J. Eagan of the American Cast Iron Pipe Company in Atlanta, William P. Hapgood of the Columbia Conserve Company in Indianapolis, and Arthur "Golden Rule" Nash from Cincinnati, who all, to the best of their understanding, worked to introduce Christian principles into their firms. But since it is so difficult to separate the sheep from the goats, the minority of devout Christian businessmen are overshadowed by the large number of businessmen who only paid lip service to Christian doctrines, who regularly went to church on Sunday and who advocated Christian ethics as the norm for business, but who, on Monday morning, were unwilling to live what they preached. Many of these nominal Christian businessmen joined a because, as one of them said in *Middletown*, "Who am I to buck an in as big as the church, and anyway it seems necessary to conform, but my pastor knows all right how little my heart is in it."[4]

Christianity can always be misused, and has often been so. People of the most different convictions have claimed to find support for their ideas in the Bible. The twenties were no different in that respect. Many businessmen held that Christianity was the necessary basis for material success; they said that the Bible was the greatest inspiration of all for the weary businessman; they claimed that Scripture showed that their ideals and methods were justified. The overall impression one gets is that, with certain exceptions, many American businessmen in the 1920s made use of religion to sell their ideals, methods, and occasionally even their products, to the largely unsuspecting American people.

RELIGION PAYS

The large majority of the business community in the twenties held that Christianity was beneficial to the individual, to his town or city, and to the American nation as a whole. This belief was not limited to the conviction that it paid off in dollars and cents to be a Christian, an argument repeated often enough, but that Christianity was the form of civilization that was the most ennobling to human beings, that bred the highest morality, and that gave rise to the most dignified cultural expressions. Christianity was seen as the form of life that best satisfied the human being spiritually and materially and that was the best foundation for a well-functioning, just, and prosperous society. In most instances, then, businessmen of the period looked upon Christianity, not as a relationship to the living God, but as a moral system and a cultural pattern.

Protestantism, many businessmen were convinced, was the cause of the steadily increasing prosperity of the American nation. Only a Christian civilization could create, as John E. Edgerton, President of the National Association of Manufacturers, said, this "land of undreamed opportunity," in which it was so easy for "a little business to grow into a big one."[5] If a nation seeks the Lord, it was argued, it will of necessity be rewarded with prosperity. But there was occasionally confusion as to what was meant by "seeking the Lord." One business supporter held that it meant to pursue "the noble ideal of equality under liberty," which in his terminology was the same as individualism and free enterprise. Referring to what Jesus says in Matthew 6:33, he continued: "All these things are being added unto us precisely because we are always seeking the Kingdom of God and his righteousness, as they are always added and must of logical necessity always be added unto any nation that seeks wholeheartedly those ideals of justice that are the very essence of the Kingdom of God."[6]

The Protestant faith created prosperity, it was felt, in part because it was inducing order. Christianity produced an economic climate that was a powerful check to disruptive social forces, or as one writer, critical of the business attitude, put it: Christianity was looked upon as "a traffic officer at the busiest corners of trade."[7] The conviction was common that, if America were to cease being a Christian nation, it would rapidly go bankrupt in every sense of the word. *The Manufacturers' Record*, a Baltimore business journal, wrote:

> Without the guiding influence of religion and the power which it has over mankind this nation would soon sink back into barbarism, and no business in it would be safe. Eliminate from any community the churches that are in it and property of all kinds would become practically worthless, and the bats and the owls would soon take possession of the city.[8]

Christianity was also conducive to prosperity, representatives of commerce felt, because it fostered cooperation and mutual respect. It was a good policy for all concerned to do unto others what you wanted them to do to you. Roger Babson, spokesman for both business and Christianity, encouraged his fellow businessmen to get a broader vision and see that all men are brothers in the sight of God. "Realize," he wrote, "that the city can be prosperous only as the farmers are prosperous, and that the West can be prosperous only as the East is prosperous. Get a broader vision; realize that the employer can be prosperous only as the wage worker is prosperous, and the wage worker is prosperous only as the employer is prosperous." In another book, Babson stated that the labor problem could never be solved until the worker's desire to produce was revived. "For this revival," he said, "we must depend upon religion," and added:

> No vote by a board of directors, or action by any official can recreate in labor a desire to produce. Such a desire cannot be developed by the use of platitudes such as "the interests of labor and capital are mutual." Only more religion in the hearts of both employers and wage workers will gradually bring both together as real co-operators.[9]

Whether such pleas to adopt the Christian faith to achieve industrial cooperation and thereby prosperity were mere talk never to be put into practice by the employers, we do not know. It seems certain, however, from the frequency of such opinions, that many people sincerely believed at least theoretically that the Golden Rule was a principle that resulted in greater material blessing for worker and employer.

To give only one more example, one may point to a short story published by *The Rotarian*, "Christ & Company,"[10] which tells the story of David Cochrane, who all his life has tried in vain to reconcile his business ethics to his Christian faith. As the story opens, he has out of charity bought a sweatshop associated with his clothing factory but up to now owned and run by another man. He is appalled to discover that the workers of this sweatshop are receiving only four dollars a week. At the same time his factory has experienced such economic difficulties that to increase the wage of the sweatshop workers would mean certain bankruptcy to the whole factory within six months. In spite of this, Cochrane decides that the only thing he can do as a Christian is to double the wage of the sweatshop workers. Quoting Matthew 7:12, he informs them of his decision, after which he goes away for months to arrange for his retirement after the expected closing of his plant. When he returns to his factory, Cochrane finds to his amazement that it is producing three times as much as when he left; far from going bankrupt, the factory is flourishing. The explanation of this mystery is in part unexpected new orders, but the primary cause for the factory's prospering is the changed attitude of the workers who have worked three times as hard in his absence only to do unto him what he had done to them. By being obedient to the Golden Rule, both workers and the employer are experiencing industrial peace and increased prosperity.

Not only was Christianity the foundation for America's national prosperity, according to the business promoters, it was also the prime determinant of individual success in business. Because of his faith in God, the Christian businessman was much more likely to succeed than were his unbelieving competitors, partly because God takes care of His own and partly because Christianity gives birth to values and characteristics that motivate the believer to achieve.

Many businessmen exhorted others to adopt religion, and by that they almost invariably meant the Protestant faith. Howard Heinz of the Heinz Company told a meeting of 200 salesmen that faith in God was "the basis of successful commercial life" and that "genuine spirituality is the first essential in a high-class salesman." Mr. Head, a banker from Omaha, similarly urged a bankers' convention at Atlantic City to realize that "religion is the foundation of business and that God rules the commercial realm."[11] In *Why I Am a Christian*, Frank Crane boomed Christianity as a good business proposition, and Roger Babson again and again preached that godliness is profitable.[12] In one of his books, Babson proclaimed:

> The best religion is that which makes its people most efficient, most productive, most useful, and most worthwhile. This is the test which men demand in business and our religion must pass the same test.... The best religion is the religion which gives the best results both to the individual and to the group. The real test of a religion is whether its followers are healthy, happy, and prosperous.[13]

There is no doubt that to Babson the religion that best met these demands was the Protestant faith.

In several instances, however, the champions of business ideals did not limit their definition of success to mean merely the acquisition of wealth. To some, success also entailed moral improvement; Christianity brought forth a new type of businessman, more honest and more concerned with the welfare of others. As one manual on business ethics put it: "The greatest asset in any trade group is the business man whose life has been cleansed, steadied and ennobled by religious communion."[14] And besides, living wholeheartedly for the Lord, in obedience and devotion, was beneficial also materially. A. E. Humphreys and Howard Cadle were two businessmen whose stories were told. On separate occasions they had been fatally ill, and in that situation each made vows to the Lord to serve Him and to devote all he had to Him if he survived. They both lived, and from that day they started to fulfill their promises to the Lord. As they did so, God blessed them even more abundantly than before, the article pointed out. Because of his obedience to his Father in heaven, A. E. Humphreys became the wealthiest man in Colorado.[15]

One of the most effective means of business success, it was observed, was prayer. A man could make more money if he prayed about his business, the dean of the University of Chicago Divinity School stated.[16] This view was repeated by representatives of commerce, Roger Babson for one. "I urge all business men," he wrote, "to learn about prayer and its possibilities. The Holy Spirit is the great undeveloped resource of religion; while prayer is the means of tapping this great undeveloped resource." He suggested that

> the successful people are consciously or unconsciously prayerful people.... If their success is not due directly to their own prayers, it is due to the prayers of a mother, father, or some friend.... Men are successful because they are religious rather than religious because they are successful. Most men are successful because, consciously or unconsciously, they are praying men.[17]

To prove his point that godliness is profitable, Babson repeatedly told his readers, in articles and books, that it was the "great outstanding testimony of religion" that the Protestant churches were filled with successful people. "We should point with pride," he wrote, "to the fact that most of the church people are prosperous and that most of the poor people are outside the church. We should be more ashamed if the church were made up of poor people and the prosperous people were outside the church." In an article called "The Business of Religion, A Sermon," he preached that any person who accepted what Jesus taught concerning honesty, courage, loyalty, and generosity could "do nothing but succeed," and he continued: "a large majority of our most successful business men are from families where these four fundamentals were constantly emphasized." In still another article, Babson asked the questions, "Do the notable men in the realm of business ... trace their origin to fathers and mothers of unmistakable piety? Is the early influence of prayer and religion a power in all kinds of success?" To get an answer to these questions, he sent out a questionnaire to business leaders in various industries. From their answers it was demonstrable, he concluded, "that the early influences of the church and praying parents are forerunners of the son's career in business, and that the son's own prayer and religion are the root of his success."[18]

In an interview, Roger Babson referred to the authority of one Professor Visher to strengthen his argument. Professor Visher had investigated the people who had been included in *Who's Who* to find out who their parents were. He found, according to Babson, "that preachers—in proportion to their numbers—

fathered 2,400 times as many eminent persons as did the unskilled laborers, who stand at the other end of the scale. The preachers fathered 35 times as many eminent persons as did the farmers; four times as many as did the business men; and twice as many as the doctors, lawyers, and other professional men."[19] The explanation was obvious to Babson: the religion of the clergyman created a climate conducive to success. *The American Magazine* decided to find out whether the Babson thesis was correct. It sent out to fifty representative "bankers, manufacturers, and other business executives" six questions concerning the faith of their parents and their own belief in God and prayer. Thirty of them—among whom were J. Ogden Armour of the Chicago meat-packing family; George F. Baker of the First National Bank; Elbert H. Gary of U. S. Steel; E. M. Statler, the hotel king; and Samuel Insull, president of the Commonwealth Edison Company—asserted that they had believing, praying parents and that they themselves were believers, if not run-of-the-mill Protestants. Only one businessman denied the importance of religion to his career. The remaining nineteen were not available or felt that the questions were too personal to be answered. The conclusion drawn by *The American Magazine* concerning the thirty affirmative answers was that "their attitude... is one of unqualified assent to Mr. Babson's claim that religion, as he defines it, is a powerful and recognized factor in all worthwhile achievement—including business success."[20] Even if Babson was the main prophet of the doctrine that it pays to be religious, he was not the only one. In a series of advertisements for elevators, William Ridgway, for instance, made public his findings that "the 'Big Boss' of almost every big long established concern 'Belongs to Church' " (see illustration 6). He listed some twenty-five major industries that were all "headed by a Churchman," among which were the Standard Oil Co., Packard Motor Car Co., General Electric Co., the Pennsylvania Railroad, Firestone Tire & Rubber Co., Procter & Gamble Co., and Sears, Roebuck & Co.[21]

Trying to explain why religion was such fertile soil for achievement and success to grow in, Babson and others sounded like disciples of Max Weber, when they explained how religion, that is, Protestantism, gave rise to a work ethic of thrift, industry, and other so-called Christian qualities. In his writings Babson gives long lists of virtues and characteristics that were a direct result of the Christian faith and that combined to make the individual efficient and thus successful. Apart from thrift and industry, these qualities were integrity, justice, charity, self-control, faith, inspiration, initiative, courage, ambition, imagination, confidence, power, vision, brotherly kindness, sympathy, meekness, honesty, usefulness, reverence, purity, and enterprise.[22] The religious man will possess at least some of these virtues, and will of necessity make a success of his life. In most instances, one gets the impression that Babson is speaking of worldly, material success, but to be fair, one must point out that now and then he sees success as a wider concept, as when he writes:

It is absolutely impossible for any individual to develop the... fundamentals of prosperity—faith, integrity, industry and brotherly kindness—without being successful in

"Uncle Billy's Bible Class"

Is what the ribald heathen call these advertisements.

You see we believe that Business and Religion mix.

We have discovered that in spite of cussin' and swearin' and gamblin' and sportin' down in the ranks among the poor old plugged under strappers, the "Big Boss" of almost every big long established concern "Belongs to Church." Here is a sample of some Steam-Hydraulickers. Every one of these is headed by a Churchman:

Standard Oil Co.
Cluett, Peabody & Co.
H. J. Heinz Co. ("57")
Crane & Co. (Dalton)
Packard Motor Car Co.
Swift & Co.
United Gas Imp. Co.
Larkin & Co. (Buffalo)
General Electric Co.
Penn. R. R.
International Harv. Co.
Standard Underground Cables Co.
John Wanamaker.
John Morrell & Co.
Christie Brown & Co. (Toronto)
Firestone Tire & Rub. Co.
Consolidated Gas Co. (N. Y.)
Remington Typewriter Co.
Lukens Steel Co.
Procter & Gamble Co. (Ivory Soap)
E. I. Du Pont de Nemours & Co.
United States Gov't.
Sears, Roebuck & Co.
United States Steel Co.
Lovell Mfg. Co.

The other day we wrote to ex-Postmaster-General Hays, who is a Presbyterian Elder, asking him to tell us what Church the members of the present Republican Administration belong to. Here is the report:

President Coolidge, Congregational
Secretary of State Hughes, Baptist
Secretary of Treas. Mellon, Presbyterian
Secretary of War Weeks, Unitarian
Atty. General Daugherty, Methodist
Secretary of Navy Denby, Episcopalian
Secretary of Interior Fall
Secretary of Agriculture Wallace, United Presbyterian.
Secretary of Commerce Hoover, Quaker
Secretary of Labor Davis, Presbyterian

So the Country is safe with old John Calvin in the Saddle!

The only thing an ad like this has to do with Ridgway Elevators is that when it came to equipping such important plants as THE BUREAU OF ENGRAVING AND PRINTING and WEST POINT MILITARY ACADEMY with Elevators Uncle Sam cried "Ridgway, come and

'HOOK 'ER TO THE BILER'"

Illustration 6

One of William Ridgway's advertisements proclaiming that it pays to be a Christian. (*The Literary Digest*, December 8, 1923.)

the highest sense of the word. I do not refer to the mere accumulation of money, but include all that a commonsense use of money can provide, namely, a necessary competence, goodly repute among one's fellows, service in the community, and, above all, that inner satisfaction which no possession of self can purchase.[23]

Other reasons why a religious person was more likely to succeed were offered as well. Just the fact that he belonged to a church was a powerful contributing factor. In the church the less fortunate met their more fortunate brothers, and the latter often gave them a helping hand. Stories like the following were not uncommon in the press. Jacob Kindleberger of Parchment, Michigan, was one of seven immigrant brothers and sisters living in extreme poverty. At the age of ten, he was at work in a paper mill sorting rags at 25 cents a day. At the age of fifteen, he was still illiterate and lived a "day-to-day, hand-to-mouth existence—eat, sleep, work," without vision or ambition. By chance he happened to visit a local church. After the service the minister took a friendly interest in him. The owner of the mill where Jacob worked was a member of the church; even he shook his hand, and gave him good advice: "Tie up with this church.... Be active, help, and the church will help you." From that day Jacob Kindleberger's life changed. He was filled with ambition. He educated himself. He worked hard and overcame tremendous obstacles. In the end he built his own paper mill with the financial help of church brethren.[24] Church belonging would also bring respect in the community which would stand a businessman in good stead in his work. *The Farm Journal Merchants Supplement* gave friendly advice to salesmen on how to succeed in selling farm implements to unresponsive farmers: "Suppose that next Saturday you say to Farmer Brown when he comes in, 'John, bring the family in tomorrow; come in about 10:30 A.M. We'll all go to church, and after church the Missis wants you and the family over to dinner.'... Now what would that mean to your business? It would create the closest feeling between you and the farmer. With this you will gain a confidence which will be so strong that it cannot be shaken."[25]

The act of tithing was also held forth as a cause of church people moving to the top more easily than the unchurched. By looking upon all their earnings as God's money and by giving away 10 percent of it, they were richly blessed also materially. Articles told of businessmen who stated that their success was directly due to the fact that they tithed. Charles Page, one of Oklahoma's great oilmen, was once down and out in Seattle. A Salvation Army worker told him to start tithing, and he gave away 15 cents of the $1.15 he owned. Since that day he tithed regularly, and he was successful in everything he undertook. Tradition said that in all his life, while drilling, he only missed oil twice. "You see," he said, "I couldn't miss, because I was in partnership with the Big Fellow and He made geology." There were also stories of the "noted Southern Lawyer" whose earnings started to increase immediately after he had adopted the principle of tithing, and about the furniture manufacturer in Grand Rapids, who was a failure once, but who had started anew, this time on a basis of tithing, and who now had become "one of the marked successes in the furniture world."[26]

The attitude of the commercial world depicted here may seem to be proof positive that Max Weber was right in his assumptions. However, one must remember that, almost without exception, all the successful businessmen dealt with were second-generation Protestants. They were not, like their parents, God's children; they were God's grandchildren. Their parents, who were believers, were in most cases not social successes. The great majority of those ministers who fathered so many successful sons were poor themselves and remain failures in the eyes of the world. This fact seems to corroborate that it is only when Protestantism has dwindled into becoming a work ethic and a system of moral rules that it gives rise to what Weber called the capitalistic spirit.

RELIGION INSPIRES

Representatives of the commercial world did not only profess a conviction that it paid off to be a Christian. Many of them also maintained that the Protestant faith offered daily guidance and inspiration to the businessman in his professional life. The greatest source of inspiration beyond any comparison was the Bible, which by many was seen as a very practical business manual. J. L. Kraft, president of the cheese company, said, for instance: "One amazing thing about the Bible is that it affords a precedent for almost any business problem which may arise in these so-called modern times. The New Testament lays down the only really practical rule of life, which, if followed, is sure to point the road to success. By success I mean a flourishing spiritually, morally, and financially."[27] Edward Bok held that it was enough to read only the first of the gospels to be truly inspired to achievement. "We turn to books of modern success as to reservoirs of hope," he wrote in *Dollars Only*. "But the greatest book of success ever written, or that ever will be written, is the book of Saint Matthew."[28] Both the Old and the New Testaments were filled, it was repeatedly observed, with sayings, events, and personalities that could teach the businessmen of America how to forge ahead in their careers.

The businessmen of the 1920s were only following the long-established Puritan tradition when they turned for inspiration to the Old Testament stories and personages. Ever since the first colonization some three hundred years earlier, Americans had expressed great admiration for the preeminence of such figures as Joseph, Moses, and David. Thus, Walter Painter was only echoing statements of past generations when he wrote that "in the Old Testament you will find some of the greatest stories of successful salesmanship that have ever been printed,"[29] even though Painter put it somewhat more bluntly than a seventeenth-century commentator would have done.

The Old Testament personages who were most often held forth as models to commerce in the twenties were, in order of Biblical chronology, Joseph,

Moses (and Jethro, his father-in-law), David, and Nehemiah. Joseph was portrayed as a man who, through foresight and wisdom, overcame adversity and rose to the top. "The successful business man is one who has sensed an unsatisfied want and found the way to fill it," one business representative wrote and gave the following example: "Joseph, the first recorded national food controller, knew that the people of the world would soon be in dire want for food and he devised the means of providing for that want. A royal garment and the signet ring of the Pharaoh were none too great reward for his perspicacity and business sense."[30] Bruce Barton also underlined that because of his foresight and organizing ability Joseph had been promoted until he was second only to the king. Joseph had made the important discovery that business runs in cycles. "Thus Joseph made the first Babson chart," Barton wrote, "showing that the era of financial inflation precedes that of depression and is of equal size and density." Babson had publicly admitted, according to Barton, that Joseph was the inspiration for his business cycle chart, which had "made [Babson] a fortune."[31] In an address before the Public Relations Section of the National Electric Light Association, Barton also made clear that Joseph had been a skillful publicity agent who had had public relations with all the other ancient nations, but who later in life had grown less careful about publicity. One of the "most staggering lines which has ever been written in a business biography," Barton claimed, was the one saying that Joseph died and "there arose a new king in Egypt which knew not Joseph." Joseph's rapid fall into oblivion showed to Barton and his listeners the need for "continuous advertising" so that the product, that is, Joseph, would not be forgotten.[32]

But even greater inspiration was to be had from Moses. Here was a man of unrivaled stature, a statesman, a salesman, a promoter. By studying his life, businessmen would be motivated to achievements they thought impossible. Moses could even lead America out of the economic depression of 1921, the industrialist Samuel M. Vauclain believed. In an address to the Associated Industries of Massachusetts in October 1921, he said:

> Don't be cowards—be brave and resolute—set the example and your friends and your employees will follow you. . . .
>
> Moses was a great leader. He was a great leader because his people followed him, and they followed him because he was brave and determined. . . .
>
> It is up to you, gentlemen of business here in New England, to set the example to all business men of this great United States, just as your forefathers did here around this old historic city some 150 years ago.[33]

A few years later the Metropolitan Casualty Insurance Company of New York published a tasteful brochure entitled *Moses, Persuader of Men*, which, according to the introduction, was published to inspire the company's agents to greater achievements. The booklet portrayed Moses as the original high pressure salesman and real estate promoter, who managed, without prospectuses, blueprints and other paraphernalia, to sell the idea of the Promised Land and make it stay sold through forty years of deferred delivery. The closing paragraph exhorted the salesmen in the following manner: "If you are engaged in the business of selling, whether it be ships or shoestrings, bridges or beads, incubators or *Insurance*, spend a little time once in a while thinking about Moses and the Faith and the Courage that made him a Dominant, Fearless and Successful Personality in one of the most magnificent selling campaigns that history ever placed upon its pages."[34] According to another businessman, Moses had had a business adviser in Jethro, his father-in-law, whose wisdom could still be an inspiration to the modern man of commerce. Jethro had pointed out to Moses that he, as a judge, was wasting his energy and time by judging both important and insignificant cases. It would be better to organize his people into groups of ten, fifty, a hundred and a thousand and to give each group its own judge, thereby freeing Moses for more demanding tasks. Jethro must consequently be seen as the world's "first counsel in organization."[35]

Other Old Testament sources of inspiration, less often referred to, were David and Nehemiah. David did not spur modern men into achievement primarily as a king and leader but as the author of the Psalms. The basic tenet of the success manuals in the twenties was that of positive thinking: you became what you thought you were. By "unthinking" negative forces, you allowed them no power. In this context the Psalms were of great use to those who aspired to success. To conquer fear, one of the worst obstacles on the road to success, one handbook advised the reader to seek help from David:

> One of the best safeguards against fear is the frequent repetition of the great stimulating twenty-third Psalm. Any one who memorizes and repeats its six short verses every day and takes its lessons to heart will conquer fear and worry and all their evil progeny. He will conquer all the enemies of his success and happiness. He will unconsciously live in complete harmony with the law of opulence.[36]

Nehemiah's rebuilding the wall of Jerusalem was also referred to as an inspirational story from which men could learn how to persevere and how to organize work. By letting each man work on that part of the wall nearest his home, Nehemiah had tied "selfishness into the great community scheme," a basic principle to all successful business. From Nehemiah's achievement it could be learned that "over a period of years, a man's life, a man's business, the community in which he lives, is what he desires it to be."[37]

If the Old Testament characters had been sources of inspiration for generations of aspiring businessmen, the New Testament, and primarily Jesus, had not been looked upon in the same light. The many attempts in the 1920s to turn Jesus into the greatest businessman of all times were part of a development new to American Protestantism. Or as one contemporary critic put it: "To become the mouthpiece of the business spirit, to glorify competitive 'service', to see Jesus as the first advertising man, and the Last Supper as the first Rotary

Club Luncheon—this is a new story for even the chameleon forms of Christianity."[38] Studying this phenomenon more closely, however, one finds that it was not primarily representatives of the church who propagated such ideas but nominally Christian leaders of the business community. Only after such biblical interpretations had been introduced by men of commerce were they occasionally echoed by churchmen.

Jesus Christ was viewed as a paragon for many types of businessmen representing widely different business mentalities. To a few, the study of Christ's sayings and doings would make businessmen more honest and thus greater. "The best man is the best businessman," uttered by Thomas Dreier,[39] could stand as a motto for this idealistic view. Other businessmen were more pragmatic. Few were as crass, however, as Dr. Frank Crane, who bluntly stated: "To me Jesus is my spiritual executive, and I ask of Him only what I ask of any other executive, 'Can He do the business?' "[40] Generally, Jesus was depicted as a model who could motivate the American businessman to gain more power and wealth. To be able to make this portrait convincing, writers often had to reinterpret, and even distort, the teachings and character of Christ. His admonishment to us to walk the second mile, for instance, is not to be followed out of altruism, but because it is a business proposition which will give us power: "History shows conclusively that real influence comes only from going the second mile. When an employer or wage worker does only what he has to do, he ends up where he begins. The creation of influence and power comes from going the second mile."[41]

The life of Jesus Christ was inspiring in a general way to all businessmen. The man meeting temporary misfortunes in his business could again become successful if he studied the teachings of Jesus. The businessman who wanted to learn the principles of leadership only had to read the Gospels. The mediocre salesman could likewise find "the key to success' in the New Testament tenets. Basic business principles, like the importance of making powerful friends, were also illustrated by the Nazarene. He befriended people while they were still uninfluential, the famous B. C. Forbes pointed out, and expected them to grow powerful as time passed. Jesus did not live in the flesh to see this development, "but the twenty centuries of history show us on a gigantic scale the process by which you in your span of life can make friends of the people about you . . . and these in time will somehow become the rich and the powerful."[42]

The words of Jesus could also show the latterday businessman how to advertise and sell his product and how to make an impact through public speaking. The New Testament verses that the propagators of such views referred to were mostly quoted out of context and applied to situations that Christ had not intended them to illustrate. To prove that Jesus was "the best salesman of all time," Fred F. French, a "nationally known real estate operator and advertiser," told the New York *Sunday World* that Jesus "said, 'Knock and it shall be opened unto you.' What He meant was 'Keep knocking until the door is opened and if it isn't opened pretty soon kick down the door.' That's my philosophy too."[43]

Not all distorted the message of Jesus so crudely; some were more sophisticated about it. To illustrate his message of positive thinking, that is, that any man who thinks thoughts of opulence and prosperity must of necessity succeed, one author quoted, "Behold I have set before you an open door which no man can shut," and went on to show that "no obstacles, no difficulties, no power on earth" but our own negative thoughts can prevent us from becoming a success.[44]

The Son of Mary was "the prince of speakers" and from Him the American businessman could learn the principles of public speaking, necessary to know if he wanted to rise in life. According to one article, Jesus had shown the advantage of the spoken word over the written; he had proved the importance of speaking in a clear, convincing, logical way to sway people's minds. By listening to the voice of the Master, the businessman would learn to speak "as one having authority," and his words would be "words of fire and [his] speech have weight among [his] fellow men."[45] One success manual also quoted the verse "My words are spirit and they are truth; and they shall not return to me void; but shall accomplish that whereunto they were sent" as an illustration to the truth of positive speech; the manual continued to draw the following erroneous parallel:

> There is a mysterious power in the spoken word, in the vigorous affirmation of a thought, which registers a profound impression on the subconscious mind, on our other self, and the silent forces within us proceed to make the thing we affirm a reality. There is a tremendous constructive power in vigorous, determined affirmation, backed by a persistent, dogged endeavour to bring about the thing we desire.[46]

The most famous of the works presenting Jesus as an inspirational figure was undoubtedly Bruce Barton's *The Man Nobody Knows* (1924), which topped the bestseller lists for months and which has since been referred to and summarized in most studies of the twenties. Barton wanted, as he said in the subtitle, to discover "the real Jesus," who according to him was the most successful businessman of all times. After the epigraph, "Wist ye not that I must be about my Father's *business*," he told the success story of Jesus Christ in seven chapters called "The Executive," "The Outdoor Man," "The Sociable Man," "His Method," "His Advertisements," "The Founder of Modern Business," and "The Master."

The Man Nobody Knows has in most cases been seen as an expression of American Protestantism as it appeared in the twenties; however, Barton's book must be understood in a different light. *The Man Nobody Knows* is not a Christian book first and foremost. It is not primarily meant to make readers come to know Christ and become His disciples.[47] This book is a success manual, written by a businessman for businessmen to inspire them to greater achievements in their worldly careers. The book is human-centered, not Christ-centered. With Christ as a model, the businessman could, in his own power and through positive thinking, rise in society. There is no mention in Barton's work of the need for conversion, repentance or submission under Christ. Jesus is a source of inspiration and no more.

Barton here tells the success story of the country boy who discovers his "inner consciousness of power," who outgrows the country town and goes to the city towards greater and greater success, which ends in no less than world dominion. Jesus is depicted as a muscular hero, an outdoor man of vigorous activity, loved and admired by women. He was definitely no milksop, but possessed perfect health, steel-like nerves, complete self-control, and a mighty arm, which was expressed, for instance, when he drove the money changers out of the temple:

> As his right arm rose and fell, striking its blows with that little whip, the sleeve dropped back to reveal muscles hard as iron. No one who watched him in action had any doubt that he was fully capable of taking care of himself. No flabby priest or money-changer cared to try conclusions with that arm.[48]

But Jesus was not only an inspiration as the perfect specimen of a man. More specifically, he epitomized the spirit and method that businessmen benefited from. By studying the life of Jesus, the executive of the twenties could learn the principles of success. "How was it that the boy from the country village became the greatest leader?" Barton asked. Jesus had had an "overwhelming" faith in himself and his mission, and the modern businessman should have an equal belief in himself and his products. Jesus had a wonderful power to pick the right men. The Bible says, "As he passed by he called Matthew," and Barton commented: "No executive in the world can read that sentence without acknowledging that here indeed is the Master" (*The Man*, p. 21). Jesus further had an unending patience, which contributed to his success. "He believed," Barton wrote, "that the way to get faith out of men is to show that you have faith in them; and from that principle of executive management he never wavered" (*The Man*, p. 28). These are only a few of the many pieces of advice that Barton, with the support of Jesus, directed to his fellow businessmen with the conviction that they would be inspired, not to follow Jesus, but to become more efficient achievers.

A book similar to Barton's, but much less well known, was Charles F. Stocking's and William W. Totheroh's *The Business Man of Syria*, published in 1923 and printed in ten editions before 1925. Written for "downcast business men" by the businessmen Stocking and Totheroh, this book presented, in some 800 pages, Jesus as the "world's most successful man of business."[49] Also like *The Man Nobody Knows*, it gives a very liberal view of the New Testament and of Jesus. The authors present "natural" or "scientific" explanations to all forms of miracles, to angels, to the Virgin birth. The crucifixion and the resurrection are not treated at all, since these, according to the writers, were merely personal experiences of Jesus and not social phenomena, and, as such, of minor interest.

Jesus Christ is seen as a paragon of human behavior, particularly of that of businessmen, and has no redemptive mission to fulfill.

The business jargon of the Stocking-Totheroh work is as obtrusive as that of Barton's book. The birth of Jesus is described in a chapter called "Peace to a Business World," and his baptism is retold under the heading of "A Consecration to Business." John the Baptist is called the "advance agent," and Jesus' talk with Nicodemus is termed the "first business interview." In "The Business Charter Given," the authors describe the "most profound business talk ever delivered," namely the Sermon on the Mount, given by "the great human Manager of 'my Father's business' to his band of representatives, whom he was about to send out on a business tour" to deliver "the goods," that is, to spread the good news.[50]

There is, however, a great difference between the works by Barton and Stocking-Totheroh. It is true that both books want to inspire businessmen to become more successful, but the authors have different definitions of success. While *The Man Nobody Knows* at bottom encouraged businessmen to earn more and more money, *The Business Man of Syria* urged its readers to transcend the mere accumulation of wealth and to overcome the demeaning forces of materialism. Jesus Christ is delineated as an ideal to be followed by American businessmen, a source of inspiration to grow spiritually and morally, to become more honest and more considerate of others. At an early age, during his "silent" years, Jesus had made a discovery that, according to Stocking and Totheroh, He wanted to pass on to the American businessmen of the 1920s:

> We know now that the man [Jesus] had discovered a tremendous "secret," the secret of true business prosperity; and he had worked out the truly successful business "method." And so, after his public dedication of himself, as symbolized by his baptism, he stood at the threshold of his real business career; he had received his education: now he was to apply it practically. He had discovered that "business" meant, as has been so well said, "the exchange of good offices." Hence it meant service, ministry, and not mere vulgar scramble for material gain, at whatever cost to self or neighbor. And so his ministry must be the attempt to persuade men to exchange their false sense of values for the real, and to learn to become a law unto themselves—by learning that all is "within"—and thus rise above chance and failure into genuine success.[51]

RELIGION JUSTIFIES

Books like Bruce Barton's *The Man Nobody Knows* served to inspire American businessmen to new exploits, but they fulfilled another function as well. They justified the ideals and the methods of modern business. By portraying Jesus as the master executive, who both in thought and in action personified the business spirit, Barton and others gave divine sanction to the commercial practices of the 1920s. What Jesus Christ had endorsed so explicitly in the Bible, the modern reader must have felt, would certainly be permissible today. More than that, businessmen of the twenties must have received the impression that they in a particular way were among the elect, since Jesus himself had chosen to work in that profession. Barton expressed this thought openly, when he wrote that Jesus "spent far more time in market-places than in synagogues. He picked His disciples from the ranks of business.... Business, in His eyes, was the machinery which God had set up for carrying on the unfinished task of creation."[52]

For almost two millennia, numerous attempts have been made to authenticate the most revered ideals of a group, movement, or culture by ascribing to them the character of Jesus. At various points in history, Jesus has been made into a monk, a soldier, a social radical, a guerilla fighter, and a hippie. In the twenties, as I have shown, he was a businessman. But as I have also shown, this image of Christ was created mainly by the business community. Many protests were raised, for instance, against the exploitation of Jesus in *The Man Nobody Knows*. *The Christian Century*, often skeptical of the intentions of business, deplored the fact that Barton had reduced Jesus to a "sublimated Babbitt' with the characteristics of the "typical Rotarian go-getter." One month later the journal charged: "Here is an attempt to claim the authority of Jesus for the pseudo-morality which underlies modern business enterprise.... Through Mr. Barton the business world looks upon Jesus and makes a frantic effort to preserve its moral self-respect in investing his life with the 'success' ideals which it so passionately cherishes." The magazine held that Barton's book revealed the hypocritical attitude of the business community. It preferred the "frank scorn of the nineteenth century business man for religious principles and Christian ethics" to the "unconscious insincerity—for it is only rarely conscious—of the modern captain of industry who veils the most predatory practices of industrial and commercial life with phrases of moral idealism."[53] Others repeated the same indictment. Jesse Rainsford Sprague wrote of *The Man Nobody Knows*: "Never, perhaps, has a writer hit upon so happy a means of elevating the ego of the business-man reader.... By depicting Jesus as a salesman Mr. Barton not only sets the seal of Divine approval upon salesmanship as an art, but contrives to convey the idea that by salesmanship one grows into the image of the Master."[54]

It was not only Bruce Barton who set the seal of Divine approval upon the business practices of the twenties. Leading manufacturers, presidents of employer organizations, government representatives, and writers of success manuals quoted the Bible and referred to the sayings and doings of God, Jesus, and leading churchmen to give sanction to what they were expounding at the moment. In this way they found support for their belief in laissez-faire capitalism and for their views of business ideals and methods.

It was believed, beyond a shadow of a doubt, by the business community of the twenties, that capitalism not only was the best of the economic systems but also created by God. The instincts of individualism and self-seeking were God-given, they further believed, and the Lord had intentionally made men unequal and divided them into masters and servants. Though he called himself a "reverent agnostic," Charles N. Fay nevertheless found that God had created man one way and that it would be wrong to try to change that:

> We human beings are urged by the socialist, and many another preacher, to deny as wrong, even vile, the most fundamental instincts of human nature; the selfish instinct, or instinct for self support, involving the right of Meum and Tuum; the instinct for justice, or individual reward proportionate to service; the instinct for love and family, involving the life of the race; the instinct of blood and country, or patriotism. We are told that we must so organize "Society" as by man-made law to correct . . . these blunders of the Almighty in the constituting human nature; and do quite away with the differences in human lot due to differences in human power.

God's creation spoke in favor of a capitalistic system, Fay argued, and so did his word. The gospels seemed "clearly to accept the great facts of private property, poverty and riches, as part of the natural order of things; and simply to lay on the rich the moral obligations of generosity and humility. Nothing in the way of neutralizing natural economic law, nothing of social redistribution of property is anywhere suggested."[55]

Capitalistic America has "a very beautiful ideal before it," Thomas Nixon Carver wrote, "an ideal that is vastly finer, more just, more righteous and withal more easily attainable than anything of which any socialist ever dreamed." In the pursuit of that ideal, Americans were achieving "an economic revolution which, in the most literal possible sense, is the exact realization of the rule, 'He that would be great among you, let him be your servant.' " Jesus never tried, according to Carver, to stir up resentment or to tell people about their rights, their wrongs, or their grievances. He only told people of their opportunities and their obligations. So, according to the Bible, the labor leaders were acting against the will of God when they went around sowing their destructive dissent.[56]

One of the business representatives who most often referred to God to give authenticity to his message was John E. Edgerton, president of the National Association of Manufacturers. Edgerton divided people into those, like himself, who were the "sound and more dependable elements" and those who were socialists and radicals. There was no doubt on whose side God was. Edgerton acknowledged in 1924 that there were undeniable tendencies toward "mob rule" in America, but he consoled his followers with the fact that "God is still in His Heaven." He believed that Americans had grown tired of "chasing the will-o'-wisps of radicalism" and were ready to return "to God, the Bible, and the fundamental principles of their forefathers." Edgerton further held that nobody could deny the fact that men had been created unequal in their earning capacities, and no change would come about until "the Great Ruler of the universe" either made all men into saints or destroyed the mental and physical inequalities by some "divine decree divinely enforced." However, all men enjoyed equality of opportunity, he held, as the parable about the talents showed. It was the difference in attitude which had made two of the servants in the parable earn "profits of one hundred per cent on their invested capital," while the third servant became a "striker" and gave up without trying. This "original striker" was probably "the real founder of our modern labour unions."[57] In this fashion Edgerton managed to exploit a parable about spiritual matters and let it illustrate and justify his own views on economic philosophy.

Other men of commerce expressed their convictions that American business in the twenties was fulfilling the commands of the Bible. Business had been chosen, as Barton said, to carry on "the unfinished task of creation." An often repeated statement was that business was adopting Christian ethics and thus improved industrial relations. The Secretary of Labor of Harding's business administration, James J. Davis, wrote that the "principles enunciated by the Man of Nazareth in His Sermon on the Mount are steadily, even though slowly, beginning to dominate, and, of course, wherever those principles dominate the world must grow better."[58] A book on business ethics proclaimed that businessmen were realizing "that 'The fear of the Lord is the beginning of wisdom,' and they want advice about the wisdom and the justice of commercial customs and transactions."[59] Many an industrialist saw himself as his brother's keeper, and even as a savior of society and mankind. Thomas Dreier turned himself into a Christ figure—maybe unwittingly—when he said: "Some time . . . I want it said of me what Isaiah wrote . . . 'He giveth power to the faint . . . and to them that have no might he increaseth strength.' "[60] This attitude was also reflected in Arthur Train's novel *The Needle's Eye*; one industrialist, Randolph McLane, at a board meeting quotes George F. Baer's statement, "The rights and interests of the laboring man will be protected and cared for, not by the labor agitators, but by the Christian men to whom God has given the control of the property interests of the country." McLane goes on to comment: "Those are my sentiments. Who are the Christian men to whom God has given the property interests of the country? They're us—us who are sitting here around this table."[61]

In business organizations like Rotary and Kiwanis, similar thoughts were common. Members often saw themselves as saviors of mankind fulfilling the commands of Jesus Christ. In the annual address of the president at the 1920 convention of Rotary at Atlantic City, Albert S. Adams quoted, "And thou shalt be called the repairer of the breach; the restorer of paths to dwell in," and continued to report

> how Rotary has constructed paths over which men might pass from the old order of selfishness and every-man-for-himself to this good day of realization that "I am my brother's keeper." How Rotary has indeed been a repairer of the breach in that we have collectively and individually made the way easier and the load lighter for those who must travel the long road with little help.[62]

Another Rotary representative maintained that the Bible "is filled with Rotary Doctrine." As an example he pointed to one of Rotary's objects, "the advancement of understanding, good will, and international peace united in the ideal service." He continued, "This is but a fulfillment of the word of the angel when he announced: 'I bring you good tidings of great joy.' 'Good tidings' in the Greek is but one word: 'Evangel.' So, fellow Rotarians, we are Evangelists."[63] The editor of *The Kiwanis Magazine* stated that the song of Moses and the song of the Lamb mentioned in Revelation 15:3 were the same as "the Song of Personal Integrity" and "the Song of Personal Sacrifice," an interpretation he applied to his own organization:

> And then I knew why KIWANIS happened into the world. For this is KIWANIS, epitomized. We are just a group of men assembled under the banner of business integrity ... agreeing with a firm resolution, that we will not live for ourselves alone but will try to help others less fortunate by personal sacrifice.... KIWANIS does square up with the Book.[64]

As it was held that capitalism was established by God and that businessmen had been chosen to do His will, so scriptural authority was used in speeches, articles, and books to support specific business ideals and methods. God was made out to be against government interference and for free competition.[65] With His word, "With what measure you mete, it shall be measured to you again," Christ had put in words the natural law of Action and Reaction, according to Babson: "The law of supply and demand, of service and reward, and other economic teachings are based upon this all-pervading principle of equal reaction. The successful man recognizes this law. Jesus would be a successful business man because he would recognize the law and work in harmony with it."[66] Such words as "As ye sow, so shall ye reap" were proof to B. C. Forbes of the existence in business of an "eternal law of compensation," which worked in the following manner: "The man who idles away his youth and early manhood, who chases pleasure instead of achievement, who prefers dalliance to diligence, who woos indulgence instead of industry, who seeks the nectar cup rather than the iron wine of success, is destined to pay the penalty of lost opportunity in after life."[67] These attempts to justify one's views of economic laws with references to Scripture were often supplemented with quotations from leading ministers and church leaders.[68]

The self-centered philosophy of the success manuals was also propped up with the help of divine approbation. According to these books, in order to make a success of himself, a person must assume an attitude of assurance and self-reliance. And to sell this message, Jesus, who preached not self-reliance but trust in Him, was turned into a spokesman for self-aggrandizement. As a typical example of this "self"-cult, and its misappropriation of scriptural values, one may quote the following:

Confidence begets confidence. A man who carries in his very presence an air of victory, radiates assurance, and imparts to others confidence that he can do the thing he attempts. An assurance of success magnetizes conditions. A man who assumes such an attitude draws to himself the literal fulfillment of the promise, "For unto every one that hath shall be given, and he shall have abundance."[69]

As proof of the need for self-assurance and the need to think large, these writers quoted "Verily, verily, I say unto you, whosoever shall say to a mountain, 'Be thou removed,' and shall not doubt it in his heart, he shall have whatsoever he sayeth" and "If ye have faith as a mustard seed, nothing shall be impossible unto you." All achievers of great things had let this tiny faith grow, they insisted, and every man could do the same, since he had in him "a spark of divine energy." One writer commented: "With what Jesus called faith and we call conceit and egotism, these doers lighted the spark, fanned it into flame, until the eye sparkled, the soul was ignited, the mind was inflamed—and 'Well done,' says Jesus, looking on. For 'unto every one that hath shall be given.' Hath what? Faith—pure and simple. To those He gives."[70]

Without self-reliance no man can succeed, they taught. But your self-reliance must be well founded, they also taught. You must "be justified in having self-reliance." When Saul of Tarsus became Paul the Apostle, he exhibited "superb self-reliance"; but he also possessed "the qualities which justified his self-reliance." The same was true of David, according to B. C. Forbes: "David would have been an unspeakable fool to have entered the lists against Goliath had he not been a crack slingshot. He had self-reliance solely because his self-reliance was justified, solely because he had made himself so adept at the sling that he knew he could hit the forehead of the swaggering giant."[71] To show how utterly Forbes here distorted the biblical message to suit his own ends, one need only refer to 1 Samuel 17:45–46, where David himself states that his trust was not in himself as a slingshot, but in "the LORD of hosts, the God of the armies of Israel," and that the Lord was the one who delivered Goliath into David's hand.

It was not enough, however, to have faith in oneself and to cultivate willpower. To succeed, this attitude must be combined with hard work and perseverance, and again the handbook writers managed to find biblical support for their ideas. The parable of the talents, which had been used to prove that capitalism is biblical, was now used as an illustration of diligence. Those who had increased their holdings had done so by means of hard work, whereas the one who loafed lost what he had. "How are you using your talents?" the author asked. "Are you zealously, industriously, painstakingly increasing them? Or are you letting them lie dormant, rusting and rotting. Opportunity can be spelled with four letters. But these letters are not L-u-c-k. They are W-o-r-k."[72] B. C. Forbes, who wrote this, was fond of epigrams, which he published in his *Forbes Magazine*, and which he later collected into a book. Many of these epigrams used the

Bible to underline truths that are not necessarily scriptural; a few concerning the importance of industry may be listed here:

" 'Watch and pray'—and work"

" 'Knock and it shall be opened' doesn't apply to knockers"

"The wages of idleness is demotion" (cf. Romans 6:23)

"Pray, yes. But when you get off your knees, don't sit down. Hustle!"[73]

In his chapter "Stick-To-Itiveness" in *Keys to Success*, Forbes demonstrated the necessity of persevering in hard work if you wanted to reach the top. As an epigraph to the chapter, he had chosen Paul's words from Galatians 6:9, "we shall reap if we faint not." Without perseverance man was doomed to remain on the lowest rung of the social ladder. The Bible was very clear on this point, one guide to business explained:

> To the persevering man nothing is difficult; we can do almost anything we make up our minds to do and resolve on doing, willingly and earnestly. "Unstable in all things, thou shalt not excel." . . . Without perseverance we are as the shifting sand which never bore a noble edifice, or that wandering star of whom the Apostle speaks: "Clouds they are without water, carried about of winds; trees whose fruit withereth, without fruit, twice dead, plucked up by the roots."[74]

The false prophets that Jude warns against in the latter quotation have in the twenties turned into all those fickle sluggards who have not understood the worth of perseverance.

RELIGION SELLS

By justifying the business practices of the twenties, religion helped sell the business spirit to the American people. On a smaller scale, religion was also employed to sell the products of manufacturers, individually and corporately. Commerce made use of the Bible, the Church, and other Protestant organizations to convince the buyers that the articles in question were worthy of being purchased.

The Protestant church was often employed, sometimes unknowingly, by business. Each year many well-meaning pastors were persuaded to preach Mother's Day sermons, one critic made clear, "and the florists, the greeting-card manufacturers, and the Western Union Telegraph Company [made] a great deal of money." Pastors were admitted all over the United States into the service clubs and the Chambers of Commerce, which added prestige to the other members and smoothed "the way for an added volume of sales." According to the same article, the new Roosevelt Hotel in New York managed to secure front-page publicity by arranging a parade along Madison Avenue, in which 100 Boy Scouts marched to the rhythm of "Onward Christian Soldiers" to deliver 1000 Bibles, given by the New York Bible Society, to the guest rooms of the hotel.[75]

The Y.M.C.A. was also manipulated in this fashion. In Indiana an annual Walk and Be Healthy Week was organized under the auspices of the Y.M.C.A. The expenses for the week were paid by the associated retail shoe dealers of the city, who knew that when people walk more their shoes are worn out faster. One dealer reported an increase of sales of 46 per cent in one year. The Y.M.C.A. also lent its Christian name and uplift status to Money in Bank Day (pushed by the banks), Pay Your Bills Day (paid for by the grocers), Mother's Day (supported by the manufacturers of stationery), and National Laundry Week (sponsored by the American laundry men.)[76]

Christianity was also pressed into service in other ways. Salesmen and advertisers discovered that references to the Bible and to the church created an aura conducive to the selling of their products. To become a good salesman or advertiser, one had to study the language of the Bible, particularly the style employed by Jesus in his parables.[77] Harry Collins Spillman, who confessed "I am a Methodist because it runs in the family like snoring and obesity," still found the Bible the most important text to study to learn sales talk. In an address to the Twenty-second Annual Convention of the Biscuit and Cracker Manufacturers Association of America, held in Chicago in 1922, Spillman stated: "The Bible is the background of the language of all the great advertising experts of the world, and all the great salesmen have read the Old Testament through and through and memorized its language."[78]

The use of religion in sales methods and advertising was a comparatively new phenomenon. Occasional instances may be found shortly after the turn of the century, but it was not until after the Great War that spirituality became a real sales argument. One source states that after the panic of 1907 a few salesmen changed their methods to include more religious emotionalism. The salesman of gold-plated andirons, for instance, now announced that his andirons were not only cheap and durable, but also that "andirons added to the spiritual atmosphere of the home, and that it was the duty of every American to endow his loved ones with the uplifting influence of a pair of beautiful gold-plated andirons in the latest mode."[79]

In the twenties this trend became more distinct. Advertisers and salesmen showed great inventiveness in pushing their products by means of references to Christian concepts. The simplest form of advertisement had a caption with a word or a phrase to catch the reader's eye and put him in the right mood. Pepsodent advertised its toothpaste under the title of "GOOD NEWS that Millions of Women Tell," and Montgomery Ward & Co. used the caption "The SINS of Price" to speak against price cutting, which sacrificed both quality and serviceability, and to sell its own quality products. Both of these advertisements were printed in a Christian magazine,[80] and it is obvious that the copywriters knew that the capitalized words of the captions above would evoke, respectively, positive and negative connotations.

Other variations of the same thing were ads headed by complete Bible quotations, as when an investment house offered its services, in *The Christian Herald* of December 5, 1925, under the legend "What Shall It Profit A Man." Similar in type were the ads that referred to biblical personages. Under the headline "When there shall be no more Marthas," one manufacturer of electrical equipment informed the readers how it lifted the household burdens of women, and a consulting firm told the story of Naaman and Elisha, entitling the ad "When You Ask an Expert, Why Not Follow His Advice?"[81]

Making references to church and Sunday school also had the desired effect of increased sales. A book manufacturer like the W. B. Conkey Company invested its products with dignity, when it printed, illustrated with a woodcut of a hymn-singing congregation, an advertisement that started: "In 1888, Conkey-made hymn-books were pushing forward with the development of civilization and progress on our Western Frontier."[82] The investment firm S. W. Straus & Co. tried a similar course of action. Under the heading of "I taught the Sunday School Class how Wise Investing helps young men succeed," it told the story of Joseph H. Hasbrouck, the president of the Penn National Bank and Trust Co. Mr. Hasbrouck had taught a Sunday school class of twenty boys on the principles of investing. Ten of these students continued to invest prudently; two of them went on to become successful businessmen. Ignoring the absurdity of teaching investment principles in Sunday school, the Straus investment firm here managed to let Sunday school sanction the investing in bonds and thereby sold its own products.[83]

There are few firsthand records of what jargon salesmen used on the road or over the phone, but one may assume with some certainty that they there as well appealed to the human need for spirituality. Edmund Wilson gives a rare description of what he calls a "real estate evangelist" during the Florida land boom. This man gave a "sermon" to prospective buyers on the three cardinal sins of fear, caution, and delay and capped his speech with, "And if Jesus Christ were alive today, he'd buy a lot right here!" This had an inspirational effect on the audience, and several people bought lots then and there.[84]

William H. Ridgway, whom I have mentioned in the beginning of this chapter, was a special case in that he sold his product in a more systematic way than others did, by means of religious advertising. Ridgway was the president of the Craige Ridgway and Son Company of Coatesville, Pennsylvania, and he sold elevators. In a series of advertisements, he emphasized the importance, not of his own product, but of religion. Every Christmas he carried a full-page ad in the trade papers headed "God Bless Us, Every One," a "little religious preachment," in which he said nothing about elevators except to wind up with his motto "Hook'er to the Biler" and to print the company's logotype. Ridgway was not ashamed of his sales methods. "I make no secret of doing business on my religion," he said, "but make the statement in our advertising, 'If religion is not a good thing to do business on, it is no good for anything else'. " He freely gave advice to others, once to a man selling harvesters, whom he told that "90 per cent of the farmers to whom he wanted to sell his agricultural machinery were men who belonged to a church and go to a church, and he could, whenever he liked, appeal to the spiritual side of his customers, and he could score every time."[85]

Commercial organizations and individual businessmen depended on the Protestant faith for their success. They appropriated Christian doctrines and values, often altering the content to suit their own purposes. Business tried in this way to appear more spiritual, more religious than it in fact was and at the same time tried to increase its sales volume. But business in the twenties not only borrowed the cloak of idealism from Protestantism; it went one step further and transformed this idealism into a religious spirit of its own. Business became what might be termed a religion.

NOTES

1. See Francis X. Sutton, et al., *The American Business Creed* (Cambridge, Mass.: Harvard University Press, 1956), pp. 5–6.
2. Thomas C. Cochran and William Miller, *The Age of Enterprise: A Social History of Industrial America* (New York: Harper & Row, 1961), pp. 310–11.
3. Jesse Rainsford Sprague, "Religion in Business," *Harper's Monthly Magazine* 155 (September 1927), pp. 431–32, 435.
4. Robert S. Lynd and Helen Merrell Lynd, *Middletown: A Study in American Culture* (New York: Harcourt, Brace and Company, 1929), p. 317.
5. Quoted from James Warren Prothro, *The Dollar Decade: Business Ideas in the 1920's* (Baton Rouge: Louisiana State University Press, 1954), pp. 28–29.
6. Thomas Nixon Carver, *The Present Economic Revolution in the United States* (Boston: Little, Brown, 1925), pp. 64–65.
7. Edwin Holt Hughes, *Christianity and Success* (Nashville, Tenn.: Cokesbury Press, 1928), p. 107. The same attitude was reflected in *Elmer Gantry*, where Sinclair Lewis lets an influential churchmember, T. J. Rigg, say that "religion is a fine thing to keep people in order—they think of higher things instead of all these strikes and big wages and the kind of hell-raising that's throwing the industrial system out of kilter." (p. 313).
8. Quoted from "Business Backing the Bible," *The Literary Digest* 76 (March 31, 1923), p. 32.
9. Roger W. Babson, *New Tasks for Old Churches* (New York: Fleming H. Revell Company, 1922), p. 135. Roger W. Babson, *Religion and Business* (New York: Macmillan Co., 1920), pp. 41, 44.
10. Charles Henry Mackintosh, "Christ & Company," *The Rotarian* 24 (April 1924), pp. 9–11, 51–56.
11. John R. Ewers, "Business is Getting Religion!" *The Christian Century* 41 (January 3, 1924), p. 19.
12. "Booming Religion as a Business Proposition," *The Christian Century* 42 (May 21, 1925), p. 658.
13. Babson, *Religion and Business*, pp. 118, 120.
14. Edgar L. Heermance, *The Ethics of Business* (New York: Harper & Brothers, 1926), p. 217.

15. Beatrice Imboden, "He Pledged Wealth, Now Has Millions," *The Christian Herald* 45 (July 29, 1922), p. 532.

16. See William E. Leuchtenburg, *The Perils of Prosperity, 1914–32*, (Chicago: University of Chicago Press, 1958), p. 189.

17. Babson, *Religion and Business*, pp. 86, 88.

18. Babson, *Religion and Business*, pp. 23–24; idem, "The Business of Religion, A Sermon," *The Christian Herald* 52 (May 4, 1929), p. 11; idem, "Do Praying Fathers Have Praying Sons? No!" in Jerome Davis, ed., *Business and the Church* (New York: Century Co., 1926), pp. 39–44.

19. "Mr. Babson Explains What He Means by Religion," *The American Magazine* 101 (March 1926), pp. 15, 203–5, 208, 210.

20. Keene Sumner, "The Kind of Parents Our Big Business Men Had," *The American Magazine* 101 (March 1926), pp. 14–15, 202–3.

21. See "Hooking Elevators to Religion," *The Literary Digest* 79 (December 8, 1923), p. 33; Walter Painter, "Give Moses a Chance," *Collier's Weekly* 76 (January 10, 1925), p. 29.

22. Babson, *Religion and Business*, pp. 14–16, 96–100, 104–5; idem, *New Tasks for Old Churches*, pp. 43–51; idem, *Fundamentals of Prosperity*, (New York: Fleming H. Revell Company, 1920), pp. 25–26.

23. Babson, *Fundamentals of Prosperity*, pp. 84–85.

24. William S. Dutton, "He Went to Church to Laugh But He Came Away to Live," *The American Magazine* 100 (December 1925), pp. 34, 163–69.

25. Quoted from Jesse Rainsford Sprague, "Putting Business Before Life," *Harper's Monthly Magazine* 155 (November 1927), p. 708.

26. William G. Shepherd, "Men Who Tithe," *World's Work* 48 (July 1924), pp. 259–63.

27. Quoted from Walter Painter, "Give Moses a Chance," *Collier's Weekly* 76 (January 10, 1925), p. 29.

28. Edward Bok, *Dollars Only* (New York: Charles Scribner's Sons, 1926), pp. 232–33. The Bible was seen as an inspirational work not only for business success but for success in general. The protagonist of Samuel Hopkins Adams's *Success* gets the advice to study the Bible, not for spiritual inspiration, but in order to become a successful writer: "And the Bible is the one book that a writer ought to read every day.... You've got to have it in your business."

29. Painter, "Give Moses a Chance," p. 29. See also William T. Doherty, "The Impact of Business on Protestantism, 1900–29," *The Business History Review* 28 (June 1954), pp. 150–53.

30. Everett W. Lord, *The Fundamentals of Business Ethics* (New York: The Ronald Press Company, 1926), p. 123.

31. Bruce Barton, *The Book Nobody Knows* (Indianapolis: Bobbs-Merrill Company, 1926), pp. 30–31.

32. Reprinted in William Phillips Sanford and Willard Hayes Yeager, eds., *Business Speeches by Business Men* (New York: McGraw-Hill Book Company, 1930), p. 418.

33. Samuel M. Vauclain, *Optimism* (Philadelphia, 1924) pp. 54–55.

34. Sprague, "Religion in Business," p. 438. See also "The Salesman Nobody Knows," *The Christian Century* 44 (July 28, 1927), p. 893.

35. E. St. Elmo Lewis, "Profitless Prosperity," in Sanford and Yeager, eds., *Business Speeches by Business Men*, pp. 462–63.

36. Orison Swett Marden, *Success Fundamentals* (New York: Thomas Y. Crowell Company, 1920), p. 266.
37. Thomas Dreier, *The Silver Lining, or Sunshine on the Business Trail* (New York: B. C. Forbes Publishing Company, 1923), p. 131.
38. John Herman Randall, *Religion and the Modern World* (New York: Frederick A. Stokes Co., 1929), p. 97.
39. Dreier, *The Silver Lining*, p. 101.
40. Frank Crane, *Why I Am a Christian* (New York: Wm. H. Wise & Co., 1924), p. 54.
41. Babson, *Religion and Business*, p. 37.
42. B. C. Forbes, *Keys to Success: Personal Efficiency* (New York: B. C. Forbes Publishing Co., 1926), p. 176. Babson, *Religion and Business*, p. 60.
43. Quoted from Jesse Rainsford Sprague, "Prosperity Without Profit," *Harper's Monthly Magazine* 158 (June 1928), p. 85.
44. Marden, *Success Fundamentals*, pp. 236–37.
45. Albert J. Beveridge, "Public Speaking," in Basil Gordon Byron and Frederic René Coudert, eds., *America Speaks: A Library of Best Spoken Thought in Business and the Professions* (New York: Modern Eloquence Corporation, 1928), pp. 21–24.
46. Marden, *Success Fundamentals*, p. 229.
47. Bruce Barton was extremely liberal in his views of Christ and the Bible. In *The Man Nobody Knows: A Discovery of the Real Jesus* (Indianapolis: Bobbs-Merrill Company, 1924), pp. 60, 70, 99, and *What Can a Man Believe* (Indianapolis: Bobbs-Merrill Company, 1927), pp. 23, 61, 146, he denied the Biblical view of Creation, the Fall of Man, the Ten Commandments, the authority of the Bible, and the need for redemption. An interesting article on the development of Barton's ideas is Leo P. Ribuffo's "Jesus Christ as Business Statesman: Bruce Barton and the Selling of Corporate Capitalism," *American Quarterly* 33 (Summer 1981), pp. 206–31.
48. Barton, *The Man Nobody Knows*, p. 37.
49. Charles Francis Stocking and William Wesley Totheroh, *The Business Man of Syria* (Chicago: The Maestro Co., 1923), Sec. I, p. 3.
50. Ibid., Sec. IV, p. 43.
51. Ibid., Sec. II, p. 35.
52. Barton, *What Can a Man Believe*, pp. 186–87.
53. "Booming Religion as a Business Proposition," p. 658; "Jesus as Efficiency Expert," *The Christian Century* 42 (July 2, 1925), pp. 851–52.
54. Sprague, "Prosperity Without Profit," pp. 85–86.
55. Charles Norman Fay, *Social Justice: The Henry Ford Fortune* (Cambridge, Mass.: The Cosmos Press, 1926), pp. 244–51.
56. Carver, *The Present Economic Revolution*, pp. 27, 171.
57. Quoted from Prothro, *The Dollar Decade*, pp. 3, 4, 15, 50.
58. James J. Davis, "Disarming in Industry," *The Christian Herald* 45 (March 11, 1922), pp. 177–78.
59. Lord, *The Fundamentals of Business Ethics*, pp. iii–iv.
60. Dreier, *The Silver Lining*, p. 42.
61. Arthur Train, *The Needle's Eye* (New York: Charles Scribner's Sons, 1924), p. 158.
62. Rotary International, *Proceedings, Eleventh Annual Convention, June 21–25, 1920* (Chicago: International Association of Rotary Clubs, 1920), p. 39.

63. Charles D. Lowry, "A Rotarian Sermon," *Educational Review* 70 (March 1925), pp. 127–28.

64. Roe Fulkerson, "My Personal Page," *The Kiwanis Magazine* 7 (April 1922), p. 11.

65. See Prothro, *The Dollar Decade*, pp. 165, 171.

66. Roger W. Babson, "What Would Jesus Do in Business?" *The Christian Herald* 52 (June 8, 1929), p. 4.

67. Forbes, *Keys to Success*, p. 61.

68. For references to the sayings of churchmen, see, for instance, Marden, *Success Fundamentals*, pp. 176, 220–21; Bok, *Dollars Only*, p. 72; Forbes, *Keys to Success*, pp. 3–4; Prothro, *The Dollar Decade*, p. 46.

69. Marden, *Success Fundamentals*, pp. 212–13.

70. Bok, *Dollars Only*, pp. 231–32, 242. See also Forbes, *Keys to Success*, pp. 146–48, and Harry Collin Spillman, "Adjusting Ourselves to a New Era in Business," in Byron and Coudert, *America Speaks*, p. 417.

71. Forbes, *Keys to Success*, p. 189.

72. Ibid., p. 57. The parable of the talents was used to prove many other things as well. One writer stated that the words "to him that hath shall be given" showed how important it was for a businessman to have a large fund of cash, because then he could easily borrow more money. See James H. Rand, Jr., *Assuring Business Profits* (New York: B. C. Forbes Publishing Co., 1926), p. 17.

73. B. C. Forbes, *Forbes Epigrams: 1000 Thoughts on Life and Business* (New York: B. C. Forbes Publishing Co., 1922), pp. 68, 77, 103, 111.

74. Grenville Kleiser, *Training for Power and Leadership* (Garden City, N.Y.: Garden City Publishing Co., 1923), p. 345; Forbes *Keys to Success*, p. 68. Kleiser further wrote that there is no finer rule in business life than "Let no corrupt communication proceed out of your mouth, but that which is good to the use of edifying." Following this rule, conversation would assume new power: "Your positive thought is stronger than the other man's negative thought, hence your positive thought will prevail" (p. 7).

75. Sprague, "Religion in Business," p. 437.

76. Jesse Rainsford Sprague, "Patronize Your Own Church People," *The New Republic* 37 (January 30, 1924), pp. 254–56.

77. Barton, *The Man Nobody Knows*, pp. 139–40, 146.

78. Spillman, "Adjusting Ourselves to a New Era in Business," in Byron and Coudert, *America Speaks*, p. 413.

79. Sprague, "Religion in Business," pp. 432–34.

80. See the October 21, 1922 and April 16, 1926 issues of *The Christian Herald.*

81. Painter, "Give Moses a Chance," p. 29.

82. *The Bookman Advertiser* 66 (March 1928), p. xix.

83. *The Christian Herald* 52 (July 6, 1929), p. 17.

84. Edmund Wilson, *The Twenties* (New York: Farrar, Straus and Giroux, 1975), p. 259. Another example of how real estate was sold by means of religion was the Southern California realtor who arranged an Easter sunrise service on the land he was about to sell. See Veronica and Paul King, *The Raven on the Skyscraper: A Study of Modern American Portents* (London: Health Cranton Limited, 1925), pp. 85–86.

85. "Hooking Elevators to Religion," p. 33.

5

Business as Religion: God and Man

When writing his seasonal greetings for the Christmas of 1922, in *The Rotarian*, the president of Rotary International made a revealing statement. He wrote:

> "On earth peace, good will toward men" will be a fact when the men who carry on the business of the world accept the responsibility which modern civilization squarely puts upon them.
>
> For the contacts of business are beyond calculation; they touch the ambitious and the humble, the dissatisfied and the satisfied. Business contact and influence are the very warp and woof of organized society. . . .
>
> One of those bloodless revolutions, which steal over us unaware, has made the work and livelihood of civilization a science and a profession. Once we talked of loyalty to religion, to party principles; now we must have loyalty to business ideals.[1]

By quoting Luke 2:14, the president first of all reflected the fact that American business and American society in general were based on Christianity and, secondly, that business capitalized on this fact by often using Christian concepts to further its own ends (as the preceding chapter made clear). What followed after the quotation from Luke, however, had little to do with what the Heavenly Host said to the shepherds. Here the president rather revealed that he thought that the babe whose birth the angels were announcing had played out its role and that the task of salvation had been taken over by business. Even if he did not say so explicitly, he indicated that the "business ideals" of that time had come to serve a religious function and to satisfy a spiritual need.

This chapter and the following one will attempt to bring more clarity to the amorphous question that the president above alluded to: Did business in the 1920s assume a religious dimension? We have seen in an earlier chapter that business enjoyed the greatest admiration and that it was regarded as the leading social force of the decade. But did this admiration turn into adoration and worship? Did business expand to become not only a social force but also a spiritual one? Did it take over functions that had earlier been restricted to Protestantism? Did the "business ideals" mentioned by the president above have a greater hold on the American people than Protestant doctrines? These are the type of questions I will try to answer, even though I am aware of the difficulties of reaching conclusive results.

In the twenties, moral values changed and no longer had a unifying influence: Protestantism lost its authority over people. As a consequence, the spiritual needs of some people atrophied, whereas the needs of others found new supplies. Religious cults and movements that offered something different from traditional Protestantism, groups such as pentecostalism, the Four Square Gospel, Jehovah's Witnesses, and New Thought, received some of the released religious energy. Many people chose to remain as nominal members of their Protestant churches while transferring their religious commitment to such nonreligious phenomena as Prohibition, science or business. Walter Lippmann commented on this development, saying that the modern man of the 1920s had ceased to believe in conservative Christianity but had not ceased to be credulous. He wrote:

> The need to believe haunts him. It is no wonder that his impulse is to turn back from his freedom, and to find someone who says he knows the truth and can tell him what to do, to find the shrine of some new god, of any cult however newfangled, where he can kneel and be comforted, put on manacles to keep his hands from trembling, ensconce himself in some citadel where it is safe and warm.[2]

As a consequence of this shift in spiritual preferences, business, as the dominant institution of the time, managed to take over many of the functions of the Protestant churches, thereby consolidating its position. When businessmen, and many outside the commercial world, started satisfying their spiritual needs, as well as their material ones, through the business ideology and fellowship, the hold of business over the general public deepened.

Whether the religious beliefs presented below only reflected the economic self-interest of their adherents, or whether they constituted sincere convictions, is difficult to know. Business may consciously have manipulated religious concepts in order to strengthen its authority and thereby profit financially. This, however, is surely too facile an explanation. Many businessmen believed sincerely in the religious beliefs incorporated into the business ideology. They believed in a well-structured universe run by a benevolent God. They were convinced He had selected business as His tool of redemption on earth, as the true spiritual force that would change the world according to His plan.

BUSINESS REFERRED TO AS RELIGION

Without defining more closely what they meant, many critics, authors, and historians in the twenties regarded business—and such variations as prosperity, success, salesmanship, and advertising—as the new religion. These observers obviously did not mean that business was an organized religion with universally agreed-upon doctrines, ritualized forms of worship, and holy places set apart for devotion, but the great frequency of such general comparisons between business and religion indicates that commentators of the time felt that business had assumed a religious dimension.

Most of these comments were of a general nature. Edward W. Bok stated that "business is our God"; *The New Republic* accused the government of worshiping the god Prosperity; and Stuart Chase declared that when Adam Smith spoke of the "invisible hand" that directed the economic development, "he little realized that he was founding what has come to be almost a new religion."[3] Some critics tried to be more specific in their comments. John Herman Randall wrote: "The cult of prosperity... has assumed in the United States all the emotional fervor of a true religion. Men worship Pluto in his temples on Wall Street; many of them have taken on the sanctified atmosphere of churches." Another critic tried to warn his readers of the "new idol," commercialism, which penetrated the spirit of the age in a very subtle way and which had "power to condition the thinking, the feeling, and the doing of great masses of men." Prosperity is both a morality and a religion, maintained Halford E. Luccock, the well-known homiletics professor at Yale, and he went on to explain what he meant:

It has its high sanctities—that the very on-going of the business of the country depends on the acceptance of the profit motive as the only sufficient guarantee of the individualistic drive necessary to industry; that whatever is good for business is good for all; that the gaining of wealth is the chief end of man; that property rights precede human rights; that profit-making must never be interfered with or at least must be very tenderly dealt with both by government and religion; that whatever disputes these dogmas is a blasphemy, a heresy to be stamped out.

Luccock saw this business-religion as the greatest threat to Christianity in America, and this view was shared by Harry F. Ward, one of the most prominent social gospel advocates of the decade, who pointed out that the ethic of Jesus had been rejected by what he called "this capitalistic industrialism":

Indeed, it has acquired some of the characteristics of a religion as changes in economic procedure and in the art of living have made some of its basic propositions to be mostly articles of faith, blindly accepted and passionately defended. As with any philosophy or religion when life moves away from it, the element of explanation decreases and that of justification increases. Now that economic institutions are changing so that the traditional body of economic doctrine no longer adequately describes them, it is the more tenaciously held by the faithful, because it supplies a sanction for established ways and a balm for the irritated conscience.[4]

The idea that business was the new religion found expression in such divergent literary forms as Hart Crane's *The Bridge*, Sinclair Lewis's *Babbitt*, John

Dos Passos's *Manhattan Transfer*, Samuel Hopkins Adams's *Success*, Waldo Frank's *The Re-discovery of America*, and numerous sentimental stories in periodicals, such as Ben Ames Williams's "None Other Gods" in *Collier's Weekly* of November 1921. All of these authors make their comments in passing without attempting a deeper analysis. Frank merely writes about success as a "cult." Adams lets his heroine say that success is a "species of religion" to her, an enthusiasm she manages to pass on to Banneker, the hero. The *Collier's Weekly* story tells of Mr. Chadwell, who initially "devoted himself to the religion of making money, and it satisfied him, left no desire of his soul unfulfilled," but who later discovers that his worship has been one of idolatry. Lewis lets Babbitt admire Zenith's only skyscraper "as a temple-spire of the religion of business, a faith passionate, exalted, surpassing common men," and Crane portrays a world where "Thomas à Ediford" has replaced Thomas à Becket, where "COMMERCE and the HOLYGHOST," "WALL STREET AND VIRGINBIRTH" are equally strong forces.[5]

Contemporary historians also recorded this tendency to view success, prosperity, and business as religious phenomena. The Beards pointed to the fact that Coolidge's system of political economy was "suffused with a moral glow," after which they quoted the president's by now classic statements that the man who builds a factory builds a temple, the man who works there worships there. Kemper Fullerton meant that money-making, which earlier had walked hand in hand with Calvinism, now was itself "almost a religion."[6] Visitors from Europe thought they saw the same thing. An English traveler, J. A. Spender, observed that "just as in Rome one goes to the Vatican and endeavors to get audience of the Pope, so in Detroit one goes to the Ford works and endeavors to see Henry Ford." After his visit, André Siegfried drew the conclusion about Americans that "the mysticism of success is perhaps their genuine religion." The well-known English author G. K. Chesterton also meditated on the American attitude toward success and came to the surprising conclusion that American businessmen were less materialistic than their European colleagues:

> But Americans do worship success in the abstract, as a sort of ideal vision. They follow success rather than money; they follow money rather than meat and drink....
>
> Thus when people say of a Yankee that he worships the dollar, they pay a compliment to his fine spirituality more true and delicate than they imagine. The dollar is an idol because it is an image; but it is an image of success and not of enjoyment.
>
> That this romance is also a religion is shown in the fact that there is a queer sort of morality attached to it. The nearest parallel to it is something like the sense of honour in the old duelling days. There is not a material but a distinctly moral savour about the implied obligation to collect dollars or to collect chips.[7]

The businessmen themselves seldom spoke of business as a religion, and for obvious reasons. They had no interest in putting the label of religion on their value system, since this might estrange large masses of not only believing but also nominal Christians. Moreover, most businessmen probably did not see their ethics and activities as religious phenomena, a lack of awareness I will have reason to come back to later. Thus, most of the linkings of business to religion came from critics impugning the business spirit of the decade or from impartial observers of the cultural climate.

Nevertheless, representatives of business occasionally revealed, as did the president of Rotary International, mentioned previously, that they viewed business as a religious force. Few were as outspoken as Edward Purinton who wrote that "the sanest religion is business." It was more common to make noncommittal reflections that suggested rather than stated a religious dimension. Elbert H. Gary, the chairman of U. S. Steel, wrote that "a standard of ethics may not serve as a substitute for Christianity, but as applied to business the two are not far apart,"—whatever he meant by that, exactly. In a book intended to boost business, Glen Buck meditated: "America is learning that there are great spiritual values in material things. And her wealth has been a high contributing factor to the process that has made her the most spiritually minded nation that has ever turned its face to the sun."[8]

Another distinct emanation of business seeing itself as a spiritual force was the vogue in the twenties of writing the decalogues and creed of various business activities. These decalogues were all based on the twentieth chapter of Exodus, and some even retained the Old Testament language of "thou shalt" and "thou shalt not," but their contents had little to do with the original Ten Commandments. In "Ten Commandments of Business," for instance, which the editor of *The Rotarian* felt was a "little business sermon that every employee might well hang over his desk," the following sentiments were expressed: "Handle the hardest job first each day. Easy ones are pleasures.... Be enthusiastic—it is contagious. Do not have the notion that success means simply making money.... Honor the chief. There must be a head to everything. Have confidence in yourself. Harmonize your work. Let sunshine radiate and penetrate." Frank Crane's "Ten Commandments of Salesmanship" were even further removed from their biblical origin:

1. Be Agreeable.
2. Know Your Business.
3. Tell the Truth.
4. Don't Argue.
5. Make It Plain.
6. Remember Names and Faces.
7. Be Dependable.
8. Don't Be Egotistic.
9. Think Success.
10. Be Human.

The Decalogue of Kiwanis was not an official document, but was found worthy of being published in its magazine. At least to this member of the business club, Kiwanis was the new redeemer:

1. KIWANIS hath brought thee out of the land of darkness; out of the house of selfishness; thou shalt prefer no other service club above KIWANIS.

2. Thou shalt not carry into KIWANIS cliques, ungenerous personalities or selfish political ambitions of any form that is in heaven above or that is in the earth beneath or that is in the waters under the earth.

3. Thou shalt not take the name of KIWANIS in vain for thine own material or business advancement....

5. Honor those things for which KIWANIS stands that thy days with the club and with its friendly fellowship may be long in the land....

9. Thou shalt not slander or bear unkind witness against thy fellow KIWANIANS or against any others.

Even though such commandments should not be taken entirely seriously, since they may have been written tongue-in-cheek, they are nevertheless revealing in that they make clear that the authors in their hearts identify business with religion. Business "creeds" were not equally common, but they did exist, and like the decalogues they revealed the conviction that commerce had a spiritual dimension. In April 1926, for instance, William E. Humphrey presented the Creed of the Federal Trade Commission of which he was a member. This was "the faith of the majority of the Commission":

We do not believe that success is a crime;

We do not believe that failure is a virtue;

We do not believe that wealth is presumptively wrong;

We do not believe that poverty is presumptively right;

We do not believe that industry, economy, honesty, and brains should be penalized;

We do not believe that incompetency, extravagance, idleness, and inefficiency should be glorified;

We do not believe that big business and crooked business are synonymous.[9]

THE EMERGENCE OF A "BUSINESS RELIGION"

All the comments listed above that endowed business with religious attributes were more or less superficial. They were generalizations, caustic denunciations or facetious observations. But the fact that this identification of business with religion was made by so many and so diverse a group of commentators is a sign that the idea was not foreign to the spirit of the age. In the 1930s or the 1960s, such comparisons and analogies were rarely made.

Whether business in fact became a religion in the 1920s is a complex question, the answer to which is dependent on what one includes in the concept of "business" and on how one defines "religion." Two basic kinds of definition of religion are the theological and the sociological ones. A theological definition would emphasize faith in an infinite, supernatural power that is in control of man's fate, feared and worshiped by finite man. G. Galloway writes in *The*

Philosophy of Religion that religion is "man's faith in a power beyond himself whereby he seeks to satisfy emotional needs and gain stability of life, and which he expresses in acts of worship and service."[10] *The New Catholic Encyclopedia* gives the following theological definition:

> From the subjective point of view, religion is a virtue that leads man to render to God the homage that is due to Him. As an objective manner of behavior and concrete manifestation of virtue, it comprises belief in one God, personal and infinite in his attributes; an attitude of absolute respect and submission; exterior acts that express this belief and this attitude in worship; and, as required by all exterior human activity, institutions to regulate that activity.[11]

In his *Psychology of Religion*, Paul E. Johnson presents a "differential," as distinct from a "general," definition of religion, in which he says that "religion is personal cooperation with a trusted Creator of Values.... Religious devotion usually refers to a superhuman being great enough to create good things."[12] In the light of such definitions, it is obvious that business in the twenties did not become a religion, even though there were supernatural elements in the worldview shared by most businessmen, a fact we will return to later.

However, if Johnson's "general" definition is applied to this question, the answer may be different. Johnson writes:

> Religion is a response to a Sustainer of Values.... Any response, whether fear or trust, any action or attitude that recognizes a power able to control values, is religion in the broad sense. Any Sustainer—or many—who can save or destroy, give or withhold what one may need or desire, is indicated. A Sustainer may be personal (as a Father) or impersonal (as a process), human (as a parent) or divine (as a Wholly Other), natural (as scientific forces) or supernatural (as magic powers), individual (as in monotheism) or societal (as in humanism) and institutional (as in Nazi devotion to the nation).... The essentials of religion are (a) desire for values, (b) conscious dependence upon a power who is able to sustain such values, and (c) responses considered appropriate to secure the values by aid from such a power.[13]

In a general characterization such as this, business in the 1920s would qualify as a religion.

Scholars have often taken the psychological or social role of religion as a starting point for their definitions. J. B. Pratt's often quoted statement said that "religion is the serious and social attitude of individuals or communities toward the power or powers which they conceive as having ultimate control over their interests and destinies."[14] Emile Durkheim held the view that "the sole characteristic that all ideas such as religious sentiments equally present seems to be that they are common to a certain number of people living together, and that, besides, they have an average intensity that is quite elevated. It is, indeed, a constant fact that, when a strong belief is held by the same community of men, it inevitably takes on a religious character. It inspires in consciences the same reverential respect as beliefs properly religious."[15] If Pratt and Durkheim, or anthropologists like Radcliffe-Brown and Malinowski, had been asked to characterize business in the 1920s, they might well have pronounced it a religious force.

Johnson stated in his general definition that the Nazi devotion to the nation could be termed religious. The same thought was expressed by Reinhold Niebuhr, when he wrote: "When national loyalty is reconstructed into an all-absorbing religion, as in modern Germany, we may witness the recrudescence of primitive religion in the modern period on a large scale."[16] Many scholars, for example, Arnold Toynbee, John MacMurray, and Jacques Maritain, have claimed that communism, like fascism, could be defined as a religion. Maritain wrote:

> Considered in its essence and its principles, communism as it exists,—above all the communism of the Soviet republics,—is a complete system of doctrine and life which claims to reveal to man the meaning of his existence, to answer all the fundamental questions which are set by life, and which manifests an unequalled power of totalitarian inclusiveness. It is a religion, and one of the most imperious quality: certain that it is called to replace all other religions; a religion of atheism, for which dialectic materialism supplies the dogma, and of which communism as a rule of life is the social and ethical expression.[17]

Business in the 1920s was not a force of the same magnitude as fascism and communism, partly because its doctrines were not propagated in a totalitarian state. Nevertheless, business ethics and business ideology exerted an influence on many Americans that differed only in degree from what took place in Germany and the Soviet Union.

Ever since the Founding Fathers (it has been argued during the last twenty years), America has developed what has variously been termed a "civil," "common," or "public" religion, similar in function, if not in commitment, to German fascism and Soviet communism. Robert N. Bellah, who initiated the debate about civil religion in 1966, argues that parallel to, but separate from, the churches in America there exists a faith in the existence of God, the life to come, the reward of virtue and the punishment of vice, and the exclusion of religious intolerance. Civil religion is most clearly noticeable on solemn occasions when civic leaders feel obliged to refer to God. Using Kennedy's inaugural address as a starting point for his discussion, Bellah points out how Kennedy spoke of God and of the obligation of Americans to carry out God's will on earth and be a light to other nations. But Kennedy

> did not refer to any religion in particular. He did not refer to Jesus Christ, or to Moses, or to the Christian church; certainly he did not refer to the Catholic church. In fact, his only reference was to the concept of God, a word that almost all Americans can accept but that means so many different things to so many different people that it is almost an empty sign.

If Kennedy was a Christian, why did he not refer to the Christian God? "He did not because these are matters of his own private religious belief and of his relation to his own particular church; they are not matters relevant in any direct way to the conduct of his public office."[18]

Civil religion in America is, in short, a worship of the "American Way of Life" and a conviction that America and Americans have been chosen to carry out God's will on earth. The ideals of the American way of life are not scrupulously observed, Will Herberg writes, "they are in fact constantly violated, often grossly. But violated or not, they are felt to be normative and relevant to 'business and politics' in a way that the formal tenets of 'official' religion are not."[19] Marie Augusta Neal limits the American way of life to mean the life-style of the dominant class and holds that "civil religion is that religious dimension associated with the life-style of the dominant class in a given society. This association gives that life-style a quality of authority and includes the power to legitimate the existing allocation and control of goods and services within the political economy."[20]

Most analysts make clear that American civil religion is based on Christianity but is "clearly not itself Christianity," as Bellah puts it. Critics further agree that civil religion is not experienced by Americans as competing with the faith of the church they belong to, although the ideals of civil religion are at great variance with their church creed. Most Americans do not even see civil religion as a separate religion. One may speculate on why many Americans are not aware of having two contrary confessions at the same time. One reason may be ignorance of the doctrines of their church. Over the years, in one poll after another, a surprisingly large majority of the American people have declared their belief in God. Consequently America has acquired a reputation of being one of the most religious countries in the world. However, when it comes to knowing more specifically what they believe in, that is, the Judeo-Christian tenets predominant in the United States, many Americans reveal a deep ignorance. Smith and Jamison drew this picture of a poll taken in 1954:

> Although 96 per cent of Americans say that they believe in God, this near-unanimity does not take them to church in the same proportion; if it did, the church buildings would be far from adequate. Nor does the high level of belief accompany a high level of information about religion; for example, 51 per cent could not name the first book of the Bible, 60 per cent could not give the names of the Holy Trinity, 66 percent did not know who delivered the Sermon on the Mount, and 79 per cent could not name one prophet mentioned in the Old Testament.[21]

One has reason to doubt the result of this poll; the stupendous ignorance shown here seems unbelievable. Nevertheless, it may be that many Americans are not aware that there is a doctrinal difference between civil religion and, for instance, the Protestant faith. Another, and more likely, reason why Americans can embrace two divergent religious beliefs is compartmentalization. As Bellah suggested previously, Kennedy would make a distinction between his private faith and his public references to God; they belonged in different compartments and were not interrelated. In the same way, many other Americans would place a watertight bulkhead between their civil religion and their Protestant, Catholic, or Jewish faith.

In the 1920s the United States adopted not a civil religion as much as a "business religion." This faith was espoused by a great number of Americans who simultaneously declared themselves to be Protestants, although the business ideals that made up the business religion in most cases ran counter to Protestant doctrine. Like a civil religion, business in the 1920s saw itself as the tool of God and the American business civilization as a model for other countries. The ideals of business were, as Herberg says of civil religion, felt to be more normative and more relevant in daily affairs than those of organized religion. The religious dimension also gave, as Neal suggested, the life-style of the dominant business class a quality of authority.

The business religion that emerged in the twenties gave a view of God and of man's position in the world that will be dealt with in the rest of this chapter. It further presented business as creating a morality of service and as offering a sense of belonging and community. Business promised redemption of society and a millennium. This business religion appropriated, as civil religion did, certain Christian values and has often been based on biblical archetypes, but it is not Christianity. It emerged as something very different from Christianity, a new faith in which the emphasis was on man rather than God, on self-reliance rather than submission, on social rather than individual salvation.

GOD AND MAN

As I have shown in the preceding chapter, and as James Warren Prothro has shown in *The Dollar Decade*, American businessmen in the twenties often referred to a Protestant God, to Christ, and to other biblical personages. Some businessmen did this because they were believing Christians; others because they knew business would benefit from such references. There is little doubt that the average businessman in the 1920s believed in God, or, at least, that he found it important to profess that he did. But he was also eager not to appear intolerant. In most cases, he vaguely referred to God as the Creator, as the Almighty and the Omnipotent, as Lord, the One and the Divine, whose "spiritual laws" could not be violated without negative effects. But he was less willing to state a belief in a specific creed. He often made a point of declaring that it did not really matter which God men believed in as long as they were working for the common good. God was the God of all men; He was a giver of good gifts to all. The editor of *The Rotarian* wrote: "When men start out to seek for spiritual values one fanatic may find them; but a council of men of all creeds, where differences were waived and the only rivalry was a healthy competition in effort for the common good, would be a more likely method of reaching the desired result."[22] A poem in the same magazine, "One Blood in Rotary,"[23] expressed the same tolerance:

> The color of the skin?
> It matters not:
> One may be dark
> or tan,
> Be yellow, white, or brown,
> Yet have a heart
> That throbs with love
> For human kind.
>
> Though we may worship Christ
> Or Jewish God;
> At Hindu temple pray,
> Or Shinto shrine
> At Buddha's feet
> Or at a Moslem mosque;—
> All hating war
> We pray for peace.
>
> The vibrant pulsing blood
> Is one in all
> And race an incident
> Of place and clime
> We meet—we fraternize—
> Together serve,
> When service calls
> in Rotary.

KIWANIS, the most prominent business club after Rotary, took a similar stand. The editor of *The Kiwanis Magazine*, Roe Fulkerson, wrote on its editorial page:

> There are no religious restrictions in KIWANIS. Each one of a large family of children wants to bring a well-beloved father a token of affection. Each thinks a different gift appropriate. Each comes in a different manner to make his offering. Each makes his present in a different language. Each offering, each manner, and each language is characteristic of the giver. Father would not have it otherwise.... We have never met God. We can not know his wishes save for his divine word common to most religions. ...If KIWANIS does nothing more to justify its existence than to increase religious toleration it will not have lived in vain.[24]

It was not uncommon in books and journals connected with the business community to print prayers to an unspecified God. These prayers either gave thanks for the gifts given by this nonsectarian divinity, like the following:

> For every joy of earth and hope of heaven
> For each good gift bestowed on us and ours,

> For inspirations sent, ambitions given,
> Ideals to climb to, wills to train, and powers
> To harness to our tasks—With one accord,
> We offer, now, our thanks, O gracious Lord.[25]

Or they asked for renewed power "to serve my fellows and my age—the power to live—the power to work—co-laborer with Thee!"[26] Or they requested, as in Thomas Dreier's prayer, new inspiration to be a willing tool:

> I would ask, too, that I be inspired to send from my heart that greatest of all prayers: "Thy will be done," thus proclaiming my faith in a Great Executive who is all-wise, all-loving, all-just, and who so manages the universe that all things work together as he would have them. This, God, is a business man's prayer.[27]

But even if most businessmen seem to have acknowledged a supernatural force, they still subscribed to an anthropocentric view of the universe.

According to the business view of the world, man was intimately dependent upon God and upon his fellowmen. He was part of an intricate pattern or plan; he was an agent and a tool set in the world to perform a special task. Life was an "inseverable web," whose strands ran "backward, upward, downward, outward," connecting man in all possible ways with "the world and the ages." As a consequence no man could live for himself alone; his self-realization had to take place "in and through society."[28] At the same time, man was presented as being self-contained. He carried his happiness, success, and salvation within him. He himself, and no other force or individual, was responsible for the outcome of his life. These two views of man, which characterized the business philosophy of the twenties, may seem to be in conflict, but this is not really so: man was the source of his own success, but the ability to succeed was a gift from God, and true success meant, not living selfishly merely for himself, but living a life of service for his fellowmen.

The American businessman of the twenties saw himself as an heir of God. And what he had inherited was not poverty, squalor, or humiliating limitations. "Lack and want have nothing whatever to do with God's children," one success manual made clear. "Your inheritance is rich, sublime." Because of this rich inheritance "you owe it to the One who has given you life, health, brains, to make something of yourself, to improve your situation."[29] Every man had been assigned a special task by God. Man had therefore no right to minimize himself or his role but should say to himself as one author suggested: "God put me here for some purpose. I am going to realize it."[30] Or as another representative of the business ideology put it:

> Every human being is sent into the world to cooperate with the Creator in working for some great motive. His powers are given him to help carry out the plan of the universe. Can there be a greater stimulus to endeavor than this? Can anything be a greater spur to self-discovery, more heartening and sustaining than the realization that one is born

for a glorious purpose, no less than to be a co-worker with God in lifting the race to greater heights?[31]

As God's heir and co-laborer, man had been given a dormant "divine spark." God had implanted a secret "seed of Divine energy" in all human beings, a potentiality and a capacity without limits. "Man has godlike possibilities," one book proclaimed. Most people, however, remained unaware all their lives of this "expression of the God within us."[32] Man had to be awakened to his own God-given potential. The best way to conquer the worst case of timidity and fear was to "recognize your own divinity, your freedom, power, and dignity as a child of God," Orison Swett Marden said in *Success Fundamentals* and stated elsewhere in the same book: "This is really the chief business of man—to learn to know himself, to realize the power that is his through his inseparable union with his Creator."[33]

As man became aware of the unlimited potential within him, his divine self became his only norm. The making or breaking of a man was contained within himself. B. C. Forbes explained in his *Keys to Success*:

Your success depends upon you.

Your happiness depends upon you.

You have to steer your own course.

You have to shape your own fortune.

You have to educate yourself.

You have to do your own thinking.

You have to live with your own conscience.[34]

But since the believers of this business religion had no written canon to follow, they were not sure how God was expressing Himself through them. John C. Tracey felt, as he wrote in *The Kiwanis Magazine*, that "the God of Love" had placed in the heart of every man "something of the love of righteousness," "a life urge that is slowly but surely driving out selfishness and moving the whole human race toward its destiny of brotherhood."[35] Preaching what he called "the gospel of self-expression," Dreier felt sure that God's commands "are sent to us in the form of desires. That which we desire to do with all our strength, that which we most love to do, is what God wants us to do."[36] Such comments as these only confirm what I have stated before: that the God referred to in these business writings is not a Christian God but a vaguely depicted Life Force.

Man was his own norm and his own source of inspiration. The most important part of man, most business ideologists agreed, was his mind. To be able to think efficiently was the basis for all success. "A man's real worth," B. C. Forbes stated, "is the quality, the value, of his thoughts, his mind."[37] This did not mean, however, that some were excluded from success by being born with less acute minds; brainpower could, and should, be developed. You had within you the ability to "bring this power under your conscious control and direction." Between the average man and the exceptional man, one writer asserted, "the chief difference in brain power is that which comes from training." Nature had put no limit to how much you could develop: "Your brain is capable of becoming just as big as you take the pains to make it. To grow it must be fed and exercised."[38] To exercise your mind, B. C. Forbes suggested, you should reserve a still time, preferably early in the morning, when you could be "absolutely alone and uninterrupted" in the woods or by a lake and just think.[39] This practice reminds one of the time set off for prayer or meditation by many religious believers.

It was essential for success to learn not only how to use your brain but how to use it in the right way, and the right way was to think positively. If you filled your mind with positive, optimistic, self-reliant thoughts, you could not help becoming a success. If, on the other hand, you filled your brain with thoughts of fear, limitation, poverty, you were bound to become a failure. One commentator testified that his life had always been rich because he had never allowed himself to think poor thoughts. He continued: "If one goes about thinking that the world is filled with crooks and schemers, the world is filled with crooks and schemers. On the other hand, if one believes that the world is filled with fine, neighborly, helpful, kindly folks, one finds people of that class in the great majority."[40] Many lives, it was held, were cursed with "self-thought poisoning" that was caused by ignorance. If all the poverty-stricken people of the world only stopped thinking of poverty, stopped dwelling on it, worrying about it, and fearing it, and instead started to think "the opulent thought, the prosperity thought," then their condition would soon be changed. Then they would no longer be shut off from the "abundant supply" that was their birthright as God's children: "The Creator did not mean that any human being should be deprived of the power to develop his Godlike possibilities. But the poverty thought has pauperized and starved more minds, narrowed more lives, stunted more divine possibilities than almost anything else."[41] Man must consequently believe wholeheartedly in himself and his possibilities; through faith everything could be accomplished. *The Kiwanis Magazine* saw this faith as an expression of the Divine Power:

All things are done through faith. Progress is only the consolidation of materialized dreams. When the time comes that men and women cease to dream new dreams and lack the faith in their mind creation, then progress has died and earth goes back to the primeval age. Faith is the divine spark in man. Without faith we are as an inanimate thing; we exist but do not grow. Faith is infectious, for how often has the faith of one person converted the multitude to his or her belief. Faith is a power without comprehension, for from that untutored savage of antiquity, armed only with mind and body strength, has come, through faith, a civilization which harnesses the very elements themselves, which taps the earth and draws her hidden minerals and makes the creatures of his dreams come true. Faith! thou powerful thing, how wonderful thou art and how few of us realize your power. There is nothing impossible through faith.[42]

The similarity is obvious between this kind of teaching and such later Christian ideas as the theology of positive thought espoused by Norman Vincent Peale and Kenneth Hagin.

But if you did not have the faith that could accomplish the impossible, if you could not think as positively about yourself and your ability as these writers suggested, what could you do then? The self-help prophets knew the answer to such skepticism. Just repeat often enough to yourself, they told their readers, that you have the ability and the faith, and you will start believing that it is true. You could "brainwash" yourself—even though that term was not used—into becoming a success. These inspirational exercises assumed the function of prayer and meditation.

In his handbook for businessmen, *Training for Power and Leadership*, Grenville Kleiser suggested that the aspiring man should set aside special time both morning and evening for meditation. Every morning the candidate should repeat the following "personal affirmations":

1. I cultivate an enthusiastic belief in myself.
2. I cultivate an enthusiasm for my work.
3. I cultivate enthusiasm for achievement.
4. I cultivate enthusiasm for the best side of things.
5. I cultivate enthusiasm for the largest possible results.
6. I cultivate enthusiasm as a daily habit.
7. I cultivate enthusiasm for my future possibilities.
8. I cultivate enthusiasm for further self-development.
9. I cultivate enthusiasm for high thinking.
10. I cultivate enthusiasm for daily progress.
11. I cultivate enthusiasm for success.
12. I cultivate enthusiasm for leadership.

This time of uplift should be combined, according to Kleiser, with "vitality-building" physical exercises—because physical fitness is also basic to success—which consisted in yoga-like movements. While doing this, the businessman should repeat silently to himself such affirmations as "I am growing in strength and endurance" and "I am developing reserve power." After he retired at night, Kleiser went on, he should suggest to his mind thoughts of what he wished to achieve:

Mentally speak to yourself as earnestly as you would discuss with another man a subject which you feel deeply. Impress upon your mind any new resolutions you have made, and positively affirm that you will fulfill them. Say to yourself, "I will make a success of this undertaking—I will concentrate my best efforts upon this particular work—I have the power to achieve it and I will do it." As your eyes grow heavy, call to your mind some helpful quotation, as "Success is due less to ability than to zeal. The man who wins is he who gives himself to his work body and soul."[43]

More important than Kleiser for advocating such self hypnotism was Emile Coué, the French psychologist who had established his Lorraine Society of Applied Psychology in Nancy and who had gained an extraordinary following in France, England, and the United States. Coué's main interest was curing the physically and mentally ill by means of "autosuggestion," but his method was applicable to all forms of improvement. Man is divided into the unconscious and the conscious self, Coué taught, into imagination and will. The unconscious or the imagination is always the stronger force of the two. Everyone can walk a plank lying on the floor, but when the plank is placed at the height of cathedral spires only the man who *imagines* that he can walk it will be able to do it. And two people in exactly the same circumstances can be, he pointed out, the one perfectly happy, the other absolutely wretched. Man is consequently ruled by his imagination, not his will, unless he learns to guide his imagination. Man can gain control over his imagination by means of "autosuggestion," which Coué defined as "the implementing of an idea in oneself by oneself."

Autosuggestion meant that a person, by repeating a thought several times, made his unconscious, his imagination, assimilate the idea presented. One could never force the imagination by the will. The result must be brought about by the unconscious; the idea must be a natural part of the unconscious. (This distinction has certain similarities to the Christian distinction between working in your own power and letting the Holy Spirit work through you.) To achieve this transformation of the idea from conscious to unconscious, the person should repeatedly persuade himself that his task was easy, that he could do it; he should ban from his thoughts such words as "difficult," "impossible," and "I cannot." He should repeat morning and night twenty times, "consecutively in a monotonous voice, counting by means of a string with twenty knots in it," the words "Every day, in every respect, I am getting better and better," a phrase which most Americans and Europeans in the twenties became familiar with and which many regularly made use of.[44]

In Sweden, Coué's philosophy was the subject of an extremely popular song, which today has become a classic. Many were aware of the religious nature of autosuggestion. In England, numerous books pointed to the similarities between Coué's ideas and religion and tried occasionally to apply the method to Christianity.[45] In *Christianity and Autosuggestion*, C. Harry Brooks and Ernest Charles pointed to the "essential harmony" between Coué's ideas and those of Christ, and argued that if the method was not Christianized it might turn into a powerful competitor: "Autosuggestion, working along a purely psychological channel, seems to set itself up in rivalry with Christianity, to be a new religion, though without a God."[46]

THE GOSPEL OF WORK AND THRIFT

God had implanted in man a divine spark and a limitless potential which He expected him to cherish and develop. God had given man a mind which He expected him to expand by means of positive thoughts. But that was not enough for man to succeed. To assure success, God had also given him work. Hard, devoted work was the divinely inspired method to transform man's potential into tangible results. But God never intended work to be a burden or a punishment for disobedience; He meant it to be a delight. Marden wrote that work was a blessing, nationally and individually, that created stability and meaning and saved people from poverty, premature death, and illness. If every "crevice" of man's mind was filled by work, his "resisting powers" would not be weakened by the fear of disease. Idleness invited worries, which wrought all sorts of havoc. Marden concluded: "God's medicine is work that we love. God's plan for man's development, his growth in mental and physical power and resourcefulness, is work."[47]

Even though all businessmen in the twenties did not explicitly refer to work as a gift from God, they all emphasized in lofty words its fundamental importance, using words and concepts that may be termed religious. Several spoke about work as a salvation or a redemption.[48] Others did not hesitate to call their message a "gospel of work."[49] Still others saw success as a "reward" for hard work. Calvin Coolidge wrote: "Any reward that is worth having only comes to the industrious. The success which is made in any walk of life is measured almost exactly by the amount of hard work put into it."[50] Work was also described as "the greatest gift life holds," the "fount" of all prosperity, and the "salt" that gives life its savor.[51] The last two examples vaguely invoke the language of the Bible, and occasionally explicit rewritings or false applications of biblical verses were used to create an inspirational tone. B. C. Forbes, for instance, wrote epigrams like "The wages of idleness is demotion" and "When tempted to dodge a stiff incline by slipping into a side-track, there's only one thing to say: 'Get thee behind me, Satan'."[52]

Other virtues, though of less importance, were still seen as necessary for the industrious man to succeed. Endurance, thrift, and cheerfulness contributed to the ultimate success. Forbes wrote that "the best time to hold on is when you reach the point where the average fellow would quit."[53] Thrift was closely allied to industry. Roger Babson referred to economic studies that clearly showed that ninety-five percent of the employers were employers because they had started saving money when young. The same studies also showed that ninety-five percent of the wageworkers were wageworkers because they systematically spent their money as fast as they had earned it.[54] In his magazine, Forbes bombarded his readers with epigrams like "Thrift lifts," "To rise, save," and "*Thrift* and *thrive* are very similar, you will note."[55] In one of his books, Forbes spoke warmly of cheerfulness as a handmaiden to industry:

> Success is the summit we all seek to attain. We can step on no escalator or elevator and be whisked up without exertion. The road is steep, steep as a ladder, and the exertion of brain and muscle is necessary to climb it step by step, painstakingly, pluckily, perseveringly.
>
> Cheerfulness is one step.
>
> Gain it early.
>
> Success in business, if not in life itself, is simply the art of pleasing.[56]

THE GOAL OF SUCCESS

One might have expected business in the twenties to teach that God's plan for man first and foremost was material gain. Surprisingly enough, this was far from the truth. The overwhelming majority of the speeches, pamphlets, articles, and books devoted to business ideology propagated an idealistic, altruistic view of man. As we have seen, the general spirit of the age spoke in favor of self-realization, individualism, and material prosperity, and business was certainly partially responsible for creating this attitude. In its doctrinal teachings, however,—if one may call them that—business rather emphasized the importance of service, honesty, the Golden Rule, and cooperation. The goal of man was to be the Good Samaritan; the truly successful man was a servant to his fellowmen. Again, we here encounter, as we did before among Protestant believers, a discrepancy between theory and practice. The business ideals of the 1920s were more sublime than those of any other segment of society, Protestantism included, and still business was a prime mover in creating a materialistic spirit. We will have reason to return to the service ideal of business in the next chapter.

That money alone never brings happiness was the universal opinion of business ideologists. The man who worked only for monetary profit was a poor man, even though he had millions in the bank. To work solely for material gain was cheap, a businessman pointed out: "A life rewarded with money alone is like the child that receives a little tinsel card as a reward of merit."[57] The ultimate goal of work was rather the satisfaction of accomplishment, the development of character, and the service to mankind. The businessman who was striving for such goals did not have to worry about profit; it would automatically come to him as a reward for work well done. One industrialist, Samuel M. Vauclain, averred:

> The money return always takes care of itself and is the least important side to be considered. I have never bothered about it. I happen to know my own salary right now because the Board of Directors of the company fixed it the other day in meeting. But until that meeting I had never quite known my annual income for perhaps twenty years past. That sounds "unbusinesslike." Is it? Why should one bother counting money if

there are more interesting things at hand to do? My salary was bound to be large enough for all proper purposes, because I was doing my work as best I knew how, and that is the world voucher for a salary.[58]

Another successful businessman, Arthur Reynolds, solemnly declared: "I have never spent time thinking about how much money I was going to get by doing one thing or by doing something else. The only thing that has ever interested me was whether I was going to *accomplish* something. . . . It is the key to happiness."[59]

True success also meant the building of character. It depended on you whether you would ultimately become a "big, generous, fully developed human being, or a diminutive shrub oak of a man"; it was in your own hands whether people would admire and respect or despise you, whether you would "win the approval or the condemnation of your Maker."[60] Marden, who wrote this, meant that if you failed to become the kind of person God intended you to become, you would never be a true success, however much money you had earned:

One of the greatest tragedies of human life is to fail to answer the call that runs in the blood, to fail to respond to the summons of the Almighty, to answer for the talent He has given you. Look around you; read history and biography, and you will find that the men and women who stand out like giants, colossal milestones on the path of civilization, are, and have always been, those who let God's purpose work in them.[61]

Business should consequently be viewed in a wider perspective. The task assigned to business was not only to supply material satisfaction, which it did so successfully, but also to care for the spiritual needs of the country. "The problem is no longer how to make more money," Edward Bok wrote, "it is the problem of what can money best accomplish. It is no longer taking something out of life; it is what you can put into it. It is taking that which came from the public and giving it back to that public for the advancement of its higher, and not for its material, life. It is appealing to the spirit rather than to the body."[62]

The inspirational message of leading businessmen, as presented in this chapter, was directed to the average American as well as the business community, in order to strengthen their belief in the righteousness of business ideals and in order to satisfy their spiritual hunger. Whether the ordinary businessman, or his fellow-Americans in the noncommercial realm, adopted these beliefs, and whether business thus actually became a quasi-religion, is difficult to know. All we can say is that those who propagated the business ideals in the 1920s were convinced that business filled a religious need, a conviction they tried to disseminate to the general public.

NOTES

1. "Bethlehem—and Twenty Centuries," *The Rotarian* 21 (December 1922), p. 285.
2. Walter Lippmann, *A Preface to Morals* (1929; reprint; New York: Time-Life Books, 1964), p. 9.

3. Edward M. Bok, "When Money Is King and Business Our God," *World's Work* 48 (September 1924), p. 479; "The Great God—Prosperity," *The New Republic* 55 (August 8, 1928), pp. 291–92; Stuart Chase, "The Dogma of 'Business First'," *Harper's Monthly Magazine* 153 (September 1926), p. 482.

4. John Herman Randall, *Religion and the Modern World* (New York: Frederick A. Stokes Co., 1929), p. 95; Joseph Jastrow, "The New Idol of the Market-Place," *Century Magazine* 93 (February 1928), pp. 491–505; Halford Edward Luccock, *Jesus and the American Mind* (New York: Abingdon Press, 1930), p. 133, see also pp. 131–34, 157–63; Harry F. Ward, *Our Economic Morality and the Ethic of Jesus* (New York: Macmillan Company, 1929), p. 31. For a discussion of the religious dimension of advertising, see J. Thorne Smith, "Advertising," in Harold E. Stearns, ed., *Civilization in the United States: An Enquiry by Thirty Americans* (London: Jonathan Cape, 1922), p. 381.

5. Hart Crane, *The Bridge*, second stanza of "The River" in "Powhatan's Daughter"; Sinclair Lewis, *Babbitt* (1922; reprint; London: Jonathan Cape, 1929), p. 22; Samuel Hopkins Adams, *Success* (Boston: Houghton Mifflin Company, 1921), pp. 96, 362, 400–401; Waldo Frank, *The Re-discovery of America* (New York: Charles Scribner's Sons, 1929), p. 93; Ben Ames Williams, "None Other Gods," *Collier's Weekly* 71 (November 1921), pp. 3, 4, 16, 22–23.

6. Charles A. Beard and Mary R. Beard, *The Rise of American Civilization*, Vol. 2 (New York: Macmillan Company, 1927), p. 700; Kemper Fullerton, "Calvinism and Capitalism," *Harvard Theological Review* 21 (July 1928), p. 168. Later historians who have commented on business as religion are William E. Leuchtenburg, *The Perils of Prosperity 1914–32* (Chicago: University of Chicago Press, 1958), pp. 187–88; Elizabeth Stevenson, *The American 1920s, Babbitts and Bohemians* (New York: Macmillan Company, 1967), p. 126; Ahlstrom, *A Religious History of the American People*, vol. 2 (Garden City, N.Y.: Doubleday and Company, 1975), p. 392.

7. The J. A. Spender quote is from Irving Bernstein, *The Lean Years: A History of the American Worker, 1920–1933* (Boston: Houghton Mifflin Company, 1972), p. 144; André Siegfried, *America Comes of Age* (London: Jonathan Cape, 1927), p. 45; G. K. Chesterton, *What I Saw in America* (London: Hodder and Stoughton, 1922), p. 110.

8. The statement by Purinton quoted from Ahlstrom, *A Religious History of the American People*, vol. 2, p. 392; Elbert H. Gary, "Higher Standard Developing in American Business," *Current History* 23 (March 1926), p. 778; Glen Buck, *This American Ascendancy* (Chicago: A. Kroch & Company, 1927), p. 59.

9. L. V. Selleck, "Ten Commandments of Business," *The Rotarian* 24 (May 1924), p. 28; Frank Crane, "Ten Commandments for Salesmen," *The American Magazine* 89 (June 1920), pp. 55, 152, 155–56, 159–60; "Ten Commandments of Kiwanis," *The Kiwanis Magazine* 11 (March 1926), p. 169; William E. Humphrey, "The Federal Trade Commission," in Basil Gordon Byron and Frederic René Coudert, eds., *America Speaks: A Library of Best Spoken Thought in Business and the Professions* (New York: Modern Eloquence Corporation, 1928), pp. 249–50. See also "Ten Industrial Commandments," *Commerce and Finance* 13 (January 16, 1924), p. 3, and "Ten Commandments by the Boss," in *The Manufacturers Trust Company Quarterly Bulletin* reprinted in James Melvin Lee, *Business Ethics: A Manual of Modern Morals* (New York: The Ronald Press Company, 1926), p. 72, and as "A Business Decalog" in Grenville Kleiser, *Training for Power and Leadership* (Garden City, N.Y.: Garden City Publishing Co., 1923), pp. 166–67. A slight variation is "Ten Demandments" in *Rotary International's Proceedings 1920* (Chicago: International Association of Rotary Clubs, 1920), p. 257.

10. George Galloway, *The Philosophy of Religion* (Edinburgh, 1914), p. 184. See also "Religion" in James Hastings, ed., *Encyclopaedia of Religion and Ethics*, vol. 10 (New York: Charles Scribner's Sons, 1918), p. 663.

11. "Religion" in *The New Catholic Encyclopedia*, (New York: McGraw-Hill Book Company, 1967).

12. Paul E. Johnson, *Psychology of Religion* (New York: Abingdon-Cokesbury Press, 1945), pp. 29–31.

13. Ibid.

14. J. B. Pratt, *The Religious Consciousness* (New York: Macmillan, 1920), p. 2.

15. Emile Durkheim, *Division of Labor*, quoted from Robert Nisbet, *The Sociology of Emile Durkheim* (London: Heinemann, 1975), pp. 169–70. For other definitions, see "Religion" in David L. Sills, ed., *The International Encyclopedia of Social Sciences*, vol. 13 (New York: Macmillan, 1968) and J. Milton Yinger, *Religion in the Struggle for Power* (Durham, N.C.: Duke University Press, 1946), pp. 6–11.

16. Reinhold Niebuhr, *Christianity and Power Politics* (New York: Charles Scribner's Sons, 1940), p. 178.

17. Jacques Maritain, *True Humanism* (London: Geoffrey Bles, 1938), p. 28.

18. Robert N. Bellah, "Civil Religion in America," in *Beyond Belief: Essays on Religion in a Post-Traditional World* (New York: Harper & Row Publishers, 1970), pp. 169–89. See also John F. Wilson, *Public Religion in American Culture* (Philadelphia: Temple University Press, 1979).

19. Will Herberg, *Protestant—Catholic—Jew: An Essay in American Religious Sociology* (Garden City, N.Y.: Doubleday & Company, 1960), pp. 76–79.

20. Marie Augusta Neal, "Civil Religion, Theology, and Politics in America," in Thomas M. McFadden, ed., *America in Theological Perspective* (New York: Seabury Press, 1976), pp. 99–122.

21. James Ward Smith and A. Leland Jamison, eds., *Religious Perspectives in American Culture* (Princeton, N.J.: Princeton University Press, 1961), pp. 124–25.

22. "Creeds and Deeds, Neither Are Sufficient in Themselves," *The Rotarian* 28 (April 1926), p. 33.

23. Tom J. Matthews, "One Blood in Rotary," *The Rotarian* 31 (December 1927), p. 26.

24. Roe Fulkerson, "Religion," *The Kiwanis Magazine* 9 (May 1924), p. 215.

25. E. H. J. Andrews, "A Grace Before Meat," *The Rotarian* 23 (December 1923), p. 12.

26. Marco Morrow, "The Prayer of a Rotarian," *The Rotarian* 27 (September 1925), p. 4. See also "A Rotarian's Prayer," *The Rotarian* 21 (December 1922), p. 309.

27. Thomas Dreier, *The Silver Lining or Sunshine on the Business Trail* (New York: B. C. Forbes Publishing Company, 1923), pp. vii–viii.

28. Harry Hibschman, "This Web of Life," *The Rotarian* 31 (October 1927), pp. 18–19, 38, 40.

29. Orison Swett Marden, *Success Fundamentals* (New York: Thomas Y. Crowell Company, 1920), p. 228.

30. Edward W. Bok, *Dollars Only* (New York: Charles Scribner's Sons, 1926), p. 234.

31. Marden, *Success Fundamentals*, p. 120. In a series of allegories about the Whydontyas, the Wishihadahs, and the Gogetits in *The Rotarian*, the religion of the admirable Gogetits also saw God in this light: "They do not rely on God to do what they will not

try themselves of their own accord. They regard God as their co-partner and so name him." *The Rotarian* 25 (September 1924), pp. 18, 46–48.

32. Bok, *Dollars Only*, pp. 223–30, 237–38; Marden, *Success Fundamentals*, p. 114.

33. Marden, *Success Fundamentals*, pp. 168, 115.

34. B. C. Forbes, *Keys to Success: Personal Efficiency* (New York: B. C. Forbes Publishing Company, 1926), pp. 3–4.

35. John C. Tracey, "Is It Necessary to 'Prove' Christianity?" *The Kiwanis Magazine* 8 (May 1923), pp. 10–11, 57.

36. Dreier, *The Silver Lining*, p. 63.

37. Forbes, *Keys to Success*, p. 13.

38. Kleiser, *Training for Power and Leadership*, p. 4; Joseph French Johnson, *Organized Business Knowledge* (New York: B. C. Forbes Publishing Co., 1923), pp. 3–4; B. C. Forbes, *Forbes Epigrams: 1000 Thoughts on Life and Business* (New York: B. C. Forbes Publishing Company, 1922), p. 80.

39. Forbes, *Keys to Success*, p. 13.

40. Dreier, *The Silver Lining*, p. 41.

41. Marden, *Success Fundamentals*, pp. 216, 220, 226–227, 255–56, 262–64.

42. "Faith," *The Kiwanis Magazine* 9 (August 1924), p. 359. In *The Self-Made Man in America: The Myth of Rags to Riches* (New Brunswick, N.J.: Rutgers University Press, 1954), Irving G. Wyllie has shown that the success manuals of the nineteenth century expressed a similar belief in man and his possibilities; see, for instance, pp. 34–35, 40, 83–84.

43. Kleiser, *Training for Power and Leadership*, pp. 253, 330, 358.

44. Emile Coué, *Self-Mastery Through Conscious Autosuggestion* (New York: American Library Service, 1922), pp. 7–26. Dreier, in *The Silver Lining*, pp. 35–36, also speaks warmly of the method of autosuggestion.

45. R. F. Horton, *The Mystical Quest of Christ*; Evelyn Underhill, *The Life of the Spirit and the Life of To-day*; H. C. Carter, *Autosuggestion and Religion*; Worcester and McComb, *The Christian Religion as a Healing Power*; The Dean of Chester, *M. Coué and His Gospel of Health*.

46. C. Harry Brooks and Ernest Charles, *Christianity and Autosuggestion* (London: George Allen & Unwin Ltd., 1923), p. 19.

47. Marden, *Success Fundamentals*, pp. 44–49. Calvin Coolidge also acknowledged that work was God's gift when he wrote: "One of the earliest mandates laid on the human race was to subdue the earth. That meant work." Calvin Coolidge, *The Autobiography of Calvin Coolidge* (New York: Cosmopolitan Book Corporation, 1929), p. 68. Samuel M. Vauclain had this to say about the joy of working:

> I have never taken a vacation. I have never needed one, and no place ever offered as many different kinds of amusement as could be found in the day's work. . . . I do not consider that I have ever really worked. It has simply been fun, and I have always been doing the sort of thing that I best liked to do. *Optimism* (Philadelphia, 1924) p. 17.

48. Harlan Hoyt Horner, "Building the Superstructure," *The Rotarian* 22 (June 1923), p. 331; Thornton Graham, the millionaire in Arthur Train's *The Needle's Eye* (New York: Charles Scribner's Sons, 1924), says to his son: "Work is the salvation of the individual and the race." (p. 131). See also Thomas Nixon Carver, *The Present Economic Revolution in the United States* (Boston: Little, Brown and Company, 1925), p. 82.

49. Vauclain, *Optimism*, p. 307; Horner, "Building the Superstructure," p. 331.

50. Coolidge, *The Autobiography*, p. 171.
51. Forbes, *Forbes Epigrams*, p. 70; Forbes, *Keys to Success*, pp. 36–38.
52. Forbes, *Forbes Epigrams*, pp. 111, 149, cf. Romans 6:23 and Matthew 16:23.
53. Forbes, *Forbes Epigrams*, p. 116.
54. Roger W. Babson, *Fundamentals of Prosperity: How to Become a Successful Business Man* (New York: B. C. Forbes Publishing Company, 1923), pp. 32–33.
55. Forbes, *Forbes Epigrams*, pp. 62, 69, 154.
56. Forbes, *Keys to Success*, p. 75.
57. Charles R. Boyce, "The Spirit of Service," *The Rotarian* 25 (July 1924), p. 5.
58. Vauclain, *Optimism*, p. 15.
59. Arthur Reynolds, "What I Consider the Most Important Thing in Business," *The American Magazine* 92 (July 1921), pp. 16, 104, 106, 108.
60. Marden, *Success Fundamentals*, pp. 153, 159.
61. Ibid., p. 159.
62. Bok, *Dollars Only*, pp. 90–91.

6

Business as Religion: Social Redemption

The greater part of the preceding chapter was devoted to the businessman's view of a supernatural God and his own relationship to that divine power. In the first part of that chapter, however, I pointed to the fact that business itself was also seen as a religious force. This chapter will continue that investigation and attempt to make clear how business was viewed as a spiritual power capable of bringing about social redemption. It will try to show how many Americans honestly believed business to be a creator of morals, brotherhood, equality, a redeemed society, and a millennium. Business had been chosen, businessmen were convinced, as God's instrument to bring forth His lasting peace on earth.

Business in the twenties described itself as altruistic and self-sacrificing. It pointed out again and again that its primary goal was neither profit nor power. Business assured the public that its deepest wish was to serve mankind, to build up, to heal, and to satisfy all man's material and spiritual needs. It was the champion of loyalty, truth, and honesty. If left alone, business promised a never-ending progress of mankind. Consequently, business looked upon itself as not merely an economic force but also as a spiritual and moral agent whose task it was to regenerate the individual and the nation.

BUSINESS—CREATOR OF MORALS

Religion produces morals; it is difficult to imagine a religion without a system of ethics. The business religion of the twenties was no exception. It gave rise to an ethical code, which certainly had its roots in Christian ethics but which was proudly looked upon by business as an indigenous product. There have been few times in American history when business ethics have been discussed by so many and in such exalted terms.

In a previous chapter, I pointed in passing to the fact that business was regarded as the civilizer that caused man to progress culturally and ethically.

Again and again, businessmen emphasized that the ascendancy of business also entailed a rise in the moral standard. Not only had business reached a hitherto unattained level of fair dealings, it also set an ideal to be emulated by other professions. American business, one writer said, was characterized by a "growing idealism that already towers high from a solid grounding of uncompromising integrity," and the President of the Chamber of Commerce of the United States, Julius Barnes, stated: "Organized industry is clearly possessing itself not only of a higher conception of efficiency in the conduct of industry, but a higher conception of the ideals properly comprised in public service."[1] It was hinted that this business idealism was as efficient as that of the churches. When B. C. Forbes wrote that "business can be as ethical as religion," he presumably also meant that it was.[2]

Possessing such high ethical standards, businessmen became "the recognized champions of right and truth" in society.[3] Business was better fitted than any other force to foster such "moral qualities" as honor, trust, loyalty, sobriety, and steadiness.[4] Glen Buck even pronounced American business "the finest achievement of mankind":

> For the first time in history the foremost activities of a great nation are running in parallels with the on-sweeping ideals of the world's straightest thinking. Our business intelligence has so far outgrown our political intelligence that it looms like a white lily on a stagnant pool. In the stress of the honest day's work we have at last convincingly demonstrated that true efficiency and high ethical standards are inseparable. And the result is a moral achievement almost unmatched in time.[5]

As I also pointed out in an earlier chapter, the business ethics of the 1920s were favorably compared, in book after book, article after article, to the moral standard of the turn of the century. The common message was, as Wigginton E. Creed phrased it in his book *Safeguarding the Future of Private Business*, that "business morality is higher today than it ever has been in the world's history."[6] Business representatives assured the American people that the old "Yankee tricks" were gone; such slogans as "let the buyer beware," "the public be damned," and "business is business" had been "put far back on the shelf" never to be brought out again. The "off-color" business practices that had been readily tolerated twenty-five years earlier had now "been abandoned altogether."[7] The chairman of U. S. Steel, Elbert H. Gary, was convinced that "undoubtedly the world is growing better" as a result of the improvement in business morals that had taken place during the last decade. In 1926, when Gary was writing, most businessmen conducted their operations on the basis that "right is superior to might" and that "morality is on a par with legality and the observance of both is essential to worthy achievement."[8]

Two poems may shed light on the development in attitude that was taking place. In 1917, *The Nation's Business* published Berton Braley's "Business Is Business":

"Business is Business," the Little Man said,
"A battle where 'everything goes,'
Where the only gospel is 'get ahead,'
And never spare friends or foes;
'Slay or be slain,' is the slogan cold,
You must struggle and slash and tear,
For Business is Business, a fight for gold,
Where all that you do is fair!"

"Business is Business," the Big Man said,
"A battle to make of earth,
A place to yield us more wine and bread,
More pleasure and joy and mirth;
There are still some bandits and buccaneers
Who are jungle-bred beasts of trade,
But their number dwindles with passing years
And dead is the code they made!"

"Business is Business," the Big Man said,
"But it's something that's more, far more;
For it makes sweet gardens of deserts dead,
And cities it built now roar
Where once the deer and the grey wolf ran
From the pioneer's swift advance;
Business is Magic that toils for man;
Business is True Romance."

"And those who make it a ruthless fight
Have only themselves to blame
If they feel no whit of the keen delight
In playing the Bigger Game,
The game that calls of the heart and head,
The best of man's strength and nerve:
Business is Business," the Big Man said,
"And that Business is to serve!"

The poem was an immediate success. During the next seven years, the editor of *The Nation's Business* received requests for reprints every week, and by 1924 more than a million copies of the poem had been sent out. First of all, this poem reflects the fact that the attitude toward business morals had started changing before the twenties. It is true, the poet asserts, that business is business, but it is more, much more. Business is responsible for the progress of humankind, and consequently is of service; it further brings pleasure and romance. In August 1924, Braley's poem was reprinted in *The Nation's Business*, this time accompanied by a new, "inspired version" written by Everett W. Lord, Dean of the College of Business Administration of Boston University:

"Business is Business," the Old Man said,
"It's warfare where everything goes,

Where every act that pays is fair
    And all whom you meet are foes.
It's a battle of wits, a heartless rush—
    It's a tearing, wearing fight;
It's a trick of the strong to win from the weak,
    With never a thought of the right."

And he schemed, and he fought, and he pushed men aside,
    While the world in contempt looked on;
It buried him deep 'neath the wealth that he claimed
    And covered his name with scorn.

"Business is Business," the Young Man said,
    "A game in which all may play;
Where every move must accord with the rules
    And no one his fellow betray.
It's wholesome and clean, and full of good-will
    It's an urging, surging game,
It's a mission to serve in your day and age,
    As a guerdon to honor your name."

And he sought and he bought, and he brought from afar,
    And he served with conscience clear;
While his praise was sung by his fellow-men
    And his service crowned with cheer.[9]

It is easy to discern how the tone has become more exalted in the latter poem, more "spiritual," if you like. In the original version, Braley acknowledged that the "jungle-bred beasts of trade" still existed, even though their power was broken; in Lord's "inspired version," the bandits and buccaneers have vanished completely. Braley also had to admit that business was business—that its first goal was profit and that it occasionally had to use rough methods—but that it also served by bringing additional blessings to humanity. In Lord's poem these blessings are no longer additional. Business has become a moral agent in itself. Its primary objective is a wholesome and clean mission to serve, not to earn money. One business manual, commenting on the two poems, contributed to their religious quality by saying that they aided "the vision of the business man who often lacks power to lift his eyes from his ledger 'unto hills from whence cometh help'."[10]

As a result of the new interest in morals, several business movements and organizations emerged, whose task was to inspire men of commerce to even greater uplift and to keep them from slipping back into shady practices. Shortly before the war, the Associated Advertising Clubs of the World had started a "Truth-in-Advertising" movement, which in the twenties, according to those involved, came to exert a widespread influence. The movement set up a standard of truth in advertising, which by 1924 had been established as law in twenty-three states. In order to enforce this law the Advertising Clubs organized its

National Vigilance Committee with a definite program "to encourage first and compel afterwards."[11]

Closely affiliated with the National Vigilance Committee were the Better Business Bureaus, which were established in most of the larger cities and which were independently operated by the local businessmen. Their purpose was to investigate and correct questionable business practices in their area, to bring any unfair practice to the attention of the "infringer," and, if that did not work, to use the cooperative pressure of bureau members to stop the practice.[12]

In 1922 the Commercial Standards Council was organized, composed of members from every business field, with the avowed object to "develop the highest commercial standards and to eliminate harmful business practices." It was to "crystallize the best sentiment of American business," to oppose any form of commercial bribery, and to work for the passage of federal legislation against corrupt trade practices.[13]

One of the main objects of the Commercial Standards Council was to formulate ethical codes for various lines of business. By doing that the Council assumed an activity that had become very fashionable in the whole of business America at that time. Most manufacturers' associations, employers' organizations, and business clubs felt obliged to write their code of ethics. Scores upon scores of such business groups publicized their sublime ideals in exalted prose. In several instances these codes were called "creeds"; as an example I may quote the Purchasing Agents' Creed:

Since I believe that the position of purchasing agents is honorable, worthy, responsible and calls forth the highest ethical principles in relationship and dealings with men, I pledge myself to emulate in all of my daily duties the lofty, yet practical, ideals set forth in the following creed:

1. I believe absolutely in honesty and sincerity—in thought, action and deed.
2. I believe in my duty to elevate the standards of my profession—by study and service.
3. I believe in the ideals embodied in the Golden Rule—"All things whatsoever that men should do unto you, do you even so unto them." Therefore, I believe in courtesy and good will toward all.
4. I believe in the "square deal," toward the company I represent, with myself, and toward the men with whom I do business.
5. I believe in a duty to refuse and renounce gifts or perquisites from those with whom I transact business.
6. I believe in enthusiasm, progressive methods, and success; in the exchange of ideas and association among fellow purchasing agents and in fulfilling all my obligations like a man.[14]

The religious tone of the moral code above was rather typical of the majority of such codes. The International President of Rotary, Glenn C. Mead, in 1921 even denied that the Rotarian Code was one of ethics and preferred to call it a "confession of faith."[15]

Thousands of firms and individual businessmen also formulated their own ethical codes. Edward A. Filene, for instance, who was the president of William Filene's Sons Company, wrote a code that he felt had obtained "somewhat general recognition": "1. A business, in order to have the right to succeed, must be of real service to the community. 2. Real service in business consists in making or selling merchandise of reliable quality for the lowest practically possible price, provided that merchandise is made and sold under just conditions."[16] Edgar L. Heermance devised his norm in a biblical style: "Thou shalt not steal thy competitor's customers, is the first commandment of business ethics.... A third commandment is that Thou shalt not run down a competitor or his goods."[17] The Golden Rule Department Store of St. Paul, Minnesota, chose to explain its moral policy through a series of more than twenty different advertisements, in which it discussed such topics as "Store-Wide Sales," "Sugar-Coated Sales," "Comparative Prices," and "Demand Truth in Advertising."[18]

The most elevated ideals advocated in these moral codes were honesty and service. Honesty, it was repeatedly stated, was a fundamental virtue without which a business could not succeed. No business, one writer said, "can be built up with any stability that is not based on the solid rock of honest trading."[19] No business house can look for success, another author explained, "if it is not known to be dependable, if its statements regarding goods and conditions cannot be accepted without qualification, if its prices are not honestly adjusted. So the business man who must try for success, finds this preeminent virtue almost forced upon him."[20] Consequently, apart from being the morally correct policy, honesty was the best method to earn more money. B. C. Forbes phrased it thus: "Honesty pays dividends both in dollars and in peace of mind."[21]

Honesty, however, was not spoken of as a goal that business should try to reach in the future but as a virtue that had already been attained by most representatives of commerce and industry. The attitude had changed radically during the last twenty-five years, it was held. Earlier, honesty had meant keeping out of jail and out of trouble. Now the honest businessman sought "not merely to avoid criminal or illegal acts, but to be scrupulously fair, upright, fearless in both action and expression."[22] The larger business had grown, the more its moral standards had improved, Owen D. Young of General Electric assured the congregation of the Riverside Church, New York, and continued: "It is safe for you to buy today, under great trade-marks, almost anything you wish without previously examining the package. You will find quantity, quality and price right. It may be no moral tribute to the managers of business. It may be only the result of their intelligence, for they know that any other practice spells ruin."[23]

Henry Ford saw reason to modify the maxim that only the honest businessman could be successful. He acknowledged that sometimes dishonest men did succeed in business. But their success was only allowed to happen when their service to mankind exceeded their dishonesty.[24] And this brings us to the by far most prevalent concept in the discussion of business morality that took place in the 1920s, the concept that business should be, and was, first and foremost, service.

Service became such a predominant business principle that it was discussed and referred to in thousands of moral codes, speeches, articles, and books during the decade. Both the language and the contents of these writings may be termed religious; business was portrayed in a devotional tone as an unselfish, sacrificial calling. God and spiritual values were often referred to; the Golden Rule was selected as the principle most worthy of emulation.

A contemporary study of business revealed that the service ideal had gradually gained prominence during the decade before 1920. Harry D. Kilson studied several American magazines issued from 1908 to 1920 in order to see how often the word *service* was used in their advertisements. He found that the number had increased five times in those twelve years. In 1920, twenty-five per cent of all advertisements included the word *service*. He also noticed a change in the meaning of the word:

> As first used, the word service denoted something gratuitous which was given in addition to the commodity, such as restroom and telephone accommodations in a department store. Service was regarded as a sort of economic second-mile which the seller furnished out of the goodness of his heart. Within recent years, however, and by the advanced sellers, service has come to be regarded not as an accessory but as a real part of the commodity, indeed, as the commodity itself.[25]

Thus, Kilson pointed out, a manufacturer of automobiles was no longer selling automobiles; he was selling transportation. Similarly, the producer of tires did not sell tires but mileage. The prevalence of the idea could further be noticed, he pointed out, by such slogans as that of the Mazda lamp: "Not the name of a thing but the mark of a service."

The service ideal had started to spread before and during World War I, and it continued to do so in the twenties. To be a servant to others was set up in the business community as the most admirable virtue of all; "service above self" and "he profits most who serves best" were highly esteemed mottoes. The road to happiness went, not through power and wealth, but through ministering to others. If you obediently served, you also fulfilled the divine mission on earth. B. C. Forbes wrote: "Don't seek things. Seek to serve. Then and then only can you become rich in mind and soul.... You can serve God only by serving men."[26] Thomas Dreier expressed a similar thought: "To be happy, say the wise men, you must express yourself completely in service to your neighbors. You must give yourself. When you are expressing all your physical, mental and spiritual energy in doing useful work, you will know what it is to be in heaven."[27] Such "inspirational" quotations as these may be multiplied.[28]

If all businessmen agreed on the importance of service, they had different views on how business could best serve. One may discern two schools of business servants, one more pragmatic, one more idealistic. The pragmatic group argued that merely by doing business, business performed the best service. Business and industry existed, it was believed, for the sole purpose of being of real service to mankind, "that we may have comfortable houses and beautiful furnishings, that we may be finely clothed and satisfyingly fed, that we may be carried from our homes and back again in security."[29] But business was not only a creator of comfort and convenience, this group reasoned; it served by simply being the backbone of society. In an article called "Business: An Opportunity to Serve Society," the president of the Georgia Railroad and Power Company, Preston S. Arkwright, wrote:

> Business not only makes the profit but conserves the profit. It accumulates the wealth. Wealth serves all mankind, no matter in whose hands the accumulated wealth may be. It raises the general standard of living. It makes possible further productive enterprise. It increases the prosperity, the comfort and the happiness of all people. It sustains government, art, literature, science and education. The making and saving of profit is, therefore, not only the motive which actuates business effort, but is, in reality, a part of the service rendered by business.[30]

Arkwright's argument above sounds like a quotation from Adam Smith, and this group of business servants was certainly dependent on the teaching of that "worldly philosopher," to adopt Heilbroner's term. If the American businessman of the twenties first of all sought "success, prosperity, or greatness for himself," he would thus be of the greatest service to his fellowmen. Business service should certainly not be "universal philanthropy."[31] It was feared that altruism in business might be carried too far. One commentator warned: "Unrestrained altruism would result in chaos; far better is the 'invisible hand' leading every man to work for the general welfare while seeking to promote his own. But there is little danger of unrestrained altruism, and most of us may for some time yet seek to cultivate the virtue without fear of developing it to excess."[32] Judging from the context, the last sentence seems, strangely enough, to be written without irony.

These disciples of Adam Smith also believed that the servant was entitled to his reward, and the greater the service, the larger the pecuniary reward. This was seen as a just law of nature, according to which, society, under the conditions of fair play, "apportions through the processes of trade a sure and fair reward to those individuals who serve it best by new inventions, or superior ability in production, or superior methods of distribution."[33] The way to get rich was to make jobs and supply needs for many other men, one book on social justice maintained and went on: "The essential thing for the common benefit of humanity is the abundant creation, organization, and wise use of durable capital. Its ownership rightly belongs to those who do the essential thing. The working class does very little of it; government does nothing at all." The same book argued that a great fortune was a sign of a great service done. The "divine intelligence" had ordered the world so wisely that "a man cannot accumulate much without supporting many." Consequently, "Vanderbilt with his railroads, Carnegie with his steel mills, Rockefeller with his oil-refineries and pipelines, Armour and Swift with their packing-houses, every one of these men gave to the nation far more than it gave him in return, *in actual wealth*—and still far more in daily abundance."[34]

The idealistic group of believers in business service agreed that business performed a great service merely through its existence, but it further insisted that service was something more. If business served only for profit, it was no true service. There should always be a consecration of one's service, these businessmen felt; true service always entailed sacrifice, the giving of oneself. This view, which was held by the majority of American businessmen at the time, was altruistic in character in that it said that business should first be concerned about the welfare of others, then about its own success. The writings of these idealistic business servants were also much more fuzzily inspirational.

As I have just said, the interest of the community should be put before the interest of the individual businessman. *Service*, one business representative preached, was the greatest word in the English language, embodying the spirit of love, brotherhood, and friendship: "Not the service that serves self, for, like lip-service, that accomplishes naught. But service in the true and intended meaning of the word—the service that labors for the interest of others, that confers an advantage, that benefits, that avails."[35] Many ethical codes also contained paragraphs of such altruistic intentions, such as the one written by the Kansas State Bankers: "Service to the public is the paramount justification for the existence of a bank."[36] The dean of New York University School of Commerce, Joseph French Johnson, was even convinced that genuine concern for others was the prime motive for every successful businessman:

> I do not believe any merchant achieved success whose first thought was, "By doing this I shall become rich." Before that was the thought, "Here is a community where people need a good shoe store," or, "the salesmen who come to this town would appreciate and patronize a better hotel," or "people are going several blocks away to buy cigars when they would stop at this corner if there were a store here."
>
> Coming before the money-making idea was the thought of rendering some benefit—of supplying better goods, or goods at a lower price, or of something that would be an improvement upon things then in use.[37]

Not seldom, the service ideal was explicitly spiritualized. Paul P. Harris, the founder of Rotary, proclaimed that the greatness of the new businessman would not be determined by his wealth, but by his "passion for truth" and his "persistent love of his fellow-men." "If he possesses these qualities," Harris wrote, "then he will be a great man because he will be a serviceable man, and the service ideal hangs as high above the dollar ideal as Heaven is above earth."[38] The implication was of course that he who serves performs a divine duty. Interviewed in 1929, Henry Ford similarly cloaked the service ideal in an aura of religious obscurity. Asked, "What is the heart of your organization," he answered that it was "spiritual" and continued: "I mean that if you will go into business with the idea of service, the spiritual will take care of itself. If you do your part honestly and try to serve others, the unseen will make the thing that you do spiritual. In a few words, my idea is that the goal of service is the seen, and the spiritual results are what we might call the unseen."[39] Ford obviously needed more than "a few words" to make clear what he had in mind; he managed, however, to add a religious dimension to his service ideal.

The central maxim that the business idealists rallied around was the Golden Rule from the Sermon on the Mount. Most businessmen of the 1920s felt that Christ's words from Matthew 7:12—"All things whatsoever ye would that men should do to you, do ye even so to them"—expressed the ideal they wanted to adhere to. The Golden Rule was not entirely new to business, it had been applied already by Richard Baxter in his *Christian Directory* (1673), but it was not until the 1920s that the rule received a widespread hearing. President Harding set the tone for the decade when he said in his inaugural address on March 4, 1921: "Service is the supreme commitment of life. I would rejoice to proclaim the era of the golden rule and crown it with the autocracy of service."[40] And the decade that followed tried to live up to Harding's words, at least in theory. Many codes of business morality included references to, or quoted verbatim, the Golden Rule, as did the Purchasing Agents' Creed reprinted previously. Shops and department stores like J. C. Penney and the Golden Rule Department Store of St. Paul, Minnesota, appropriated the name as an emblem. The Chicago Engineering Works School advertised itself as "The Golden Rule School," and factories like the Nash textile company of Cincinnati, Ohio, were also designated by the same maxim.

What we are meeting here is a rather typical phenomenon in the creation of a civil religion. A large group of influential people appropriate a specifically Christian concept and proceed unwittingly to divest it of its specificity so that it may suit non-Christians as well. At the same time, the concept in question retains its religious aura, which adds to its authority and dignity. Cut loose from its Christian context, the Golden Rule in most cases came to mean a maxim of noncommittal humanitarianism that Christian, Jewish, agnostic, atheistic, and indifferent businessmen could all subscribe to.

Whenever businessmen and industrialists wanted to convince the public of their good intentions, they loosely referred to the Golden Rule. President John E. Edgerton of the National Association of Manufacturers said, for instance, that his organization stood "and will continue to stand openly and courageously for the eternal principles of right, reason, and justice enshrined in the constitution of our republic, in the Golden Rule, and as construed and applied by those whose names and deeds have made this country the greatest among nations on the earth."[41] And Frank E. Hering, managing editor of the *Eagle Magazine*, wrote that it was "most encouraging to the lover of humanity to note the ever-widening influence of this Golden Rule in the business relations of both individuals and nations."[42] John D. Rockefeller, Jr., tried to be more specific, but one still gets the impression that his advice to a group of young men is merely high-sounding rhetoric and not meant to be applied in everyday practice:

If I were to sum up in a few words what I have been endeavoring to say to you in regard to the personal relation in industry, I should say, apply the Golden Rule.

Every human being responds more quickly to love and sympathy than to the exercise of authority and the display of distrust. If in the days to come, as you have to do with labor, you will put yourself in the other man's place and govern your actions by what you would wish done to you, were you the employee instead of the employer, the problem of establishment of the personal relation in industry will be largely solved, strife and discord as between labor and capital will give place to cooperation and harmony, the interests of both will be greatly furthered, the public will be better served, and through the establishment of industrial peace, a great stride will have been taken toward the establishment of peace among nations.[43]

When businessmen tried to define more closely the Golden Rule, they either drowned, like Rockefeller, in blurry eloquence, or they felt forced to compromise with the ideal. In many cases they did both. Dr. Arthur Holmes, president of Drake University and friend of business, felt that the Golden Rule was an impulse in human nature imbedded in man's thinking. He was convinced that "a human being can no more excise the Golden Rule from his science, estheticism, religion, and ethics and still escape agnosticism, superstition, cubism [!] and anarchy, than he can throw away the multiplication table and still expect to calculate his profits." Trying to apply the rule to business, he saw two principles. The modern businessman applied the Golden Rule when he imagined himself in the position of his customers. To be successful, the salesman had to know the needs of different groups of clients. The sales expert put himself in the place of the public when he advised the businessman to launch a product:

On his ability to judge what they want the manufacturer, first, risks a huge sum for an advertising campaign; and secondly, risks a huge sum in the manufacturing and marketing of his product. The whole vast project involving possibly millions, risking possibly the ruin of the firm, revolves around the central pivot of the Golden Rule, which demands as its first essential that a man shall put himself in the other's place.

The other application of the Golden Rule that Holmes discerned was this: "Do what you would like to have done if you were in the same position as the other man." You do not treat, Holmes meant, a baby, an octogenarian, or a savage as you yourself would be treated. "Imagine yourself old, then act; imagine yourself a savage, and ask what you would want; then act.[44] Imagine yourself a worker, he might have added, and ask what you would want then. Presumably Holmes would have felt that the worker, like the savage, would have been satisfied with less than the industrialist.

Other business representatives openly stated that if the Golden Rule was to be applied to business it had to be modified. Owen D. Young said that the Golden Rule supplies all that a man of business needs "in principle": "Yet if you ask me to apply the Golden Rule to a bank rate, I find it amazingly difficult to do. It is like telling me to apply the multiplication table to the design and manufacture of a steam turbine."[45] The writer of a book on business ethics similarly stated that business is so complex that an absolute application of the rule was impossible. "The only practical solution, therefore," he wrote, "is often a sort of compromise, to 'do good to all men.' When that is impossible the only practical solution is to 'do the greatest good to the greatest number' of those involved in the business under consideration."[46] So, even if most businessmen firmly expressed their faith in the Golden Rule as an ideal, few tried to live by it. A Methodist pastor in a Southern city sent out two thousand letters to businessmen asking the question: "Can a man be successful in business to-day and practice the Golden Rule?" Only three percent of the replies were in the affirmative. The others were more or less certain that Christ's maxim would not work well in their daily business activities.[47]

A few men of commerce—but they were few indeed—disapproved of the sanctimoniousness of the business idealists. They felt that all this talk of the Golden Rule, of ethics and service, was only dust thrown into the eyes of the public. The code of the "credal type" like the Golden Rule, one commentator pointed out, suffered from the same weakness as the gentlemen's agreement. "The public does not know what it has to expect of the industry. A fringe of unscrupulous men are able to hide behind the vagueness of the standard."[48] The word "ethics" had been abused so much that it had lost much of its real meaning. "It has been used as a hypocritical cloak to cover crooked practice," one businessman charged, and continued: "It has been worked overtime by some folks trying to restrict the activities of competitors with no thought of applying it to their own practices." The same was true of the word *service*: "Now you see the word attached to all sorts of expedients for private gain—yes, even as an excuse for exorbitant charges."[49]

Why not admit the simple truth, these businessmen asked, that business is based on profit and competition? In the professions, they held, service was prior to monetary considerations, but business was differentiated from the professions mainly by the fact that "profit always has been and is always bound to be, the motive of business enterprise." The businessman should assert his Americanness by stating his belief in the "doctrine of selfishness" instead of stumbling into "bleary sentiment" when trying to define service. When businessmen lose sight of the fact that business is based on profit, one author wrote, and sentimentally assert that "service is above profit," their statements are meaningless or misleading. "No business man," he concluded, "need be ashamed of the fact that his business is earning a profit; and often big profits are the result of good business management. But when he asserts that he is in business primarily 'to serve the public,' he is liable to repeat the experience of the jackdaw that painted himself white and tried to associate with doves."[50]

THE CIVIC CLUBS: FAITH AND FELLOWSHIP

I have had reason off and on in the preceding pages to refer to the ideals of such civic clubs as Rotary and Kiwanis. These organizations, and at least a dozen more like them, served in the twenties as tools of business to instill its moral codes, discussed above, and its spiritual ideals into the members and to create among them a sense of community. These business clubs, or service clubs as they also were called, took over many of the functions that the Protestant churches had filled before. As the churches were no longer seen as natural gathering points, particularly by men and more especially by businessmen, the business luncheon clubs started to fill the needs for fellowship that these men experienced.[51] The clubs also saw themselves as a new religious force that would accomplish what other religions had failed to do.

The larger of these business clubs were founded shortly before or during the war—Rotary, the oldest of them, saw the light in Chicago in 1905—but it was only in the 1920s that they dramatically increased their membership. By 1928, Rotary and Kiwanis each counted more than a hundred thousand members; ten years after its birth in 1917 the Lions' Club had over fifty thousand men on its roll. Those who were not admitted into the large, prestigious clubs, started their own. The twenties saw the growth of numerous service clubs, some of which were called Civitan, Cosmopolitan, Newcomers, Optimist, Thirteen, Conopus, Cooperative, Exchange, City, Gyro, and Mercator.

It is obvious from their proceedings and magazines that at least the two largest of the business clubs, Rotary and Kiwanis, saw themselves as spiritual or religious forces. Rotary did not openly pronounce itself a religion; that would only have offended a number of members. But it was safe to say that Rotary was *like* a religion or that it was a spiritual force, and this was asserted again and again in speeches and articles (see illustration 7). The president of Rotary International, Donald A. Adams, said, for instance, in 1925: "Rotary is a spiritual force. Mark my word, I did not say a religious force. I said a spiritual force. On no other grounds can I account for the way it has gripped thousands of lives and changed them from selfish existences into lives of helpful and unselfish service."[52] Others did not make the distinction between spiritual and religious, whatever Adams meant by that, but felt as another commentator put it a year later: "I find in Rotary a *religious* spirit. By that I do not mean a preference for any particular creed, but a deep and reverent regard for the things of the spirit. And apparently though not a religious institution yet it holds an important place as a school where one may lay a lasting foundation for religion to build on." Rotary makes every member a better man who works, not for himself, but for others, this same Rotarian claimed, and continued:

Illustration 7

"The Spirit of Rotary." (*Rotary International Proceedings 1920*. Used with permission.)

Hence Service above Self. And the moment you say "Above Self" your acts begin to partake of a religious atmosphere, because after all, what is religion? The Latin word *relegare* expresses it clearly. To bind back, knit closely; in other words to re-establish closer relations between the creature and the Creator, and between man and fellow-man. And this Rotary is certainly striving after and is succeeding in accomplishing.[53]

Editorials in *The Rotarian* were not seldom devoted to the spiritual dimension of the club. They could be more facetious comments like the following:

You say that religion means loving your neighbor. In my whole business experience I have never found yet where taking an honest interest in the welfare of my neighbor, whether he was a competitor or an employee or a customer, ever cost me a nickel. Rotary has adopted the motto, "He profits most who serves best." It is gospel truth, man. And it is good business. And by your own definition I am inclined to think it is religion.[54]

Other editorials adopted a lyrical, at times bombastic, tone, but the message was the same: "The Rotarian spirit is uniting men in a faith and an order that shall endure. It is a great tidal wave of confidence that is moving upon the face of the earth. It is beating the sword of violence into a symbol of service. It is the welding instrument of nations. It is a great force that is rolling this old world a little nearer heaven."[55]

The same eagerness to define the club as a religious movement characterized Kiwanis. Leading Kiwanians time after another emphasized that their organization was more than a club or a "meeting ground"; it was a crusade infused with divine ideals and blessed by the Supreme Being. They were careful, however, to present this Divinity in such indistinct terms that all members, irrespective of church belonging, could identify with it. Roe Fulkerson, the editor of *The Kiwanis Magazine*, wrote, for instance, in his "Personal Page" that the spirit of Kiwanis was pleasing to "the Great Musician": "But it is also our hope that when the music we offer Him ascends in sweetness and in harmony, through the vaulted reaches of the stars to that far place where He makes the music of the spheres, He is pleased with what we play and moved to set aside yet one more joy for us, when we, too, come to read the eternal score."[56] George H. Ross, former president of Kiwanis International, proclaimed that it was the inspiring ideals of Kiwanis that "light the candle of understanding in our hearts, that wake the chords of the soul to the music of the stars and tune the ear to catch the 'Great Accent';[57] and H. W. Riggs, governor of the Pacific Northwest district, explained that Kiwanis meant "a conscious or unconscious working in harmony with the Divine Spirit in the universe for the realization of that type of life which feels it a privilege to work with and for the other fellow. If conscious, there is intense satisfaction in knowing that we are in tune with the Infinite—if unconscious, must come a gradual awakening to a sublime outlook on life."[58]

To observers outside the clubs, their religious dimension was also obvious.

These voluntary associations had a prototype according to Max Weber, in the sects. The civic clubs were only secularized versions of Protestant denominations: "They stem, indeed, from the sects in the homeland of genuine yankeedom, the North Atlantic states." The Lynds also noticed how, as the Protestant churches in Middletown lost their influence, other "centers of 'spiritual' activity" grew up in the community, the civic clubs that were "marked sources of religious loyalty and zeal." The Protestant churches obviously also became aware of the competition, which was experienced as difficult to come to grips with since the business clubs offered approximately the same things as the churches. A troubled Methodist wrote about the luncheon clubs:

> They are useful, fellowshipful organizations, for the most part emphasizing 'Service'—but it is a *quid pro quo*, by no means the lavish service of others without hope of return, which the founder of Christianity enjoined. They do so near fill the need and in such a characteristic Main Street way they so parody the Church of other days, that they leave many participators immune to organized Christianity. Efforts to interest them in the church do not "take".[59]

As I have pointed out before, the business clubs of the twenties advocated far-reaching religious tolerance. The civic clubs claimed to be spiritual forces but shunned identification with any particular faith. Rotary was proud of "cutting squarely across religious lines and admitting men to its membership utterly regardless of faith or creed." It declared that "There is room upon earth for Jew and Christian, for Musselman and Buddhist, and there is room in Heaven for all of them too."[60] As a consequence of this attitude, the civic clubs did not only refer to Judeo-Christian beliefs to establish their own spirituality, but often pointed to analogies with other religions. Kiwanis likened its beliefs to those of Yoga Ramacharaka and referred to the laws of Karma; Rotary identified its ideals with the spirit of Ormazd, the essence of truth, law, and goodness in Zoroasterism.[61] Those who did not subscribe to any particular faith were assured that "every man has a religion.... Every man has a faith, though he may claim not to have. Even doubt is a form of faith—faith in the opposite. Psychologically speaking, doubt and faith are the same."[62] Men of all beliefs or nonbeliefs were consequently welcome in the business clubs. Rotary and Kiwanis were the new spiritual forces that unified contentious elements, that made peace. "There is no other agency in all the world," one writer claimed, "so surely calculated as Rotary to reduce a spiritual truce to a permanent religious peace."[63]

The nonsectarian religious movement of the business clubs felt that it was the latter-day fulfillment of earlier religions, particularly the Judeo-Christian ones. The luncheon clubs, it was believed, had helped create a spirit of cooperation and brotherly love that had not existed before. "Had an Optimist, Co-operative, Exchange, Lions, Kiwanis, or a Rotary club flourished in the days of Exodus with old Moses as president," one Rotarian wrote, "they would have reached the promised land in forty days instead of forty years. Would not any of these clubs in the days of Sodom and Gomorrah have saved those cities? Abraham could not even find ten charter members to start a club." The teaching of Christ—that it is more blessed to give than receive, that he who would be greatest among you let him be your servant—had lain fallow for nineteen hundred years "in the bosom of humanity struggling for expression"; these teachings had been accepted in theory "as a beautiful Utopian dream, but always and for ever repudiated in practice and in action." Since the first service clubs started to come into existence, however, there had begun "to dawn a new consciousness" that the Sermon on the Mount was practical and workable. "The existence of the Service clubs today," the Rotarian concluded, "is only an answering and an affirmative echo to the truth that was taught and rejected nineteen centuries ago."[64] The Kiwanis had been one of "the biggest factors" in creating such a new spirit of brotherly love, the editor of *The Kiwanis Magazine* proclaimed, that the parable of the Good Samaritan was no longer applicable to modern American society:

> Today if a man journeying from one city to another fell among thieves, the next passerby would do what the Good Samaritan did. But no newspaper would give the kindly act a paragraph. It is the usual thing. Any one would do it. It is no longer unusual or news. If a passerby failed to do what the Good Samaritan did it would be so unusual that it is likely the newspapers would make a headline of it.[65]

Representatives of the business clubs were convinced that their organizations had succeeded where the Protestant churches had failed. They did not say it in so many words, but they questioned, for instance, whether a system of ethics that could pretend only to apply to the Day of Rest was not only a "system of words," while the Kiwanian moral system, the "doctrine of Brotherhood," was applicable principally to work days.[66] Most people have neglected the fundamentals of religion, another article held. But a Kiwanian need not fear neglecting the important things in life; he is driven by "a tender force" that leads compellingly: "KIWANIANS are fortunate above other men in having, in the ideals of our organization, a blazing sun of inspiration to shed its radiance upon their hearts."[67] Members of the civic clubs were warned not to make the mistake that organized religion had made, to take refuge in "smug respectability," but should offer those in need "two kinds of salvation," remedial salvation to the man who is down and out and "preventive" salvation to the as yet unwrecked youth. "We who are strong," the writer asserted, "are necessarily the agents of redemption."[68]

In many instances the belief that the civic clubs had replaced Christianity as the redemptive force was only implied, but the message was still clear enough. When the Rotary International *Proceedings* of 1920 stated that "Rotary is the seed of Faith in our fellowmen, Hope in our community, and Charity to all," they said implicitly that the basic Christian concept of 1 Corinthians 13:13 had been fulfilled by the service club.[69] When Kiwanis wrote its battle hymn to the tune of "Onward Christian Soldiers," calling it "Onward in Kiwanis!", it was actually saying that Kiwanians were the new crusaders:

> May Kiwanis lead us
> To each brave ideal,
> May the tasks that need us
> Find us quick and leal;
> For our God and nation,
> Home and children, too,
> Forward, then in consecration,
> Where there's work to do!
>
> Onward in Kiwanis,
> Whither God has willed,
> Hailing as our brothers
> All who work and build![70]

And when Frank H. Lamb's allegory *The Heart of the World*, which won the trophy for the best Rotary play of 1922, ended with an adaptation of John Oxenham's well-known hymn, "In Christ There Is No East or West," the underlying message must have been obvious:

> In Rotary, there's no east or west,
> To it no south or north,
> But one great fellowship of love,
> Throughout the whole, wide earth.
>
> In Rotary true hearts everywhere,
> Their high communion find.
> Its service in the golden cord
> Close-binding all mankind.
>
> Join hands then, brothers of the faith,
> Whatever your race may be;
> Who serves Rotary as a son,
> Is surely kin to me.
>
> In Rotary meet both east and west,
> In it meet south and north.
> All nations one in Rotary,
> Throughout the whole, wide earth.[71]

In the organization of the business clubs, in the arrangement of their weekly meetings, and in their communal activities, they resembled, and were presumably modeled on, the Protestant churches, or they sought their inspiration in biblical patterns. Rotary, for instance, like most of these service clubs, had an organization based on a representation plan where only the best single representative from each business or profession was invited to join the club. The founder of Rotary, Paul P. Harris, explained why he chose to introduce such a structure:

All are agreed that in some good way the benefits of Rotary must be made available to all people. The words "Go ye into the world and preach the gospel to every people," have not lost their savor, but the church has its divinity schools and we have our Rotary. The limited-representation plan imposes heavy obligations upon members. It is a challenge to ourselves. It is the most satisfactory means we have as yet discovered of accomplishing the various purposes we have in mind.[72]

These various purposes were obviously to preach not the gospel of Jesus Christ but that of Rotary. Harris ended his article: "There is a soul stream in Rotary, may it be kept ever pure."

In their gatherings, the luncheon clubs offered, apart from the spiritual atmosphere, a sense of community, a need that had earlier been satisfied by the churches. Here the member could meet his brethren, call them by their first names or nicknames, make valuable professional contacts, and relax in their genial company. Rotary described the benefits of being a member in the following manner:

Making the acquaintance of men you ought to know. Genuine, wholesome goodfellowship. Developing true and helpful friends. Enlightenment as to other men's work, problems and successes. Education in methods that increase efficiency. Stimulation of your desire to be of service to your fellow men and society in general. Business returns that come from enlarging your acquaintance and inspiring confidence in you and your business.[73]

Observing the fellowship of the Middletown service clubs, the Lynds noticed that this "combination of utilitarianism and idealism, linked with social prestige and informal friendliness" was "almost irresistible" to the Middletowners, and pointed also to the similarity to church belonging:

These genial, bantering masters of the local group find here some freedom from isolation and competition, even from responsibility, in the sense of solidarity which Rotary bestows. For some members the civic clubs have displaced lodges and churches as centers of loyalty and personal and class morale: "Rotary and its big ideal of Service is my religion," said one veteran church and Sunday School worker of Middletown. "I have gotten more out of it than I ever got out of the church. I have gotten closer to men in Rotary than anywhere else, except sometimes in their homes."[74]

As in the churches, the fraternization of the clubs also meant, it was held, an improvement of the individual member's morals and of his willingness to show his innermost feelings. Men are loathe to admit, one Rotarian wrote, "that sentiment is part of their being." It was only in the church and in the civic clubs that they were allowed to "give full play to their emotions."[75]

The fellowship of the weekly luncheons was characterized by rituals intended to build up loyalty to the club and its ideals. The member was expected to attend the meetings every week. Every new member had to go through initiation rites that could be rather extreme, as the following description shows: "The new members were placed at children's tables in the middle of the room. Each one had an express cart, and each was provided with a balloon, a bib, and a little cap tied under the chin. They were allowed to eat bread and milk, and after being ridden around in their little carts by their sponsors, they were introduced and had to sing a song, dance a jig or tell a story."[76] Community singing was a regular part of the program, often combined with body exercises, and the tinkling accompaniment on glass and china. Favorite songs were "Old MacDonald Had a Farm," "Lil' Liza Jane," "Jingle Bells," and the "Anvil Chorus." When one writer suggested that, while singing "Lil' Liza Jane," the men should "rise hurriedly, throwing up their arms in the air camp-meeting style," he may have been closer to the source of this activity than he imagined.[77] Rotary claimed it had changed the attitude of men: "Men rarely sang before the days of Rotary if they were cold sober. All too often, their singing and their religious propensities were in their wife's name. Rotary has clearly shown that there is a lot of fun and real melody left in the world and has set business and professional men singing and laughing."[78] The linking of "singing" and "religious propensities" in this quotation is interesting. Is the reader to understand implicitly that Rotary has managed to satisfy men's religious needs as well?

Part of the luncheon program was always openly "spiritual" in nature. Inspirational addresses were given by members of the club or by invited professional speakers, occasionally also by a "live-wire" minister who made "a point of honor to be the last man in the room a stranger would identify as being of the cloth."[79] These addresses often emphasized the credo of the club, the Six Objects of Rotary, for instance, which every Rotarian was expected to know, not in "a parrot-like verbatim way," but in order to be able to explain to others the essence of Rotary.[80] In exceptional cases the clubs had religious services of their own, as Kiwanis had at their annual meeting in 1926, when Edmund F. Arras, past president of Kiwanis International, served as preacher. He started his sermon by saying: "By this, the first religious service ever officially conducted by KIWANIS International, His Majesty's Theatre of this beautiful City of Montreal becomes a KIWANIS shrine, dedicated for this occasion to 'One God,' by the unity of all sects and all denominations under the universal creed of the 'Golden Rule'." In the rest of his sermon, Arras, by quoting the Bible, Hindu scripture, and Abraham Lincoln, continued to make a case for tolerance and humanitarianism. "The final achievement of all religions and all creeds is happiness," he told his congregation. "Real spirituality is found in true happiness which comes from hope, optimism and cheerfulness. . . . If we determine each day to tune in only good cheer, love, hope, joy and health, we will soon learn to turn the dials of our thoughts against the thieves of happiness, commonly known as despondency, hatred, selfishness, envy and jealousy." If we only learn to be kind, cheerful, and grateful, was his final message, this world will become a "Garden of Eden."[81] Kiwanis also outlined an educational program meant to "restimulate" the "lukewarm or back sliding KIWANIAN," thereby adopting terms one usually associates with the Protestant churches. The program consisted in services on the occasion of accepting new members into the club, in monthly meetings devoted to the ideals of Kiwanis, in five-minute "testimonies" from dedicated Kiwanians, and in pamphlets to be used in the organization's "extension work."[82] As in the churches, the leaders in the civic clubs told the members that their beliefs must be expressed in deeds. "The hands which help are better than the lips which pray. 'Faith without works is dead'," Kiwanis taught. Rotary explained that belonging to a Rotary club and being a Rotarian was not necessarily the same thing: "Rotary is not a mere creed to be recited though beautiful its rendition; nor merely a song to be sung, though sweet be the singing. Rotary is a life to be lived. Your individual responsibility to Rotary is to live Rotary."[83]

BUSINESS—BREEDER OF BROTHERHOOD

The civic clubs gave their members a sense of consanguinity not unlike the one the churches gave. But this feeling of fraternity should not be limited to the service clubs, businessmen felt. Business, they held, also brought into being a brotherhood among men, irrespective of nationality, race or station. Here the parallel to Christianity is obvious, which teaches that "There is neither Jew nor Greek, there is neither bond nor free, there is neither male nor female: for ye are all one in Christ Jesus." The business spirit, as it was formulated in the twenties, likewise claimed to be the source of true democracy.

The capitalistic system, it was pointed out, was by far superior to any other system in creating equality among men. Wherever capitalism had been permitted to develop freely, famine had been abolished, which was a basis for social equality. The weaknesses within the system, like the inequality of wealth, were only of a superficial and temporary nature. "In fact," one writer explained, "where capitalism is given a chance to develop freely, unhampered by social and political obstacles, it tends to eliminate its own inequalities and secure not only great abundance for everybody, but to distribute the best things of life more evenly than any other system has ever succeeded in doing."[84]

Business declared that it had, more or less, abolished industrial strife by reducing the differences between employer and employee, by making them see that they were partners in the same enterprise. Workers had been given higher wages, opportunities for education and advancement, and access to labor-saving devices in home and factory, which had changed their attitude. "They are happy people," one industrialist assured his readers. "It is a joy to live with them, to associate with them. You have no desire to go beyond them when you understand them; and they are loyal, not only to the place they work in, but to the country, to their families, to themselves." The old order of enmity and distrust, this writer explained, had given place to the new order of friendliness and confidence:

> The old days of master and workman have passed. I thank God that they have. Today, as a matter of fact, we have no master and workman. More and more the trend of progress, of economics, of supply and demand in the largest sense of the term, is eliminating the cut and dried division between the two. Instead of the master and the workman, we have two workers, one the superior of the second by virtue of years of labor and ability, it is true, but the second conscious of the fact that the same job or a similar job is open to him if he proves his strength. Masters have themselves become workmen under the supervision of those more skilled in the getting together of the means to make an organization grow and prosper.[85]

The honor for ending the conflicts between capital and labor, Booth Tarkington wrote, should go to the "modern business man, practical, hard-thinking and generously imaginative," who had understood that the interests of the two were one: "With an enlightenment ever increasing, he is more and more taking labor for his partner; and thus not only recognizes that such a partnership is profitable to both, but, with an open and generous mind, gives his emphatic sanction to an old belief of our fathers that every human being has a natural right to 'life, liberty, and the pursuit of happiness'."[86] Even if many workers presumably had difficulties recognizing this picture of their working conditions, some labor leaders said they did, like William P. Clarke, the president of the American Flint Glass Workers Union, who stated that "the American manufacturer and business man has to-day a closer contact with the men who work for and with him than ever before. He is not taking this interest just because it pays him financially to do it—although it does—but because we are enjoying in business a friendliness among men, a desire to know the best in each other, such as we have never known before."[87]

Not only were capital and labor working in brotherly harmony, business made clear, they had also assumed each others' identities. A pet idea put forward by the mighty in the twenties was that the capitalist was a laborer and the laborer had become a capitalist. Consequently, as Elbert H. Gary of U. S. Steel wrote, "There is no standard for drawing an exact line between labor and capital."[88] The result of this "economic revolution," one professor of economics pointed out, was a world of harmony, where no classes, and consequently no class consciousness, disturbed the peace. Workers had become capitalists when they opened savings accounts, bought stock or life insurance, and started labor banks. In theory at least, labor could control capital: "Any day the laborers decide to do so, they can divert a few billions of savings to the purchase of the common stock of industrial corporations, railroads, and public service companies, and actually control considerable numbers of them."[89] The professor did not explain how many such savings accounts would be necessary, nor how such a unified action could be organized in practice.

So, business leaders were eager to underline that there was only a difference of degree between themselves and their employees; they were brothers-in-arms united in their fight for a better world. The president of the Chamber of Commerce of the United States, John W. O'Leary, said that the number of stockholders in the industries had doubled in two decades:

A capitalist and a car for every family seems to be our goal. One consequence of this has been that the line of demarcation between capital and labor has been obliterated. It exists now only in a few fevered minds. There has come a realization that the interests of the worker and his employer are identical, and that they must prosper or languish together. We are all, it may fairly be said, capitalists as well as laborers, consumers as well as producers.[90]

Alfred P. Sloan was proud that General Motors in part was owned by workers. He told the story of a steel worker from Pittsburgh who had told him in a letter how he step by step had bought more and more stock in the company, and Sloan commented: "It was especially pleasant to feel that words of mine had had some influence in the evolution of this wage-earner into a modest capitalist."[91]

In the same way that business created friendship between labor and capital, it was the source of fraternity also among competing businessmen. A generation earlier, businessmen pointed out, competitors had looked upon each other with suspicion, and had often resorted to "unscrupulous trade practices" that developed into a "state of real warfare." Not so anymore. The businessman of the twenties, if one is to believe his own statements, had made it a rule to cooperate with his competitors, to exchange ideas and business methods, and to solve problems together. It was regarded as "discreditable to make false or disparaging statements about one another," or to seek "advantage by underhand or dishonorable methods." "A meeting of the trade or commercial association," one business representative said, "might be mistaken for a love feast, and a chamber of commerce lunch for a big family party."[92]

BUSINESS—SAVIOR OF SOCIETY

It was generally believed in the business community that the welfare capitalism of the decade would redeem society. If left alone, business would continue what it had started, to remedy social ills, to establish justice among men, and to raise humanity to a more elevated level. As Walter Rauschenbusch and the Social Gospel movement had wanted to Christianize the social order, business in the twenties saw as its goal to create an Edenic society. Business could assume this central role, because it was the hub of the social wheel. Preston S. Arkwright, president of the Georgia Railway and Power Company, listed some of the functions that made business into a redemptive force:

It organizes, systematizes, manages, and directs all human effort. It develops the natural resources, opens the mines, refines the raw products, manufactures the materials and conducts the services of exchange, transportation, and distribution. It gathers and disseminates the information. It provides the means for intercourse between peoples the world around. . . . It founds the cities. It supplies machinery, vehicles, tools, conveniences, the food, shelter, clothing, materials, . . . implements, appliances, comforts, conveniences, luxuries, and amusements.[93]

To reach its goal, business intended first of all to work for the "material advancement of the entire race." It was pointed out again and again that America had become the richest nation on earth and that its working classes were the most prosperous. "By ingeniously developing new ways of greatly multiplying man-power, and at the same time lessening drudgery," one commentator wrote, "we have literally lifted the nation by its own boot-straps. And in the process a keener, cleaner manhood has been developed."[94] But business was responsible for more than the country's economy, it was argued, it should also be an authority in directing the general welfare of the nation. "If our civilization is to survive," one businessman preached, "business must not only maintain its present ideals, but must proceed to improve upon them and practice them until the entire world is saturated with the new spirit." The commentator continued:

Business must use its tremendous power and influence in support of the finer fruits of our civilization. Business must see to it that our institutions of learning are not only adequately supported financially, but that they teach the younger generations the finer qualities of character, as well as the material facts of commerce, industry, science and the arts.[95]

The business clubs were also convinced that they had been selected to be saviors of society, and they clothed their message, as always, in an overtly religious style. The service clubs had been chosen to lead businessmen in a divine crusade against the evil forces of this world, as the following Rotary allegory explains:

And it came to pass in those days that the Spirit of Good moved over the face of the waters of industry and commerce and breathed into the hearts of men the inspiration of a new hope and a larger consciousness.

And almost immediately there was a great awakening, and the Spirit of Good said, "Go to now and start a movement that will deliver my people from the bondage of war, ignorance, hatred, prejudice and petty jealousies."

And the people did as the Spirit commanded and gathered together men from every vocation of life; in many cities and countries gathered the men together in bands, until the movement spread to the four corners of the earth . . .

And it came to pass as they became wise-hearted men, they were filled with the spirit of humility, and gave to all men their due; neither did they tear down the work of any man nor build for themselves any graven image; for the manner of their living was a monument unto them to the end of time.

And the Spirit of Good blessed and multiplied them and gave them for an inheritance freedom from the bonds of hatred and prejudice and from the ravages of war to this day. Selah.[96]

Kiwanis announced that there was only "one recipe, one solvent, one cure, one saving hope for humanity," and that was the spirit that was embodied in Kiwanis. The Kiwanian spirit was nothing but "applied Christianity," as differentiated from "dogmatic Christianity": "KIWANIS is so broad that it includes Hebrew, Roman Catholic, Protestant, and men of no faith at all."[97] Rotary also felt that it could save the world where others had failed: "Rotary can redeem a lazy world by work. Rotary can regenerate a selfish, dishonest world by square dealing.... Rotary can recreate a prejudiced world by tolerance.... Rotary can restore peace to a war-torn world by unselfishness."[98]

The method to bring about this social salvation, most businessmen argued, was that of mass production and mass consumption. The self-perpetuating process they advocated looked something like this: men saved money, which they did not hoard, but invested productively; the results of this investment were new jobs and—since more employers bid for a worker's services—higher wages; other results of the investment were more goods and therefore lower prices; the higher wages and the lower prices made it possible for men to invest more and more, which created new jobs and more goods, higher wages and lower prices, and so on. Many in the twenties hailed mass production, as one commentator put it, "as the economic messiah, which, by reducing the price of goods and at the same time raising wages, is to redeem the world from poverty."[99]

To meet possible objections, it was pointed out that mass production did not make man a slave to the machine. It was rather the other way around. Men had to work less hard than before. Nor did the machine "kill the soul" of the worker, it was held. There is always room for creativity, and besides, "most workers prefer to perform a simple, specialized, repetitive operation. It leaves their mind free to ruminate on other things. They do not abhor monotony, but desire it." Nor did the machine lead to unemployment. All those who had been "released" by the machine had found "more remunerative and pleasanter tasks."[100] Mass production also resulted in shorter work hours, which gave the masses more leisure time to be used for education or the enjoyment of "the good things of life." Mass production did not lead to vulgarization and ugliness, businessmen were eager to point out, but rather to beauty. Mass production strove to make the product as simple as possible, they explained, and "simplicity usually makes for beauty." Because of the higher salaries, better artists could be hired for designing products. By lowering the prices, mass production made beauty accessible to the people, and, "by creating an appreciation for beauty where it did not exist before, [made] the world a much better place to live in."[101]

A BUSINESS MILLENNIUM

American society has always been characterized by a strong belief in the future and in itself as a Promised Land. During different periods of American history, the executive forces behind this optimism have varied—religion, reformism, nationalism—but the faith in America's future and its special mission has not changed. In the twenties, business was seen as the source from which a new age and a new land would spring. Business would create what the churches and the "radicals" had failed to do, a New Canaan that was to last for at least a thousand years.

The friends of business in the 1920s often referred to the ideal state they planned to build in religious or mythical terms. They called it simply "the Promised Land," or "heaven on earth" or compared it to the vision of the Holy City that John had had on Patmos. They referred to the millennial era about to begin as "the Golden Age" or "that day 'foretold by prophets and by poets sung'."[102] Calvin Coolidge declared that the new age was already at hand, saying that "we have seen the people of America create a new heaven and a new earth. The old things have passed away, giving place to glory never before experienced by any people of our world."[103] Other business representatives felt that the Promised Land had not yet been entered, but that it was within easy reach:

> We are like a chosen people on a dividing ridge between the desert, through which we have just come with pain and struggle, and the promised land, in the hope of which we have been sustained in the terrible journey. We stand facing the desert, thinking desert thoughts, forming desert words, when all the time at our backs, in plain sight and even seen occasionally over our shoulders, there lies the land of milk and honey. We progress backward, crab fashion, down the easy slope, mumbling about sand and dryness, the need of provision for desert life, the dangers of travel, and the sins and sorrows of a homeless folk, when we might run like children, shouting joyfully, down into grassy, well watered valleys, privations forgot, hearts full of an opulent tomorrow.[104]

Many men of commerce expressed their conviction that American society, because of the accomplishments of business, was about to enter a millennial age, characterized by ever increasing prosperity, improved education and healthcare, brotherhood, and righteousness.[105] In this future realm there would be neither masters nor slaves, only those who were their own masters "though the slaves of honor," as one businessman expressed it in his meditation on the future called "The Land Where Dreams Come True." He went on to etch out the following picture:

> Courtesy is their religion and truth their law. They waste no strength in jealousy, no time in vanity, and no thought in avarice. Their golden cities are built in confidence and studded with monuments to service. They treasure health as a foundation for happiness, learning as the basis of true perspective, and find in wealth a lever wherewith

to shift obstacles from the path of the common good. Their morality is derived from within and their piety is dependent on conviction.[106]

The implication is that this is what American society will look like in the future if only business is left alone to continue its regenerative work.

These pictures of the future were also expressed in fictional form. One may, for instance, mention a short story called "The Land of Illusion" published in *Munsey's Magazine*. Multimillionaire Jerry Travis goes up in an airplane for the first time in his life and manages to fall into the ocean. When he regains consciousness, he is in a different world, which he assumes is a "land of illusion." Here food is plentiful for all, housing is comfortable, all men are well educated. There is no unemployment, and everybody is working at a vocation "which is best suited to his or her capabilities." The distribution of wealth is fair in this country, but it is not a socialistic but a capitalistic one, whose goal is "the greatest good benefiting the greatest number, regardless of either race or station." The point of the story is that Travis discovers that this is no land of illusion; indeed, it is the "land of fulfillment."[107]

The illustrations that accompany these writings on the future underlined their spiritual dimension. "The Land Where Dreams Come True" was illustrated with a drawing of a marble-white city in the distance, behind which a radiant sun was rising. The buildings were a blend of skyscrapers and Greek temples. Elevated on a hill, shining white, the city reminded the reader of the New Jerusalem coming down from above. The *Munsey* story was illustrated with a similar city, but here the skyscrapers and smokestacks made entirely clear that this was an American city built by commerce and industry. The illustration of an article on "To-morrow's Business Man" depicted a businessman who through opened portals was allowed to see future society while two angelic creatures offered him a wreath and a scepter for work well done. He was overawed by what he saw through the opening: a city with soaring skyscrapers, funnels of ocean liners, and chimneys of factories. This was heaven on earth created by the humble and service-minded American businessman.[108]

The prerequisite for the New Canaan was the complete abolishment of poverty, and this goal was about to be fulfilled, leaders of the nation felt. Again they expressed their feelings in spiritual terms that reveal that they saw the dawning new age as the consummation of God's plan. President Hoover said—one year before the Crash—that "we in America today are nearer to the final triumph over poverty than ever before in the history of any land.... We have not yet reached the goal, but, given a chance to go forward with the policies of the last eight years, we shall soon with the help of God be in sight of the day when poverty will be banished from this nation.[109] The president of the Chamber of Commerce of the United States, Julius H. Barnes, was also of the conviction that America was within reach of "the goal of many centuries of social effort—the utter and absolute elimination of poverty." America's "chief glory," he felt, would rest in history on the fact that it had defeated poverty and thereby led the way for the rest of the world to universal happiness.[110] The succeeding president of the Chamber of Commerce, John W. O'Leary, implied that business as a spiritual force was accomplishing what Christianity had not managed to do. Jesus Christ had said that "ye have the poor always with you," but O'Leary now felt that America very soon would be able to "refute the ancient dictum that the poor we have always with us."[111] The well-known business leader Edward A. Filene made exactly the same point when he wrote that it showed "supine acquiescence" to assume that "the poor are always going to be with us"; the responsibility of the businessman, he held, was not to alleviate poverty but to abolish it.[112]

By establishing heaven on earth in America, American business would also spread the good news to the rest of the world and thereby accomplish its salvation as well. America would become the true city upon a hill, an exemplary to be studied and emulated by all other nations. Henry Ford expressed this conviction by saying that "the essential principles of Americanism are the goal toward which all civilization is striving," and by pointing out that the United States was created as a "nursery," presumably by God, in which the principles of free enterprise could be brought to full growth, so that "all nations of the earth might see, and seeing, know, the practical nature of liberty in all things."[113] Many versions of the same message were preached: America would bring prosperity and progress to the world, it would establish a new moral code of service and cooperation, it would abolish wars and international strife.[114] And America in this case was the same as business. "Is it not a fact," one businessman asked, "that the responsibility of our entire civilization rests today squarely on the shoulders of business? Business is the dominant world activity. It knows no limitation of boundary or shoreline. It ignores all frontiers and challenges all nations and all peoples. Business is international. Business commands respect."[115]

The business clubs felt a similar desire to spread their "gospel to the whole world," in order to "unite all nations." The spirit of Rotary and other civic clubs would prove to all mankind that "co-operation is better than competition," that it is "better to give than to receive," that the Golden Rule can be put into daily practice. As Jeremiah experienced God not in thunder but in the still, small voice, the world would find that the "still, small voice" was now inhibited by the Rotarian spirit, which would make wars obsolete and establish a universal brotherhood. The ideals of the service clubs would "make possible a peaceful world of neighborly nations," the president of Rotary International, Harry H. Rogers, wrote. "If we have 'good will toward men' of every nation," he concluded, "we can confidently look forward to 'Peace on Earth'."[116]

In *The Rotarian* of April 1928,[117] there was a picture that embodied many of the phenomena dealt with here. The drawing showed a businessman, presumably a Rotarian, standing behind the globe of the world, his arms encircling it in a protective gesture, arranging a piece of cloth on which was written "Business Ethics." To the left the reader could see a city with skyscrapers showing great similarity to cathedrals, to the right he could see tall chimneys and smokestacks and below a freighter at full speed. The message was clear: The businessman, particularly if he belonged to a civic club, would save the world by applying his ideals and would establish a new social order, a New Canaan, based on capitalistic principles.

NOTES

1. Glen Buck, *This American Ascendancy* (Chicago: A. Kroch & Co., 1927), pp. 7–8; Julius H. Barnes, *The Genius of American Business* (New York: Doubleday, Page & Company, 1924), p. 77.

2. B. C. Forbes, *Forbes Epigrams: 1000 Thoughts on Life and Business* (New York: B. C. Forbes Publishing Company, 1922), p. 150; see also James Warren Prothro, *The Dollar Decade: Business Ideas in the 1920's* (Baton Rouge: Louisiana State University Press, 1954), p. 92.

3. Everett W. Lord, *The Fundamentals of Business Ethics* (New York: The Ronald Press Company, 1926), p. 8.

4. Edward W. Bok, "When Money Is King and Business Our God," *World's Work* 48 (September 1924), p. 480. In this article, however, Bok is simultaneously critical of the crass money-worship that he felt also existed in business.

5. Buck, *This American Ascendancy*, p. 7.

6. Wigginton E. Creed, *Safeguarding the Future of Private Business* (Boston: Houghton Mifflin Company, 1923), p. 1.

7. Ed R. Kelsey, "The Human Note in Business," *The Rotarian* 31 (December 1927), p. 25; Caspar S. Yost, "A Business Code of Ethics," *World's Work* 43 (March 1922), pp. 471–73; Henry M. Robinson, *Relativity in Business Morals* (Boston: Houghton Mifflin Company, 1928), pp. 22–25.

8. Elbert H. Gary, "Higher Standards Developing in American Business," *Current History* 23 (March 1926), pp. 775–79.

9. The two poems by Berton Braley and Everett W. Lord were reprinted in full in James Melvin Lee, *Business Ethics: A Manual of Modern Morals* (New York: The Ronald Press Company, 1926), pp. 7–9.

10. Ibid., p. 9.

11. Herbert W. Hess, "History and the Present Status of the 'Truth-in-Advertising' Movement," *The Annals of the American Academy of Political and Social Science* 101 (May 1922), p. 211; Lee, *Business Ethics*, pp. 84, 88–89; H. J. Donnelly, "The Truth-in-Advertising Movement as It Affects the Wealth-Producing Factors in the Community," *The Annals of the American Academy of Political and Social Science* 115 (September 1924), pp. 162–66.

12. William J. Reilly, "Ethics in the New Professions," *The Kiwanis Magazine* 9 (August 1924), p. 359; Edgar L. Heermance, *The Ethics of Business* (New York: Harper & Brothers, 1926), pp. 69–70; Harold H. Maynard and Walter C. Weidler, *An Introduction to Business* (New York: The Ronald Press Company, 1925), pp. 553–54.

13. William Haynes, "Better Ethical Standards for Business," *The Annals of the American Academy of Political and Social Science* 101 (May 1922), pp. 221–23; Reilly, "Ethics in the New Profession," pp. 358–59.

14. Purchasing Agents' Creed quoted from Lee, *Business Ethics*, p. 60. See also

"The Rotary Code of Ethics for Business Men of All Lines," *The Rotarian* 30 (February 1927), p. 4; Reilly, "Ethics in the New Profession," p. 359; F. M. Feiker, "The Profession of Commerce in the Making," *The Annals of the American Academy of Political and Social Science* 101 (May 1922), pp. 203–5.

15. Glen C. Mead's statement appeared in the July, 1921 issue of *The Rotarian*, according to Chesley R. Perry, "The Rotary Code of Ethics," *The Rotarian* 22 (January 1923), p. 20.

16. Edward A. Filene, "A Simple Code of Business Ethics," *The Annals of the American Academy of Political and Social Science* 101 (May 1922), pp. 223–24.

17. Heermance, *The Ethics of Business*, pp. 35–39.

18. Several of these advertisements are reprinted in Lee, *Business Ethics*, pp. 64, 77, 86, 114, 164.

19. Ralph Frost, "Modern Business: Its Pleasures and Penalties," *The Rotarian* 28 (May 1926), p. 24.

20. Lord, *The Fundamentals of Business Ethics*, pp. 40–41. See also Roger W. Babson, *Fundamentals of Prosperity* (New York: Fleming H. Revell Company, 1920), pp. 16–17; Frank Crane, "The Truth in Business," *The Rotarian* 20 (March 1922), p. 101; Donnelly, "The Truth-in-Advertising Movement as It Affects the Wealth-Producing Factors in the Community," *The Annals of the American Academy of Political and Social Science* 115 (September 1924), p. 162.

21. B. C. Forbes, *Keys to Success: Personal Efficiency* (New York: B. C. Forbes Publishing Company, 1926), p. 113.

22. Ibid., p. 107.

23. Owen D. Young and Gerard Swope, *Selected Addresses* (General Electric Company, 1930), p. 258.

24. Henry Ford, *Today and Tomorrow* (London: William Heinemann, 1926), pp. 3–4.

25. Harry D. Kilson, "The Growth of the 'Service Idea' in Selling," *Journal of Political Economy* 30 (April 1922), pp. 417–19.

26. Forbes, *Forbes Epigrams*, pp. 146, 150.

27. Thomas Dreier, *The Silver Lining or Sunshine on the Business Trail* (New York: B. C. Forbes Publishing Company, 1923), p. 8.

28. Telling examples are, for instance, Preston M. Nolan, *Business First* (Chicago: Raymond Publishing Company, 1928), p. 55: "As nothing else in life, will this serve you. Opportunity, wealth, fame—beyond even these, will it bring you power: the ability to help others. So may you know the joy of Service, the peace of Brotherhood—the exaltation of having truly lived and well." C. H. E. Boardman, "A Life to Be Lived," *The Rotarian* 27 (November 1925), p. 5: "Service is eternal—its influences never cease. In ever-widening circles its vibrations spread beyond the horizon that borders the unknown seas. No one has ever been able to measure the ultimate force and effect of even the simplest act of courtesy to a chance passerby."

29. Buck, *This American Ascendancy*, pp. 11–12.

30. Preston S. Arkwright, "Business: An Opportunity to Serve Society," *The Rotarian* 21 (August 1922), p. 74.

31. Thomas Nixon Carver, *The Present Economic Revolution in the United States* (Boston: Little, Brown and Company, 1925), p. 181.

32. Lord, *Fundamentals of Business Ethics*, pp. 56–57.

33. Barnes, *The Genius of American Business*, p. 13. Roger W. Babson wrote in *Religion*

and Business (New York: Macmillan Co., 1920), (p. 25): "Under a free competitive system . . . wealth naturally gravitates to those people who use it for the good of the community rather than to those who use it only to satisfy their own selfish and sensual desires."

34. Charles Norman Fay, *Social Justice: The Henry Ford Fortune* (Cambridge, Mass.: The Cosmos Press, 1926), pp. 13–14, 63.

35. Edward W. Bok, *Dollars Only* (New York: Charles Scribner's Sons, 1926), p. 47. See also Creed, *Safeguarding the Future of Private Business*, pp. 34–35.

36. Heermance, *The Ethics of Business*, pp. 138–39.

37. Joseph French Johnson, *Organized Business Knowledge* (New York: B. C. Forbes Publishing Co., 1923), p. 10. See also Samuel M. Vauclain, *Optimism* (Philadelphia, 1924), pp. 28–29.

38. Paul P. Harris, "Barometers of Success," *The Rotarian* 23 (July 1923), p. 13.

39. Cameron Wilkie, "If You Talk for an Hour with Henry Ford," *The Christian Herald* 52 (July 20, 1929), pp. 4–5.

40. Quoted from Will H. Hays, "Teamwork," in Basil Gordon Byron and Frederic René Coudert, eds., *America Speaks: A Library of Best Spoken Thought in Business and the Professions* (New York: Modern Eloquence Corporation, 1928), p. 188.

41. Quoted from Prothro, *The Dollar Decade*, p. 81.

42. Frank E. Hering, "Are We on the Way?" *The Kiwanis Magazine* 7 (February 1922), p. 12. See also Forbes, *Forbes Epigrams*, pp. 24, 33, 103.

43. John D. Rockefeller, Jr., "The Personal Relation in Industry," in Byron and Coudert, eds., *America Speaks*, pp. 389–90.

44. Arthur Holmes, "Business Must Have the Golden Rule,", *The Christian Herald* 45 (February 11, 1922), pp. 101–2; see also L. W. Fifield, "The Golden Rule in Business," *The Kiwanis Magazine* 10 (August 1925), pp. 315, 339.

45. Young and Swope, *Selected Addresses*, pp. 255–56.

46. Lee, *Business Ethics*, p. 61.

47. "The Golden Rule in Business," *The Nashville Christian Advocate* 87 (February 19, 1926), p. 227.

48. Heermance, *The Ethics of Business*, pp. 21–23.

49. John O. Knutson, "The Cash Value of Ethics," *The Rotarian* 32 (April 1928), p. 8.

50. William Feather, *The Ideals and Follies of Business* (Cleveland: The William Feather Company, 1927), pp. 78–79; Carl F. Taeusch, *Professional and Business Ethics* (New York: Henry Holt and Company, 1926), p. 258.

51. This is also the explanation for the tremendous growth in the 1920s of the secret lodges. Contemporary calculations showed that there might have been eight hundred active secret orders with thirty million members, a figure that surely seems too high. Some of these orders, like Woodmen, the Knights of Pythias, the Odd Fellows, and the Daughters of Rebekah, were believed to have more than half a million members each. Other orders were the Maccabees, the Red Men, the Prophets, the Watchmen, the Stags, the Owls, and the Eagles. See Charles Merz, *The Great American Band Wagon* (New York: The John Day Company, 1928), pp. 23–29. Babson wrote in his foreword to *Religion and Business* that he recognized that "there is much real religion apart from the churches and that many lodges and other organizations are as much dispensers of religion as are the churches themselves."

52. Donald A. Adams, "Keeping Rotary Rotary," *The Rotarian* 27 (October 1925), p. 5.

53. L. S. Balutha, "Creeds and Deeds: Neither Are Sufficient in Themselves," *The Rotarian* 28 (April 1926), p. 33. Garet Garett explicitly defined Rotary as a religion with an "evangel of service above profit," see *The American Omen* (New York: E. P. Dutton & Co., 1928), p. 183.

54. Hugh Allen, "Your Friends—Who Are They?" *The Rotarian* 23 (October 1923), p. 5. Other articles proclaimed that the Rotarian service idea was "almost a religion" and that its motto was "impregnated with the missionary spirit as ever was any religious movement in history." See Miles H. Krumbine, "Some Fundamental Aims of Rotary," *The Rotarian* 21 (November 1922), p. 230, and Calvin O. Davis, "Some Guide-Posts for New Members," *The Rotarian* 24 (February 1924), pp. 23–24.

55. Sherwood Snyder, "Humanity's Love Story," *The Rotarian* 30 (February 1927), p. 5.

56. Roe Fulkerson, "My Personal Page," *The Kiwanis Magazine* 9 (May 1924), p. 205.

57. George H. Ross, "The Ideals and Objects of Kiwanis," *The Kiwanis Magazine* 11 (February 1926), p. 55.

58. H. W. Riggs, "One Process of Progress," *The Kiwanis Magazine* 7 (June 1922), pp. 51–52. Even such playful comments as the following are revealing in that they identify Kiwanis as a religious expression: "And it came to pass that the spirit of KIWANIS didst descend upon the city of Fargo.... And there was much joy and much cheer, to say nothing of much song, in the hearts of those who were selected to aide by the Spirit of KIWANIS." "Scripture Lesson from the Book of Kiwanians at Ortonville, Minnesota," *The Kiwanis Magazine* 8 (December 1923), p. 299.

59. Max Weber, "The Protestant Sects and the Spirit of Capitalism," in H. H. Gerth and C. Wright Mills, eds., *From Max Weber* (London: Routledge & Kegan Paul, 1970), p. 311; Robert S. Lynd and Helen Merrell Lynd, *Middletown: A Study in American Culture* (New York: Harcourt, Brace and Company, 1929), p. 407; Lewis Thurber Guild, "The Church on Main Street," *The Methodist Quarterly Review* 78 (April 1929), pp. 205–6.

60. Harlan Hoyt Horner, "Building the Superstructure," *The Rotarian* 22 (June 1923), pp. 332, 372.

61. Roe Fulkerson, "Editorials," *The Kiwanis Magazine* 8 (December 1923), p. 282; James H. MacLennan, "Builders of the New Kiva," *The Kiwanis Magazine* 9 (July 1924), p. 297; Harlan H. Horner, "The *Something Else* in Rotary," *The Rotarian* 21 (February 1922), pp. 58–61, 90–91.

62. Louis L. Mann, "Getting the Most out of Life: Rotary Philosophy as an Antidote to an Old Disease," *The Rotarian* 32 (May 1928), pp. 14–15, 60–61.

63. Horner, "Building the Superstructure," pp. 332, 372. See also Balutha, "Creeds and Deeds: Neither Are Sufficient in Themselves," pp. 59–61.

64. Stewart C. McFarland, "Service and Cooperation," *The Rotarian* 24 (May 1924), pp. 17–18.

65. Fulkerson, "Editorials," *The Kiwanis Magazine* 8, p. 283.

66. Henry S. Dennison, "Kiwanianism Can Never Be Devil's Scripture," *The Kiwanis Magazine* 8 (December 1923), pp. 268, 304.

67. Roe Fulkerson, "My Personal Page," *The Kiwanis Magazine* 8 (December 1923), p. 272.

68. Henry J. Elliott, "Paralysis or Power?" *The Kiwanis Magazine* 9 (January 1924), pp. 13, 44.

69. Rotary International, *Proceedings: Eleventh Annual Convention, June 21–25, 1920*, p. 401.

70. *The Kiwanis Magazine* 9 (July 1924), p. 324.

71. Frank H. Lamb, "The Heart of the World: An Allegory in One Act," *The Rotarian* 21 (August 1922), pp. 68–69.

72. Harris, "Barometers of Success," p. 13.

73. Rotary International, *Proceedings 1920*, p. 431.

74. Lynd and Lynd, *Middletown*, pp. 302–5.

75. Maynard and Weidler, *An Introduction to Business*, p. 561; Kelsey, "The Human Note in Business," p. 56.

76. Feather, *The Ideals and Follies of Business*, pp. 95–96.

77. Kenneth S. Clark, "Mr. Jones Will Lead Us!" *The Rotarian* 21 (August 1922), pp. 76–78, 111.

78. Kelsey, "The Human Note in Business," p. 56.

79. Bruce Bliven, "The Babbitt in His Warden," *The Forum* 80 (December 1928), pp. 899–903.

80. Adams, "Keeping Rotary Rotary," p. 5; Raymond J. Knoeppel, "Rotary States Its Case," *The Forum* 80 (December 1928), pp. 953–54.

81. "The Radio of Life," *The Kiwanis Magazine* 11 (July 1926), pp. 376–77, 407–8, 422.

82. O. Samuel Cummings, "Stimulating the Backslider," *The Kiwanis Magazine* 7 (April 1922), pp. 17–18.

83. "The Editor's Uneasy Chair," *The Kiwanis Magazine* 7 (February 1922), pp. 22–23; Boardman, "A Life to Be Lived," p. 5. An interesting book about the business clubs in the early 1930s is Charles F. Marden's *Rotary and Its Brothers: An Analysis and Interpretation of the Men's Service Club* (Princeton: Princeton University Press, 1935), which corroborates many of the points made in my study.

84. Carver, *The Present Economic Revolution*, p. 209.

85. Vauclain, *Optimism*, pp. 288, 301. See also Edward A. Filene, "Why Men Strike," in Byron and Coudert, eds., *America Speaks*, pp. 163–164.

86. Booth Tarkington, "Rotarian and Sophisticate," *The World's Work* 58 (January 1929), p. 44.

87. Quoted in Kelsey, "The Human Note in Business," p. 25.

88. Gary, "Labor," in Byron and Coudert, eds., *America Speaks*, p. 180.

89. Carver, *The Present Economic Revolution*, pp. 9–10, 13–14, 89, 93–94. See also Thomas Nixon's Carver's "Employee and Customer Ownership," in Byron and Coudert, eds., *America Speaks*, pp. 73–74.

90. John W. O'Leary, "Twenty-five Years of American Prosperity," *Current History* 23 (February 1926), p. 702.

91. Alfred P. Sloan, "Modern Ideals of Big Business," *The World's Work* 52 (October 1926), pp. 695–96.

92. Heermance, *The Ethics of Business*, p. 17; Lord, *The Fundamentals of Business Ethics*, p. 102; Maynard, *An Introduction to Business*, pp. 540–41.

93. Arkwright, "Business: An Opportunity to Serve Society," p. 74.

94. Henry S. Nollen, "Business—Social Service," *The Rotarian* 25 (September

1924), pp. 19, 59–61; Fay, *Social Justice*, p. 3; Buck, *This American Ascendancy*, pp. 12–13.

95. Knutson, "The Cash Value of Ethics," p. 60. See also Fay, *Social Justice*, p. 30.

96. McFarland, "Service and Cooperation," p. 18.

97. Leon C. Prince, "The History of the Spirit of Kiwanis," *The Kiwanis Magazine* 9 (January 1924), p. 48.

98. Horner, "Building the Superstructure," pp. 330–32, 372. See also Guy Gundaker, "Follow the Star of Rotary," *The Rotarian* 23 (December 1923), p. 5, and Harris, "Barometers of Success," p. 12.

99. A. Lincoln Filene, "The Fallacy of an Industrial Panacea," *The Atlantic Monthly* 143 (May 1929), p. 632; Feather, *The Ideals and Follies of Business*, pp. 32–35; Filene, "A Simple Code of Business Ethics," p. 227; Edward A. Filene, *The Way Out: A Forecast of Coming Changes in American Business and Industry* (Garden City, N.Y.: Doubleday, Page & Company, 1924), pp. 33–34.

100. Edward A. Filene, "Mass Production Makes a Better World," *The Atlantic Monthly* 143 (May 1929), pp. 625–31; O'Leary, "Twenty-five Years of American Prosperity," p. 702; Garett, *The American Omen*, pp. 52–53; Barnes, *The Genius of American Business*, p. 74.

101. Filene, "Mass Production Makes a Better World," p. 631.

102. "The Promised Land," *Collier's Weekly* 75 (October 10, 1925), p. 24; Dreier, *The Silver Lining*, pp. 83–84; Harry R. Fitzgerald, "Is Industrial Democracy the Answer?" *The Rotarian* 23 (September 1923), p. 45 "The Editor's Uneasy Chair," *The Kiwanis Magazine* 7 (May 1922), p. 36; Elliott, "Paralysis or Power?" pp. 12–13; Hering, "Are We on the Way?" p. 12.

103. Calvin Coolidge, *The Autobiography of Calvin Coolidge* (New York: Cosmopolitan Book Corporation, 1929), pp. 137–138.

104. Rexford Guy Tugwell, et al., *American Economic Life and the Means of Its Improvement* (New York: Harcourt, Brace and Company, 1925), p. 590.

105. See Vauclain, *Optimism*, p. 11; Filene, *The Way Out*, pp. 30–31, 65–66; William Leavitt Stoddard, "Our Era of Prosperity," *The Outlook* 146 (July 13, 1927), p. 356.

106. Arthur Melville, "The Land Where Dreams Come True," *The Rotarian* 24 (January 1924), p. 4.

107. Emmet F. Harte, "The Land of Illusion," *Munsey's Magazine* 72 (May 1921), pp. 607–16.

108. Edward W. Bok, "To-morrow's Business Man," *The Rotarian* 25 (October 1924), p. 7.

109. Quoted from Prothro, *The Dollar Decade*, p. 225.

110. Barnes, *The Genius of American Business*, p. 22.

111. O'Leary, "Twenty-five Years of American Prosperity," p. 699.

112. Quoted from Morell Heald, "Business Thought in the Twenties: Social Responsibility," in Gerald D. Nash, ed., *Issues in American Economic History* (Lexington, Mass.: D. C. Heath and Company, 1972), p. 380.

113. Ford, *Today and Tomorrow*, pp. 250–52.

114. Glenn Frank, "Welding the World Together," *The Rotarian* 30 (January 1927), p. 5; Julius H. Barnes, "Teamplay Between Government and Industry," in Byron and Coudert, eds., *America Speaks*, p. 38; Vauclain, *Optimism*, pp. 114–15; Feiker, "The Profession of Commerce in the Making," p. 207; Barnes, *The Genius of American Business*, p. 16.

115. Knutson, "The Cash Value of Ethics," p. 59.

116. Albert S. Adams, "Annual Address," in Rotary International, *Proceedings 1920*, pp. 43–44; Boardman, "A Life to Be Lived," p. 5; Harry H. Rogers, "Good Will," *The Rotarian* 29 (December 1926), p. 5.

117. *The Rotarian* 32 (April 1928), p. 8.

Conclusion

The picture I have given of the American 1920s as being completely dominated by the business culture is, as I have pointed out before, only partially correct. To a large extent it is true that business was dominant because other social institutions willingly let business have the ruling position. However, this situation did not prevent business, when its authority did not suffice, from exerting its power directly; business leaders did not hesitate, when they thought it necessary, to use economic leverage. Most Protestant churches voluntarily adjusted to the dominant business culture; they often made the business ideals and methods their own. Again, one must be aware, however, that there were exceptions to this predominant attitude. A number of individuals and churches refused to conform to the business values. I think it illuminating to study in greater detail an incident that took place in Detroit in 1926, which will show how business forced, rather than inspired, the churches to act in a certain way, and how some of these churches resented and rebelled against the business pressure.

THE BATTLE OF DETROIT

The Detroit of 1926 was proud, prosperous, and powerful. It was the home of the automobile. It was the headquarters of the most admired man in the United States, Henry Ford. To a degree unknown in most other cities, its life was molded by the preferences and prejudices of business. The leaders of Detroit were solidly anti-union men; they were proud of having made Detroit into a shining example of an open-shop city.

The majority of the Detroit Protestant churches were influenced by the city's predominant business spirit. They were eager to use business as a model for their organization and activities. They were happy to listen to the advice of the many businessmen who were members of their churches. But there were also a small number of churches that were not equally willing to conform.

In the fall of 1926, this world of peaceful coexistence suffered a disturbance that forced business to resort to a pressure and a power it usually did not need to exert in order to make the churches toe the line.[1] The American Federation of Labor had decided to hold its annual convention in Detroit in October. It had been a tradition that the Protestant churches in the A.F.L. convention invite leaders of the Federation to speak on the spiritual aspects of the labor movement. The Federal Council of Churches suggested that this tradition be upheld in Detroit. The Detroit council of churches invited the more than 150 local ministers to a meeting to discuss the proposal. Eighteen came, and they tentatively decided to extend five invitations to labor leaders. Somewhat later the Y.M.C.A. of Detroit invited William Green, the secretary of the A.F.L., to speak in the regular Sunday afternoon meeting on October 10.

The business community saw the presence of the American Federation of Labor as a threat to the open shop policy it had so successfully established in Detroit. It had carefully prepared itself for the October convention. In late July *The Detroit Saturday Night* published a special, open shop number that praised the present industrial policy and denigrated all forms of unionism. In September business put pressure on the churches. On September 14, 1926, the Associated Building Employers of Detroit wrote a letter to the members of the association asking them to talk to the ministers of certain churches about "why these ministers take upon themselves the bringing of unionism into the church pulpit." On September 27, *The Detroiter*, the official organ of the Detroit Board of Commerce, published a full-page, open letter addressed "To Detroit churchmen." The letter charged that inviting labor leaders to Detroit churches was "part of the program of the American Federation of Labor to make Detroit a closed-shop city" and that the men invited were "admittedly attacking our government, and our American plan of employment."

The business campaign was a great success. Individual laymen put pressure on their ministers. Church boards discussed the issue anew. When the Detroit council of churches called a new meeting, only six pastors came. Later, in the heat of the fight, only two or three ministers held fast to their original position. Three of the five invitations to labor leaders were withdrawn. *The Detroit Saturday Night* congratulated the churches and their ministers upon their good sense.

The Y.M.C.A., under pressure as well, called a board meeting. The board consisted of Charles B. Warren, president of the Michigan Sugar Company; Chester Culver, secretary of the Employers' association; C. B. Van Dusen, president of the Kresge Company; and Paul King, who had managed Truman H. Newberry's campaign for a Senate seat, a campaign that became a symbol of money in politics. The board decided that William Green should not speak at the Y.M.C.A. meeting. C. B. Van Dusen, president of the board, is reported to have explained to Green that the Y.M.C.A. had a large building program under way that must not be jeopardized. Businessmen of Detroit—the Fords, the Fishers, and the Kresges—had pledged two and a half million dollars to the Y.M.C.A. building program. Green understood.

The local churches and the Y.M.C.A. had failed to withstand the pressure from business. To save the face of the Protestant churches, the Federal Council of Churches took action. It organized a Sunday afternoon mass meeting at the First Congregational Church of Detroit, in which Dr. Worth M. Tippy of the Federal Council openly condemned the behavior of business and tacitly accused the local churches of submissiveness. In his speech Dr. Tippy turned to the board of commerce and protested against the "affront" that it had offered to the churches of Detroit; he admonished the Detroit churches to remember that "the independence of the pulpit is its most vital possession," and he assured the A.F.L. representatives that, in spite of what had happened in Detroit, the Protestant churches were "manifestly sympathetic to labor."

From what happened in Detroit in 1926, we can learn how business in the twenties occasionally misused its position and forced the churches into submission. But we can also see how certain ministers and church organizations refused to give up their independence. The Battle of Detroit was widely publicized in the denominational press, most of which denounced business for having gone too far. As I have shown, the Federal Council of Churches leveled a direct attack against the business interests. And in Detroit itself, there were a couple of ministers who withstood the business intimidation. One of the ministers was Reinhold Niebuhr, who was later to become one of the most influential churchmen and theologians in American history.

At the time of the trial of strength, Reinhold Niebuhr was pastor of Bethel Evangelical Church in Detroit. He was then a liberal advocate for the social gospel; his move toward a neo-orthodox position would come later. In his *Leaves from the Notebook of a Tamed Cynic*,[2] which reflects Niebuhr's life in the 1920s, we get the picture of a man who deplores the lack of social awareness in most congregations and the presence of "suavity and circumspection" that characterize the average parson. It is clear from the *Notebook* that others look upon him as a controversial figure because of his liberal social message, but it is equally clear that his liberalism does not extend as far as questioning such fundamental issues as the divinity of Christ. He wanted to free Protestants from the traditional "individualistic ethic" and awaken their social conscience; at the same time he saw this work as a force of "decadence" and longed for "religious naiveté" and "a proper appreciation of the mystical values in religion."

Reinhold Niebuhr was a man of conviction and courage. During the 1926 controversy, he did not let himself be intimidated, nor did he condemn the ministers who were. It was not surprising at all to him that the churches had retreated in the way they did. He knew business was king of Detroit. "There are few cities," he wrote at the time, "in which wealth, suddenly acquired and proud of the mechanical efficiency which produced it, is so little mellowed by social intelligence." The business leaders of the city were "hard-boiled realists" who "used their power in the city to prevent any discussion of the character of their power and the method of its preservation." He further knew that most of the churches were not "sufficiently liberal" to dare go against the dictums of business. And what was true of the Detroit churches was true of all American churches: "The churches of America are on the whole thoroughly committed to the interests and prejudices of the middle classes." Niebuhr was mildly surprised, however, at the fact that business saw the labor convention as a threat to the established order. He had attended several sessions of the convention, and the men there had impressed him "as having about the same amount of daring and imagination as a group of village bankers."

Reinhold Niebuhr did not hesitate to criticize even "the hero of the average American," Henry Ford. Niebuhr accused Ford of being a hypocrite. Ford had a reputation of being one of the world's leading humanitarians; Niebuhr meant that there was no true basis for this reputation, which was only the "wonderful triumph of astute publicity." Niebuhr scrutinized one of Ford's philanthropic schemes after another. Ford had boasted that he paid such high wages that there was no need in his company for unemployment and old age insurances. Niebuhr pointed out that Ford's wages may have been adequate at one time but that by 1926 they had become so hollowed out that workers had difficulties surviving on them. Ford had introduced a widely heralded, five-day week. Niebuhr pointed out that this had been done, not for the benefit of the workers, but in order to adjust production to the decreased demand for Ford automobiles. Ford had further made public that he was going to do something about the crime problem by employing five thousand boys between 16 and 20 years of age to keep them out of mischief. Niebuhr charged that Ford was doing this at a time when hardly any of his workers were working full time and when many were being discharged. The net result, according to Niebuhr, was that Ford was only substituting young men for old men. In a final attempt to analyze Ford's character, Niebuhr wrote:

> It is difficult to determine whether Mr. Ford is simply a shrewd exploiter of a gullible public in his humanitarian pretensions, or whether he suffers from self-deception. My own guess is that he is at least as naive as he is shrewd, that he does not think profoundly on the social implications of his industrial policies, and that in some of his avowed humanitarian motives he is actually self-deceived. The tragedy of the situation lies in the fact that the American public is, on the whole, too credulous and uncritical to make any critical analysis of the moral pretensions of this great industry.[3]

But men like Niebuhr were rare in the American 1920s. Consequently, the Protestant churches of the decade had little to say and had little impact on social life. This identity crisis, or "religious depression" as Handy has called it,[4] lasted into the 1930s, when the churches regained some of their authority.

THE CRASH AND AFTER

The business dominance of the 1920s was broken in October 1929. But the shift of authority away from business to other social institutions was not as abrupt as is occasionally held. The decline in business prestige was a gradual one from 1929 to approximately 1932. Immediately after the Crash, the authority of business was not severely shaken. Business assured the public that what had happened was only a temporary setback and that America's financial system was basically sound. The amazing prosperity would come back within a year. Looking into *Reader's Guide to Periodical Literature 1929–1932*, one is struck by the large number of articles overflowing with optimism, carrying such titles as "Better Times Coming," "Blue Sky Ahead," "Business Revival," "Why Prosperity Will Return," and "Right Now Is the Time to Begin to Get Rich."[5]

But as the business volume shrank and the wholesale prices declined, as the commercial failures and the bank closures rose, as the national income declined and the unemployment rose, the American public lost faith in the businessman's ability to overcome the crisis. Many of the assumptions upon which the American people had depended, Frederick Lewis Allen pointed out, were wrecked in the Depression, a few of which were "the assumption that the big men of Wall Street were economic seers, business forecasters could forecast, and business cycles followed nice orderly rhythms; and the assumption that the American economic system was sure of a great and inspiring growth."[6]

During a period of three years, the reputation of the American businessman was virtually demolished. From his venerated position in the twenties, he fell to an object of "public hostility, suspicion, and ridicule," as George Mowry puts it.[7] Historians agree that the businessman's fall from grace was unusually rapid and heavy. Mowry speaks about the businessman's "social bankruptcy." John Kenneth Galbraith says that the businessman's "credit for wisdom, foresight, and, unhappily also, for common honesty underwent a convulsive shrinkage." Thomas Cochran calls this change from veneration to distrust "cataclysmic."[8]

The businessman was not only a victim of economic forces but contributed actively to his own downfall through his inflexible stance. Up to 1933 he continued to propagate the individualistic business ideals of the 1920s. In 1932, the president of the National Association of Manufacturers, to take a flagrant example, ascribed the Depression and the growing unemployment to mass laziness.[9] Such insensitivity to the problems at hand not surprisingly led to business becoming alienated from the rest of American society. After 1933 business started realizing that it had no ready solutions; it withdrew into self-doubt and frustration. During the rest of the decade and the following one as well, business lost its voice. It did not have the confidence to propagate its business creed as it had done during the golden days of the 1920s.[10]

As business was forced down from its dominant position, other social sectors grew more influential. Government, under the New Deal, regained an authority it had not enjoyed since the prewar years. Roosevelt promised in his inaugural address to drive the money-changers from the temple, i.e. to oppose the business influence that had undermined the American economy. As a result, agriculture, banking, and business were supervised through government regulation. Labor also gained more of a hearing. Unions grew at a remarkable pace; the United Textile Workers of America, for instance, grew from 50,000 in 1933 to 300,000 by mid–1934. Government and labor were no longer dependent on business ideals or methods; now they were in a position where they could dictate the conditions.[11] A similar process of liberation from dependence on business domination took place among the Protestant churches.

Business ceased being the lodestar to the churches. In the 1930s there was little talk in the denominational press of business methods and organization in the churches. In the preceding decade numerous articles had been written on "Religion and Business"; the *Reader's Guide to Periodical Literature* lists no such articles for the period 1929–1932.

Many churchmen expected that this loss of faith in the business community and its ideals would lead to what Frederick Lewis Allen calls "the consolations and inspirations of religion."[12] Their expectations were not fulfilled; there was no massive revival within the Protestant churches. As Hudson says, the secularism of the 1920s had become "so pervasive that a general revival was impossible."[13] However, there were signs that the Protestant churches no longer were willing to adapt to the dominant social sector. Several individual developments show that the churches were eager to strengthen their identity and to gain an authority they had lacked for so long.

Many expressions of a modest awakening in the churches may be mentioned. The number of Bible institutes started growing again, radio evangelism became more active, fundamentalist congregations became increasingly numerous, denominations like the Southern Baptists began urging their members to rekindle their religious fervor as an antidote to the Depression, and the Oxford Group gained a hearing in the United States.[14] The two major signs of renewal, however, were the move among some influential churchmen toward a neo-orthodox position and the renaissance of the Social Gospel movement.

As the Depression deepened and the business dominance lost its grip, many Protestants felt that the churches in the 1920s had compromised with the world. H. Richard Niebuhr held that the church was "imperiled not only by an external worldliness but by one that has established itself within the Christian camp." The church, he meant, had retreated and then made a pact with the enemy "in thought, in organization, and in discipline." Niebuhr dismissed the modernists of the 1920s as being obsolete and irrelevant and urged the churches to return to Scriptures and the "prophetic note." Richard's brother Reinhold shared his view of the illness of the church and the possible remedy. Reinhold Niebuhr wrote in 1934:

> We borrowed our criteria of evaluation from the world around us—a world gone mad in its worship of mere size. And we were guilty of the incredible folly of supposing that

'Christ's church was of this world,' to be judged by the world's standards, to be modeled on the world's ways, to walk in the world's procession, and to keep step to the crashing discord of its brazen shams.

Niebuhr moved toward a more orthodox view of man as not being perfectible, but as suffering under original sin. The Niebuhr brothers were joined in their neo-orthodox stance by many influential theologians like John C. Bennett, Walter Horton, Henry Van Dusen, and Samuel McCrae Cavert.[15]

The other distinctive feature of the Protestant churches of the Depression was the revival of the Social Gospel. In the twenties the Social Gospel had suffered from an attitude of "adjustment and acquiescence to 'things as they are'." By 1932 many of the churches that before the Crash had endorsed business values turned much more militant in their advocacy of the Social Gospel. Their reform spirit was not only directed to the secular world but turned inward to question, for instance, the economic morality of the church.[16]

The final pattern that emerges from this study is that the American 1920s were characterized by an orientation towards business domination, but that such a domination was not unique to this period. As I have pointed out, this prominent position of business in American society has always been a feature distinguishing the United States from, for instance, European societies. Nor was the willingness of the Protestant churches to adopt the business spirit unique to the decade after WWI; examples of such an accommodating attitude can be mentioned from the latter half of the nineteenth century as well as from the 1980s.

What was peculiar to the business civilization in the 1920s was rather, first of all, the deliberateness with which business sold itself to the American public and the apparent success of its campaign. Seldom before or since had business so consciously made use of publicity to reform its image. Furthermore, many traits of the image business tried and largely managed to create were unique to the period. Never to the same extent had business portrayed itself as such a selfless, service-minded, redemptive moral force. The way business chose to create this image was also new, namely, the use of religious terms and concepts in order to elevate business to a spiritual level, a state that managed to forge together two forces that have been fundamental to the shaping of American society—and that to Europeans have been an unlikely constellation—business and religion.

NOTES

1. For a presentation of the "Battle of Detroit," see Hubert C. Herring, "Business Cracks the Whip!" *The Christian Century* 43 (October 21, 1926), pp. 1292–1294; "The Battle of Detroit," *The Christian Century* 43 (October 21, 1926), pp. 1287–1289; "The Church and Labor," *The Nashville Christian Advocate* 94 (November 12, 1926); "The Detroit Churches Reply," *The Nashville Christian Advocate* 94 (November 26, 1926), p. 1497.

2. Reinhold Niebuhr, *Leaves from the Notebook of a Tamed Cynic* (New York: Richard R. Smith, Inc., 1930), pp. 104–136.

3. Reinhold Niebuhr, "How Philanthropic Is Henry Ford?" *The Christian Century* 43 (December 9, 1926), pp. 1516–1517. See also Reinhold Niebuhr, "Ford's Five-Day Week Shrinks," *The Christian Century* 44 (June 9, 1927), pp. 713–714.

4. Robert T. Handy, "The American Religious Depression 1925–1935," *Church History* 24 (March 1960), pp. 3–16.

5. I. F. Marcosson, "Better Times Coming," *Saturday Evening Post* 203 (November 29, 1930), pp. 3–5; "Blue Sky Ahead," *Collier's Weekly* 88 (December 12, 1931), p. 62; "Business Revival," *Saturday Evening Post* 203 (July 12, 1930), p. 20; M. S. Rukeyser, "Why Prosperity Will Return," *Review of Reviews* 81 (May 1930), pp. 46–51; J. G. Lonsdale, "Right Now Is the Time to Begin to Get Rich!" *The American Magazine* 110 (October 1930), pp. 18–19.

6. Frederick Lewis Allen, *Since Yesterday 1929–1939* (New York: Bantam Books, 1965), p. 125.

7. George E. Mowry, *The Urban Nation, 1920–1960* (New York: Hill and Wang, 1965), p. 69.

8. Ibid., p. 69; John Kenneth Galbraith, *The Great Crash 1929* (Boston: Houghton Mifflin Company, 1955), p. 149; Thomas C. Cochran, *The American Business System: A Historical Perspective, 1900–1955* (New York: Harper & Row, 1962), p. 140. See also Thomas C. Cochran, *American Business in the Twentieth Century* (Cambridge, Mass.: Harvard University Press, 1972), pp. 112, 124.

9. See Mowry, *The Urban Nation*, p. 69.

10. See Francis X. Sutton, et al., *The American Business Creed* (Cambridge, Mass.: Harvard University Press, 1956), pp. 395–396.

11. See, for instance, Alfred D. Chandler, *The Visible Hand: The Managerial Revolution in American Business* (Cambridge, Mass.: Harvard University Press, 1977), pp. 493–495.

12. Allen, *Since Yesterday*, p. 126.

13. Winthrop S. Hudson, *Religion in America* (New York: Charles Scribner's Sons, 1965), p. 362. See also Robert S. Lynd and Helen Merrell Lynd, *Middletown in Transition: A Study in Cultural Conflicts* (New York: Harcourt, Brace & World, 1937), pp. 302–308.

14. See Sydney E. Ahlstrom, *A Religious History of the American People* (Garden City, N.Y.: Doubleday and Company, 1975), Vol. 2, pp. 410–411; James J. Thomson, Jr., *Tried as by Fire: Southern Baptists and the Religious Controversies of the 1920s* (Macon, Ga.: Mercer University Press, 1982), pp. 207–209; Hudson, *Religion in America*, p. 362; Allen, *Since Yesterday*, pp. 126–127.

15. See Martin E. Marty, *Righteous Empire: The Protestant Experience in America* (New York: The Dial Press, 1970), pp. 234–239, and Donald B. Meyer, *The Protestant Search for Political Realism, 1919–1941* (Berkeley, Cal.: University of California Press, 1960), pp. 217–269.

16. See Paul A. Carter, *The Decline and Revival of the Social Gospel: Social and Political Liberalism in American Protestant Churches 1920–1940* (Ithaca, N.Y.: Cornell University Press, 1956), pp. 127, 144–147.

Note on Method

The principle used for the selection of primary sources has been a combination of representativeness and variety. I have tried to draw on mainstream sources, thereby avoiding, with certain exceptions, extreme, unrepresentative minority views. The material for investigation has been chosen in order to portray the representative, predominant majority opinion. But within this limitation I have selected widely varied forms of sources with the intention of creating a composite picture of American business and religion in the twenties. I have not limited this study to the writings of one trade organization or one Protestant denomination, as other scholars have done, but instead I have included many such social units. The selection of sources has not been limited to the professional view of business or the Protestant churches, but includes material that expresses more popular and more general views, such as popular periodicals, nondenominational Protestant journals, novels, plays, biographies, and contemporary cultural histories and critiques. The sources finally selected came from an extensive body of material. The selection amounts to some 250 books and over 500 articles, most of which are directly concerned with the relationship between business and Protestantism in the American 1920s.

The question of reliability and representativeness of the primary material needs to be addressed. There are several dangers of misrepresentation in employing the material selected. First, there is the danger of overemphasizing the importance of the research problem at hand. To give one example: I have, in selecting articles that would show the Protestant attitude toward business, studied numerous annual volumes of several Protestant journals. The overwhelming majority of the articles in these journals was not devoted to expressions of how the Protestant churches looked upon business and its ideology, but to entirely different matters such as doctrinal and denominational issues. By presenting the Protestant attitude to business in the concentrated form that this study does, one runs the risk of giving the impression that Protestant thought and action in the twenties were exclusively concerned with what business thought and did, which obviously they were not. The same danger holds for the study of business ideals and their dissemination.

Another possible source of error is the heterogeneous structure of the United States.

It is a large country. What is true of Protestantism in Tennessee may not be true in New England. The ideals of the Ohio business community may differ from those of California. The sources used in this study express more the views of the eastern half of the American continent, with a particular emphasis on the northeastern and southern states, because it was in these areas that the mainstream business and Protestant institutions were located. There is also the difference between country and city to be kept in mind. Rural areas are generally more conservative and less willing to adopt new ideals than urban ones. The views expressed in this study come primarily from urban persons and organizations. One can safely assume that the rural part of America was less affected by the value changes discussed in this study.

The variety of American Protestantism, referred to here, must also be taken into account. To be as representative as possible, I have included material from "high status" as well as "low status" churches, from doctrinally modernist/liberal as well as doctrinally conservative churches, from reformist/Social Gospel churches as well as nonreformist churches. Nevertheless, the majority of the voices speaking in this study belong to middle-class, doctrinally liberal, nonreformist Protestant groups.

One might ask to what extent the individual voices that here express their views are representative of the larger group, business or Protestantism. Many of the writers of articles and books cited in this study are not official spokesmen of their group; very often they merely present their own views. One can nevertheless assume that most of these writers express views, given a small degree of variation, that are sanctioned by the influential stratum of their group. Too extreme views would not be published in journals and books printed by denominations and business organizations. I have not tried to account for every single person's background and beliefs but have rather assumed that the screening of editors has created an acceptable representativeness. It may seem from the picture I draw that I think there is a monolithic business view and an equally monolithic Protestant opinion, but this of course is not true. However, in all these sources studied there is such a homogeneity in the major themes that I have no hesitation in stating that the picture I present is both reliable and representative of the major tendencies in the twenties. In order to let readers judge for themselves, numerous quotations from primary sources have been included to document my argument.

Bibliography

PRIMARY SOURCES

Periodicals

The American Lutheran	1923–1928
The American Magazine	1920–1929
The American Mercury	1924–1928
Annals of the American Academy of Political and Social Science	1920–1929
The Atlantic Monthly	1920–1929
The Bookman	1920–1929
The Century Magazine	1924–1928
The Christian Century	1923–1927
The Christian Herald	1922–1929
Church Management	1923–1929
Collier's Weekly	1920–1929
Commerce and Finance	1924
Current History	1920–1929
Current Opinion	1923
The Delineator	1923–1924
The Dial	1920–1929
Educational Review	1924–1925
The Forum	1922–1928
Harper's Monthly Magazine	1920–1929
Harvard Theological Review	1920–1929

Homiletic Review	1922–1923
Journal of Political Economy	1922
The Kiwanis Magazine	1922–1929
The Literary Digest	1920–1929
The Menorah Journal	1928
The Methodist Quarterly Review	1922–1929
The Missionary Review of the World	1920–1929
Munsey's Magazine	1921
The Nashville Christian Advocate	1926–1928
The Nation	1925
The Nation's Business	1929
The New York Christian Advocate	1920–1927
The Outlook	1920–1929
The Presbyterian Survey	1924–1926
The Red Book Magazine	1921
The Religious Herald	1924–1928
The Review of Reviews	1923–1929
The Rotarian	1921–1929
The Saturday Evening Post	1924–1929
Southern Churchman	1925–1927
The Survey	1924–1928
System	1927
The World's Work	1920–1929
The World Tomorrow	1921–1929

Literary Works

Adams, Samuel Hopkins. *Success*. Boston: Houghton Mifflin Company, 1921.

Anderson, Sherwood. *Dark Laughter*. 1925. Reprint. New York: Liveright, 1970.

———. *Poor White*. 1920. Reprint. New York: The Modern Library, 1926.

Boyd, Thomas. *Through the Wheat*. New York: Charles Scribner's Sons, 1923.

Crane, Hart. *The Bridge*. 1930. Reprinted in *The Collected Poems of Hart Crane*. New York: Liveright, 1933.

Cummings, E. E. *The Enormous Room*. 1922. Reprint. New York: Liveright, 1950.

Dos Passos, John. *Manhattan Transfer*. 1925. Reprint. Boston: Houghton Mifflin Company, 1953.

———. *U.S.A.*, New York, 1930, 1932, 1936. Reprint. New York: Modern Library, 1938.

Douglas, Lloyd C. *Magnificent Obsession*. New York: P. F. Collier & Son Corporation, 1929.

Dreiser, Theodore. *An American Tragedy*. New York: Boni and Liveright, 1925.

Eliot, T. S. *The Waste Land.* 1922. Reprint. London: Faber & Faber, 1959.
Faulkner, William. *Sartoris.* 1929. Reprint; New York: New American Library, 1953.
———. *The Sound and the Fury.* 1929. Reprint. New York: Random House, 1956.
Fitzgerald, F. Scott. *The Great Gatsby.* 1925. Reprint. New York: Charles Scribner's Sons, 1953.
———. *This Side of Paradise.* 1920. Reprint. New York: Dell, 1948.
Green, Paul. *The Field God and In Abraham's Bosom.* New York: Robert M. McBride & Co., 1927.
Hemingway, Ernest. *The Sun Also Rises.* New York: Charles Scribner's Sons, 1926.
Kaufman, George S., and Marc Connelly. *Beggar on Horseback.* New York: Boni and Liveright, 1924.
Lewis, Sinclair. *Arrowsmith.* New York: Harcourt, Brace and Company, 1925.
———. *Babbitt.* 1922. Reprint. London: Jonathan Cape, 1929.
———. *Elmer Gantry.* New York: Harcourt, Brace and Company, 1927.
———. *Main Street.* New York: Harcourt, Brace and Company, 1920.
Norris, Charles G. *Pig Iron.* New York: E. P. Dutton and Company, 1925.
O'Neill, Eugene. *The Hairy Ape* (1922), *The Emperor Jones* (1920), *Desire under the Elms* (1924) in *Ah, Wilderness and Other Plays.* Harmondsworth: Penguin Books, 1966.
———. *Lazarus Laughed and Dynamo.* London: Jonathan Cape, 1929.
———. *Strange Interlude.* 1928. Reprinted in *Three Plays.* New York: Vintage Books, 1958.
Pollock, Channing. *The Fool.* New York: Samuel French, 1922.
———. *Mr. Moneypenny.* New York: Brentano's, 1928.
Stribling, T. S. *Teeftallow.* Garden City, N.Y.: Doubleday, Page & Company, 1926.
Suckow, Ruth. *The Folks.* New York: Farrar & Rinehart, 1934.
Tarkington, Booth. *Alice Adams.* 1921. Reprint. New York: New American Library, 1961.
———. *The Plutocrat.* Garden City, N.Y.: Doubleday, Page & Company, 1927.
Train, Arthur. *The Lost Gospel.* New York: Charles Scribner's Sons, 1925.
———. *The Needle's Eye.* New York: Charles Scribner's Sons, 1924.
Wright, Harold Bell. *God and the Groceryman.* New York: D. Appleton and Company, 1927.

Other Primary Sources

Adams, James Truslow. *Our Business Civilization.* New York: Albert & Charles Boni, 1929.
Atkins, Gaius Glenn. *Religion in Our Times.* New York: Round Table Press, 1932.
Babson, Roger W. *Business Fundamentals: How to Become a Successful Business Man.* New York: B. C. Forbes Publishing Company, 1923.
———. *Fundamentals of Prosperity.* New York: Fleming H. Revell Company, 1920.
———. *New Tasks for Old Churches.* New York: Fleming H. Revell Company, 1922.
———. *Religion and Business.* New York: Macmillan Co., 1920.
Barnes, Julius H. *The Genius of American Business.* New York: Doubleday, Page & Company, 1924.
Barton, Bruce. *The Book Nobody Knows.* Indianapolis: Bobbs-Merrill Company, 1926.
———. *The Man Nobody Knows: A Discovery of the Real Jesus.* Indianapolis: Bobbs-Merrill Company, 1924.

———. *What Can a Man Believe?* Indianapolis: Bobbs-Merrill Company, 1927.

Beard, Charles A., and Mary R. Beard. *The Rise of American Civilization*. Vol. 2. New York: Macmillan Company, 1927.

Bok, Edward W. *Dollars Only*. New York: Charles Scribner's Sons, 1926.

Brooks, C. Harry, and Ernest Charles. *Christianity and Autosuggestion*. London: George Allen & Unwin Ltd., 1923.

Brown, William Montgomery. *Communism and Christianism*. Galion, Ohio: Bradford-Brown Educational Co., 1927.

Bryce, James. *The American Commonwealth*. Rev. ed. New York: Macmillan Company, 1919–1920.

Buck, Glen. *This American Ascendancy*. Chicago: A. Kroch & Company, 1927.

Byron, Basil Gordon, and Frederic René Coudert, eds. *America Speaks: A Library of Best Spoken Thought in Business and the Professions*. New York: Modern Eloquence Corporation, 1928.

Cabot, Richard C. *Adventures on the Borderlands of Ethics*. New York: Harper & Brothers, 1926.

Carver, Thomas Nixon. *The Present Economic Revolution in the United States*. Boston: Little, Brown and Company, 1925.

Chandler, Warren A. *Current Comments on Timely Topics*. Nashville, Tenn.: Cokesbury Press, 1926.

Chase, Stuart. *Prosperity, Fact or Myth*. New York: Charles Boni, 1929.

Chesterton, G. K. *What I Saw in America*. London: Hodder and Stoughton, 1922.

Coolidge, Calvin. *The Autobiography of Calvin Coolidge*. New York: Cosmopolitan Book Corporation, 1929.

Coué, Emile. *Self-Mastery Through Conscious Autosuggestion*. New York: American Library Service, 1922.

Crane, Frank. *Why I Am a Christian*. New York: Wm. H. Wise & Co., 1924.

Crawford, Julius Earl. *The Stewardship Life*. Nashville, Tenn.: Cokesbury Press, 1929.

Creed, Wigginton E. *Safeguarding the Future of Private Business*. Boston: Houghton Mifflin Company, 1923.

Cushman, Ralph S. *The Message of Stewardship*. New York: Abingdon-Cokesbury Press, 1922.

Davis, Jerome, ed. *Business and the Church*. New York: Century Co., 1926.

———. *Christianity and Social Adventuring*. New York: Century Co., 1927.

Day, Clive. "Capitalistic and Socialistic Tendencies in the Puritan Colonies." *Annual Report of the American Historical Association for the Year 1920*. Washington, D.C.: Government Printing Office (1925): 225–235.

Diefendorf, Dorr Frank. *The Christian in Social Relationships*. New York: The Methodist Book Concern, 1922.

Diffendorfer, Ralph E. *The Church and the Community*. New York: Interchurch World Movement of North America, 1920.

Dreier, Thomas. *The Silver Lining, or Sunshine on the Business Trail*. New York: B. C. Forbes Publishing Company, 1923.

Eddy, Sherwood. *Facing the Crisis: A Study in Present Day Social and Religious Problems*. New York: George H. Doran Company, 1922.

———. *Religion and Social Justice*. New York: George H. Doran Company, 1927.

Fay, Charles Norman. *Social Justice: The Henry Ford Fortune*. Cambridge, Mass.: The Cosmos Press, 1926.

Feather, William. *The Ideals and Follies of Business*. Cleveland: The William Feather Company, 1927.

Filene, Edward A. *The Way Out: A Forecast of Coming Changes in American Business and Industry*. Garden City, N.Y.: Doubleday, Page & Company, 1924.

Fiske, George Walter. *The Changing Family: Social and Religious Aspects of the Modern Family*. New York: Harper & Brothers, 1928.

Forbes, B. C. *Forbes Epigrams: 1000 Thoughts on Life and Business*. New York: B. C. Forbes Publishing Company, 1922.

———. *Keys to Success: Personal Efficiency*. New York: B. C. Forbes Publishing Company, 1926.

Ford, Henry. *Today and Tomorrow*. London: William Heinemann, 1926.

Forging Ahead in Business. New York: Alexander Hamilton Institute, 1929.

Fosdick, Harry Emerson. *Christianity and Progress*. New York: Fleming H. Revell Company, 1922.

———. *The Living of These Days: An Autobiography*. New York: Harper & Brothers, 1956.

———. *The Meaning of Service*. New York: Association Press, 1921.

Frank, Waldo. *The Re-discovery of America*. New York: Charles Scribner's Sons, 1929.

Gabriel, Ralph H., ed. *Christianity and Modern Thought*. New Haven: Yale University Press, 1924.

Galpin, Charles Josiah. *Empty Churches*. New York: The Century Co., 1925.

Garett, Garet. *The American Omen*. New York: E. P. Dutton & Co., 1928.

Grant, Percy Stickney. *The Religion of Main Street*. New York: American Library Service, 1923.

Hart, Albert Bushnell, ed. *The American Year Book 1925–1929*. Garden City, N.Y.: Doubleday, Doran & Co., 1926–1930.

Heermance, Edgar L. *The Ethics of Business*. New York: Harper & Brothers, 1926.

Hughes, Edwin Holt. *Christianity and Success*. Nashville, Tenn.: Cokesbury Press, 1928.

Johnson, Joseph French. *Organized Business Knowledge*. New York: B. C. Forbes Publishing Co., 1923.

King, Veronica and Paul. *The Raven on the Skyscraper: A Study of Modern American Portents*. London: Heath Cranton Limited, 1925.

Kirchwey, Freda, ed. *Our Changing Morality: A Symposium*. New York: Albert & Charles Boni, 1924.

Kleiser, Grenville. *Training for Power and Leadership*. Garden City, N.Y.: Garden City Publishing Co., 1923.

Krutch, Joseph Wood. *The Modern Temper: A Study and a Confession*. New York: Harcourt, Brace & Co., 1929.

Kyne, Peter B. *The Go-Getter: A Story That Tells You How to Be One*. New York: Cosmopolitan Book Corporation, 1922.

Lee, James Melvin. *Business Ethics: A Manual of Modern Morals*. New York: The Ronald Press Company, 1926.

Lippmann, Walter. *A Preface to Morals*. 1929. Reprint. New York: Time-Life Books, 1964.

Lord, Everett W. *The Fundamentals of Business Ethics*. New York: The Ronald Press Company, 1926.

Luccock, Halford Edward. *Contemporary American Literature and Religion*. New York: Abingdon Press, 1934.

———. *Jesus and the American Mind*. New York: Abingdon Press, 1930.
Lynd, Robert S., and Helen Merrell Lynd. *Middletown: A Study in American Culture*. New York: Harcourt, Brace and Company, 1929.
———. *Middletown in Transition: A Study in Cultural Conflicts*. New York: Harcourt, Brace and World, 1937.
Machen, J. Gresham. *Christianity and Liberalism*. 1923. Reprint. Grand Rapids, Mich.: Wm. B. Eerdmans Publishing Company, 1974.
McKee, Henry S. *The ABC's of Business*. New York: Macmillan Company, 1922.
Mackenzie, W. Douglas. *Christian Ethics in the World War*. London: Andrew Melrose Ltd., 1918.
Magary, Alvin E. *Character and Happiness*. New York: Charles Scribner's Sons, 1924.
Marden, Orison Swett. *Success Fundamentals*. New York: Thomas Y. Crowell Company, 1920.
Maynard, Harold H., and Walter C. Weidler. *An Introduction to Business*. New York: The Ronald Press Company, 1925.
Mazur, Paul M. *American Prosperity: Its Causes and Consequences*. New York: Viking Press, 1928.
Mencken, H. L. *Selected Prejudices*. New York: Alfred A. Knopf, 1927.
Merz, Charles. *The Great American Band Wagon*. New York: The John Day Company, 1928.
Miller, Spencer, and Joseph F. Fletcher. *The Church and Industry*. New York: Longmans, Green and Company, 1930.
Nash, Arthur. *The Golden Rule in Business*. New York: Fleming H. Revell Company, 1923.
Niebuhr, Reinhold. *Does Civilization Need Religion? A Study in the Social Resources and Limitations of Religion in Modern Life*. New York: Macmillan Company, 1927.
———. *Leaves from the Notebook of a Tamed Cynic*. New York: Richard R. Smith Inc., 1930.
Niese, Richard Beall. *The Newspaper and Religious Publicity*. Nashville, Tenn.: Sunday School Board of the Southern Baptist Convention, 1925.
Nolan, Preston M. *Business First*. Chicago: Raymond Publishing Company, 1928.
Ogburn, William F., ed. *Recent Social Changes in the United States Since the War and Particularly in 1927*. Chicago: University of Chicago Press, 1929.
Page, Kirby. *Jesus or Christianity*. Garden City, N.Y.: Doubleday, Doran & Company, 1929.
Page, Kirby, ed. *Christianity and Economic Problems*. New York: Association Press, 1924.
———. *Recent Gains in American Civilization*. New York: Harcourt, Brace and Company, 1928.
Penney, J. C. *J. C. Penney: The Man with a Thousand Partners*. New York: Harper & Brothers, 1931.
———. *View from the Ninth Decade*. New York: Thomas Nelson & Sons, 1960.
Poling, Daniel A. *An Adventure in Evangelism*. New York: Fleming H. Revell Company, 1925.
Rand, James H., Jr. *Assuring Business Profits*. New York: B. C. Forbes Publishing Co., 1926.
Randall, John Herman. *Religion and the Modern World*. New York: Frederick A. Stokes Co., 1929.
Rascoe, Burton. *We Were Interrupted*. Garden City, N.Y.: Doubleday & Company, 1947.

Recent Social Trends in the United States. Report of the President's Committee on Social Trends. 2 vols. New York: McGraw-Hill Book Company, 1933.

Robinson, Henry M. *Relativity in Business Morals*. Boston: Houghton Mifflin Company, 1928.

Rotary International. *Proceedings: Eleventh Annual Convention, June 21–25, 1920*. Chicago: International Association of Rotary Clubs, 1920.

Sanford, William Phillips, and Willard Hayes Yeager, eds. *Business Speeches by Business Men*. New York: McGraw-Hill Book Company, 1930.

Siegfried, André. *America Comes of Age*. London: Jonathan Cape, 1927.

Söderblom, Nathan. *Från Uppsala till Rock Island: En Predikofärd i Nya Världen*. Stockholm: Svenska Kyrkans Diakonistyrelses Bokförlag, 1924.

Stearns, Harold E., ed. *Civilization in the United States: An Enquiry by Thirty Americans*. London: Jonathan Cape, 1922.

Stocking, Charles Francis, and William Wesley Totheroh. *The Business Man of Syria*. Chicago: The Maestro Co., 1923.

Taeusch, Carl F. *Professional and Business Ethics*. New York: Henry Holt and Company, 1926.

Tarbell, Ida M. *The Life of Elbert H. Gary: The Story of Steel*. New York: D. Appleton and Company, 1925.

———. *Owen D. Young: A New Type of Industrial Leader*. New York: Macmillan Company, 1932.

Tocqueville, Alexis de. *Democracy in America*. 2 vols. 1835, 1840. Reprint. New York: Vintage Books, 1945.

Torrey, R. A. *The Power of Prayer*. 1924. Reprint. Grand Rapids, Mich.: Zondervan Publishing House, 1971.

Trimble, Henry Burton. *The Christian Motive and Method in Stewardship*. Nashville, Tenn.: Cokesbury Press, 1929.

Tugwell, Rexford Guy, *et al. American Economic Life and the Means of Its Improvement*. New York: Harcourt, Brace and Company, 1925.

Vauclain, Samuel M. *Optimism*. Philadelphia, 1924.

Ward, Harry F. *Our Economic Morality and the Ethic of Jesus*. New York: Macmillan Company, 1929.

Whitley, Jesse T. *Filled with Messages from Thee*. Richmond, Va.: Whittet & Shepperson, 1923.

Winchester, Benjamin S., ed. *The Handbook of the Churches*. Baltimore, Md.: J. E. Stohlmann, 1927.

Young, Owen D., and Gerard Swope. *Selected Addresses*. General Electric Company, 1930.

SECONDARY SOURCES

Ahlstrom, Sydney E. *A Religious History of the American People*. 2 vols. Garden City, N.Y.: Doubleday and Company, 1975.

Allen, Frederick Lewis. *The Lords of Creation*. New York: Harper & Brothers, 1935.

———. *Only Yesterday*. New York: Harper & Brothers, 1931.

———. *Since Yesterday 1929–1939*. 1940. Reprint. New York: Bantam Books, 1965.

American Heritage 16 (August 1965). Special Issue: The 20's.

ernard. *Social Stratification: A Comparative Analysis of Structure and Process*. New ork: Harcourt, Brace & World, 1957.

oren, ed. *The Culture of the Twenties*. Indianapolis, Ind.: Bobbs-Merrill Company, 1970.

, Robert N. *Beyond Belief: Essays on Religion in a Post-Traditional World*. New York: Harper & Row, 1970.

Bendix, Reinhard, and Seymour M. Lipset, eds. *Class, Status, and Power: Social Stratification in Comparative Perspective*. New York: The Free Press, 1966.

Bernstein, Irving. *The Lean Years: A History of the American Worker 1920–1933*. Boston: Houghton Mifflin Company, 1972.

Braeman, John, and Robert H. Bremner, and David Brody, eds. *Change and Continuity in Twentieth-Century America: The 1920's*. Columbus: Ohio State University Press, 1968.

Brody, David, ed. *Industrial America in the Twentieth Century*. New York: Thomas Y. Crowell Company, 1967.

Carter, Paul A. *The Decline and Revival of the Social Gospel: Social and Political Liberalism in American Protestant Churches 1920–1940*. Ithaca, N.Y.: Cornell University Press, 1956.

———. *The Other Part of the Twenties*. New York: Columbia University Press, 1977.

———. *The Twenties in America*. New York: Thomas Y. Crowell Company, 1968.

Cawelti, John G. *Apostles of the Self-Made Man: Changing Concepts of Success in America*. Chicago: The University of Chicago Press, 1965.

Chandler, Alfred D., Jr. *The Visible Hand: The Managerial Revolution in American Business*. Cambridge, Mass.: Harvard University Press, 1977.

Cochran, Thomas C. *American Business in the Twentieth Century*. Cambridge, Mass.: Harvard University Press, 1972.

———. *The American Business System: A Historical Perspective 1900–1955*. New York: Harper & Row, 1962.

———. *Basic History of American Business*. Princeton, N.J.: D. Van Nostrand Company, 1959.

———. *Business in American Life: A History*. New York: McGraw-Hill Book Co., 1972.

———. *Challenges to American Values: Society, Business, and Religion*. New York: Oxford University Press, 1985.

———. *Social Change in Industrial Society*. London: George Allen & Unwin, 1972.

———. *200 Years of American Business*. New York: Basic Books, Inc., 1977.

Cochran, Thomas C., and William Miller. *The Age of Enterprise: A Social History of Industrial America*. New York: Harper & Row, 1961.

Cole, Arthur H. *Business Enterprise in Its Social Setting*. Cambridge, Mass.: Harvard University Press, 1959.

Conkin, Paul D. *The New Deal*. New York: Thomas Y. Crowell, 1967.

Coser, Lewis A. *The Functions of Social Conflict*. New York: The Free Press, 1956.

Cowley, Malcolm. *A Second Flowering: Works and Days of the Lost Generation*. New York: Viking Press, 1973.

———. *Exile's Return: A Literary Odyssey of the 1920s*. New York: Viking Press, 1951.

Curti, Merle. *The Growth of American Thought*. New York: Harper & Brothers, 1943.

Dahrendorf, Ralf. *Class and Class Conflict in Industrial Society*. Stanford, Cal.: Stanford University Press, 1959.

Diamond, Sigmund. *The Reputation of the American Businessman*. Gloucester, Mass.: Peter Smith, 1970.
Diggins, John P. *The American Left in the Twentieth Century*. New York: Harcourt Brace Jovanovich, 1973.
Doherty, William T. "The Impact of Business on Protestantism, 1900–1929." *The Business History Review* 28 (June 1954): 141–53.
Douglass, Elisha P. *The Coming of Age of American Business: Three Centuries of Enterprise, 1600–1900*. Chapel Hill, N.C.: University of North Carolina Press, 1971.
Ehrmann, Henry W., ed. *Interest Groups on Four Continents*. Pittsburgh: University of Pittsburgh Press, 1960.
Elias, Robert H. *"Entangling Alliances with None": An Essay on the Individual in the American Twenties*. New York: W. W. Norton & Co., 1973.
Fass, Paula S. *The Damned and the Beautiful: American Youth in the 1920's*. New York: Oxford University Press, 1977.
Faulkner, Harold Underwood. *American Economic History*. New York: Harper & Row, 1960.
Frazier, E. Franklin. *The Negro Church in America*. New York: Schocken Books, 1966.
Furniss, Norman K. *The Fundamentalist Controversy 1918–1931*. New Haven: Yale University Press, 1954.
Galambos, Louis. *The Public Image of Big Business in America, 1880–1940*. Baltimore, Md.: Johns Hopkins University Press, 1975.
Galbraith, John Kenneth. *The Great Crash 1929*. Boston: Houghton Mifflin Company, 1955.
Gatewood, Willard B., Jr. *Controversy in the Twenties: Fundamentalism, Modernism, and Evolution*. Nashville, Tenn.: Vanderbilt University Press, 1969.
Geismar, Maxwell. *Writers in Crisis: The American Novel Between Two Wars*. Boston: Houghton Mifflin, 1942.
Gerth, H. H., and C. Wright Mills, eds. *From Max Weber*. London: Routledge & Kegan Paul, 1970.
Goldman, Eric F. *Rendezvous with Destiny*. New York: Vintage Books, 1955.
Goodman, Paul, and Frank O. Gatell. *America in the Twenties: The Beginnings of Contemporary America*. New York: Holt, Rinehart and Winston, 1972.
Griswold, A. Whitney. "Three Puritans on Prosperity." *The New England Quarterly* 7 (1934): 475–93.
Grob, Gerald N., and George Athan Billias, eds. *Interpretations of American History: Patterns and Perspectives*. Vol. 2. New York: The Free Press, 1967.
Hall, Thomas Cuming. *The Religious Background of American Culture*. Boston: Little, Brown, and Company, 1930.
Handlin, Oscar, ed. *This Was America*. Cambridge, Mass.: Harvard University Press, 1949.
Handlin, Oscar, and Mary F. Handlin, *The Wealth of the American People*. New York: McGraw-Hill Book Company, 1975.
Handy, Robert T. "The American Religious Depression 1925–1935." *Church History* 24 (March 1960): 3–16.
Hastings, James, ed. *Encyclopaedia of Religion and Ethics*. New York: Charles Scribner's Sons, 1918.
Heald, Morrell. *The Social Responsibilities of Business: Company and Community, 1900–1960*. Cleveland: The Press of Case Western Reserve University, 1970.

Heilbroner, Robert L. *The Worldly Philosophers: The Lives, Times and Ideas of the Great Economic Thinkers*. New York: Simon and Schuster, 1961.
Herberg, Will. *Protestant—Catholic—Jew: An Essay in American Religious Sociology*. Garden City, N.Y.: Doubleday & Company, 1960.
Hicks, John D. *Republican Ascendancy 1921–1933*. New York: Harper & Brothers, 1960.
Hoffman, Frederick J. *The Twenties. American Writing in the Postwar Decade*. New York: The Free Press, 1965.
Huber, Richard M. *The American Idea of Success*. New York: McGraw-Hill Book Company, 1971.
Hudson, Winthrop S. *American Protestantism*. Chicago: University of Chicago Press, 1961.
———. *Religion in America*. New York: Charles Scribner's Sons, 1965.
Huthmacher, J. Joseph. *Trial by War and Depression: 1917–1941*. Boston: Allyn and Bacon, 1973.
International Encyclopedia of the Social Sciences. Edited by David L. Sills. New York: Macmillan, 1968.
Johnson, Paul E. *Psychology of Religion*. New York: Abingdon-Cokesbury Press, 1945.
Jones, Peter d'A. *The Consumer Society: A History of American Capitalism*. Baltimore, Md.: Penguin Books, 1965.
Kolko, Gabriel. *The Triumph of Conservatism: A Reinterpretation of American History, 1900–1916*. Glencoe: Free Press, 1973.
Krooss, Herman E. *American Economic Development: The Progress of a Business Civilization*. Englewood Cliffs, N.J.: Prentice-Hall, 1974.
———. *Executive Opinion: What Business Leaders Said and Thought on Economic Issues, 1920–1960s*. Garden City, N.Y.: Doubleday & Company, 1970.
Krooss, Herman E., and Charles Gilbert. *American Business History*. Englewood Cliffs, N.J.: Prentice-Hall, 1972.
Leighton, Isabel, ed. *The Aspirin Age 1919–1941*. New York: Simon and Schuster, 1949.
Lens, Sidney. *The Labor Wars: From the Molly Maguires to the Sitdowns*. Garden City, N.Y.: Doubleday & Company, 1973.
Lenski, Gerhard E. *Power and Privilege: A Theory of Social Stratification*. New York: McGraw-Hill Book Co., 1966.
———. *The Religious Factor: A Sociologist's Inquiry*. Garden City, N.Y.: Doubleday Anchor, 1963.
Leopold, Richard W., Arthur S. Link, and Stanley Coben, eds. *Problems in American History*. Englewood Cliffs, N.J.: Prentice Hall, 1966.
Leuchtenburg, William E. *The Perils of Prosperity, 1914–32*. Chicago: University of Chicago Press, 1958.
Lindert, Peter H., and Jeffrey G. Williamson. "Three Centuries of American Inequality." *Research in Economic History* 1 (1976): 69–117.
McConnell, Grant. *Private Power and American Democracy*. New York: Vintage Books, 1966.
McFadden, Thomas M., ed. *America in Theological Perspective*. New York: Seabury Press, 1976.
McGuire, Joseph W. *Business and Society*. New York: McGraw-Hill Company, 1963.
Marden, Charles F. *Rotary and Its Brothers: An Analysis and Interpretation of the Men's Service Club*. Princeton: Princeton University Press, 1935.
Maritain, Jacques. *True Humanism*. London: Geoffrey Bles, 1938.

Marty, Martin E. *Righteous Empire: The Protestant Experience in America*. New York: The Dial Press, 1970.
May, Henry F. *Protestant Churches and Industrial America*. New York: Harper & Brothers, 1949.
———. "Shifting Perspectives on the 1920's." *Mississippi Valley Historical Review* 43 (December 1956): 405–427.
Mead, Sidney E. *The Lively Experiment: The Shaping of Christianity in America*. New York: Harper & Row, 1963.
Merz, Charles. *The Dry Decade*. Garden City, N.Y.: Doubleday, Doran Co., 1931.
Meyer, Donald B. *The Protestant Search for Political Realism, 1919–1941*. Berkeley, Cal.: University of California Press, 1960.
Miller, Perry. *American Character: A Conversion*. Santa Barbara: University of California Press, 1962.
Miller, Robert Moats. *American Protestantism and Social Issues, 1919–1939*. Chapel Hill: University of North Carolina Press, 1958.
Miller, William, ed. *Men in Business: Essays in the History of Entrepreneurship*. Cambridge, Mass.: Harvard University Press, 1952.
Miller, William R., ed. *Contemporary American Protestant Thought, 1900–1970*. Indianapolis, Ind.: The Bobbs-Merrill Company, 1973.
Mills, C. Wright. *The Power Elite*. New York: Oxford University Press, 1956.
Minton, Bruce, and John Stuart. *The Fat Years and the Lean*. New York: International Publishers, 1940.
Mowry, George E. *The Urban Nation 1920–1960*. New York: Hill and Wang, 1965.
Nash, Gerald D., ed. *Issues in American Economic History*. Lexington, Mass.: D.C. Heath and Company, 1972.
Nash, Roderick. *The Nervous Generation: American Thought 1917–1930*. Chicago: Rand McNally & Company, 1970.
Nevins, Allan, ed. *America Through British Eyes*. New York: Oxford University Press, 1948.
The New Catholic Encyclopedia.New York: McGraw-Hill Book Company, 1967.
Niebuhr, H. Richard. *The Kingdom of God in America*. New York: Harper & Row, 1959.
Niebuhr, Reinhold. *Christianity and Power Politics*. New York: Charles Scribner's Sons, 1940.
Nisbet, Robert A. *The Sociology of Emile Durkheim*. London: Heinemann, 1975.
Noggle, Burl. "The Twenties: A New Historiographical Frontier." *Journal of American History* 53 (September 1966): 299–314.
Nye, David E. *Henry Ford: "Ignorant Idealist"*. Port Washington, N.Y.: Kennikat Press, 1979.
Olmstead, Clifton E. *History of Religion in the United States*. Englewood Cliffs, N.J.: Prentice-Hall, 1960.
Pachter, Marc, ed. *Abroad in America: Visitors to the New Nation 1776–1914*. Reading, Mass.: Addison-Wesley Publishing Company, 1976.
Parker, Richard. *The Myth of the Middle Class: Notes on Affluence and Equality*. New York: Harper & Row, 1972.
Perrett, Geoffrey. *America in the Twenties*. New York: Simon and Schuster, 1982.
Pratt, J. B. *The Religious Consciousness*. New York: Macmillan, 1920.
Primer, Ben. *Protestants and American Business Methods*. UMI Research Press, 1979.

Prothro, James Warren. *The Dollar Decade: Business Ideas in the 1920's*. Baton Rouge: Louisiana State University Press, 1954.

Raucher, Alan R. *Public Relations and Business 1900–1929*. Baltimore, Md.: Johns Hopkins Press, 1968.

Rayback, Joseph G. *A History of American Labor*. New York: The Free Press, 1966.

Ribuffo, Leo. "Jesus Christ as Business Statesman: Bruce Barton and the Selling of Corporate Capitalism." *American Quarterly* 33 (Summer 1981): 206–31.

Riesman, David. *The Lonely Crowd: A Study of the Changing American Character*. New Haven: Yale University Press, 1950.

Rischin, Moses, ed. *The American Gospel of Success: Individualism and Beyond*. Chicago: Quadrangle Books, 1965.

Schlamm, William S. "European Business Is Different," *Fortune* 41 (February 1950): 97–99, 184–86, 188.

Schlesinger, Arthur M., Jr., *The Crisis of the Old Order, 1919–1933*. Boston: Houghton Mifflin Company, 1957.

Shannon, David A. *Between the Wars: America 1919–1941*. Boston: Houghton Mifflin Company, 1965.

Slosson, Preston William. *The Great Crusade and After, 1914–1928*. New York: Macmillan Company, 1930.

Smith, James Ward, and A. Leland Jamison, eds. *Religious Perspectives in American Culture*. Princeton, N.J.: Princeton University Press, 1961.

Soule, George. *Prosperity Decade*. New York: Rinehart & Company, 1947.

Spiller, Robert E., *et al. Literary History of the United States*. New York: Macmillan Company, 1963.

Stevenson, Elizabeth. *The American 1920s: Babbitts and Bohemians*. New York: Macmillan Company, 1967.

Sutton, Francis X., *et al. The American Business Creed*. Cambridge, Mass.: Harvard University Press, 1956.

Sweet, William Warren. *The Story of Religions in America*. New York: Harper & Brothers, 1930.

Tawney, Richard Henry. *Religion and the Rise of Capitalism*. London: John Murray, 1926.

Thomson, James J., Jr. *Tried as by Fire: Southern Baptists and the Religious Controversies of the 1920s*. Macon, Ga.: Mercer University Press, 1982.

Urofsky, Melvin I. *Big Steel and the Wilson Administration*. Columbus: Ohio State University Press, 1969.

Viner, Jacob. *Religious Thought and Economic Society*. Durham, N.C.: Duke University Press, 1978.

Watts, Emily Stipes. *The Businessman in American Literature*. Athens, Ga.: University of Georgia Press, 1982.

Weber, Max. *The Protestant Ethic and the Spirit of Capitalism*. New York: Charles Scribner's Sons, 1958.

———. *The Theory of Social and Economic Organization*. New York: Oxford University Press, 1947.

Weinstein, James. *The Corporate Ideal in the Liberal State. 1900–1918*. Boston: Beacon Press, 1968.

Wiebe, Robert H. *Businessmen and Reform: A Study of the Progressive Movement*. Cambridge, Mass.: Harvard University Press, 1962.

Wilson, Edmund. *The Twenties*. New York: Farrar, Straus and Giroux, 1975.

Wilson, John F. *Public Religion in American Culture.* Philadelphia: Temple University Press, 1979.

Wyllie, Irving G. *The Self-Made Man in America: The Myth of Rags to Riches*. New Brunswick, N.J.: Rutgers University Press, 1954.

Yinger, J. Milton. *Religion in the Struggle for Power: A Study in the Sociology of Religion.* Durham, N.C.: Duke University Press, 1946.

Index

About the Author

ROLF LUNDÉN is Professor of American Studies at Uppsala University in Sweden. He has published two literary studies on Theodore Dreiser and is a frequent contributor to *American Literary Scholarship*, *American Literature*, and other literary journals.